INTEGRATED

INTEGRATED

The Lincoln Institute, Basketball, and a Vanished Tradition

JAMES W. MILLER

UNIVERSITY PRESS OF KENTUCKY

Copyright © 2017 by The University Press of Kentucky

Scholarly publisher for the Commonwealth,
serving Bellarmine University, Berea College, Centre College of Kentucky,
Eastern Kentucky University, The Filson Historical Society, Georgetown
College, Kentucky Historical Society, Kentucky State University, Morehead State
University, Murray State University, Northern Kentucky University, Transylvania
University, University of Kentucky, University of Louisville, and Western
Kentucky University.

Editorial and Sales Offices: The University Press of Kentucky
663 South Limestone Street, Lexington, Kentucky 40508-4008
www.kentuckypress.com

Cataloging-in-Publication data available from the Library of Congress

ISBN 978-0-8131-6911-8 (hardcover : alk. paper)
ISBN 978-0-8131-6947-7 (epub)
ISBN 978-0-8131-6946-0 (pdf)

This book is printed on acid-free paper meeting the requirements of the American
National Standard for Permanence in Paper for Printed Library Materials.

Manufactured in the United States of America.

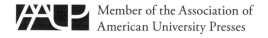
Member of the Association of
American University Presses

To Dad, who introduced my brother and me
to Lincoln Institute and basketball,
while teaching us that a man's worth
is measured by what's inside and not outside

Contents

Foreword

I first met Jim Miller when he came to work for the Kentucky Department of Public Information in 1968, when I was its commissioner. (In those years, cabinet heads in the state government were called commissioners, not secretaries, as they are today.) Jim was a summer intern from the University of Kentucky College of Journalism, and he joined the department's staff of writers. During an early-morning staff meeting, I went around the room asking our writers what they were working on that day. One by one, each described the story he or she was working on, but when I got to the intern, Jim listed about five things. This prompted me to interrupt and remind him that I only wanted to know his project for *today*. "That *is* today," he responded.

Years later, I ran into Jim in New Orleans when he was the director of athletics at the University of New Orleans (UNO). I was making a presentation to the athletic directors of the Sun Belt Conference, which had its headquarters in New Orleans, and Jim reminded me of our Kentucky connection. We met again at a convention of the National Association of Collegiate Directors of Athletics, and he did me one of the biggest favors of my career: he suggested that I interview his brother, Jerry, for a position in state government when I became Kentucky's secretary of commerce in 2008. Jerry became chief financial officer of the Commerce Cabinet and then commissioner of parks (another job I had held in 1969–1970). Today, Jerry is a well-respected state representative from Louisville.

Jim had left UNO by the time I saw him next, at the 2012 Final Four. He asked me to look at a book he was writing called *Where the Water Kept Rising*, which chronicled the devastating effects of Hurricane Katrina on New Orleans, the UNO Athletic Department, and Jim's family personally.

It was a great story of personal resilience, crisis management, and how an organization can maneuver through hardship.

So more recently, when he asked me to look at another book he was writing about African American high school basketball in the early years of desegregation, I jumped at the opportunity. *Integrated: The Lincoln Institute, Basketball, and a Vanished Tradition* is a terrific history of a school that was kept alive during difficult social and economic times by the drive and resilience of one man: Whitney Young Sr. A member of Lincoln Institute's first class of 1912, Young returned as a teacher and then became the school's principal, instilling in his students the value of hard work while respecting the discipline that comes from athletics.

When the US Supreme Court declared segregation illegal, Young, by then the president of Lincoln Institute, faced the new reality with pragmatism and with the best interests of his students at heart. But he knew the decision meant the eventual end of Lincoln Institute and the many other African American schools across Kentucky that gave members of an oppressed minority their only opportunity at an education.

This book takes me back to my own experiences with African American athletes and friends. In my early years in Ashland and then in Lexington in the 1950s, I played semiprofessional baseball with a team that consisted of me, four other white players, and a group of outstanding black players such as John "Scoop" Brown, William "Bunny" Davis, and future major leaguer Bill White, who, after a great career, would become president of the National League.

Later, I was involved with the publishing of two books about African American sports. *Transition Game* (2001) is the story of S. T. Roach and how he helped pave the way for black athletes in the commonwealth as a coach at Dunbar High School in Lexington. *Shadows of the Past* (2006) is the definitive history of the Kentucky High School Athletic League, written by Louis Stout, a former KHSAL star and the first African American commissioner of Kentucky high school athletics.

Integrated is a worthy addition to that literature. The years when both black and white students and their parents were experiencing the transition from segregation to integration and inclusion constitute a transformative period in our history. Jim Miller brings this history to life through the recollections of former Lincoln Institute students and athletes and his own personal memories of events he witnessed, having grown up only five miles from the school. This is a fascinating story that you will find as entertaining and informative as I did.

Jim Host
Founder
Host Communications

Introduction

The US Supreme Court's 1954 decision in *Brown v. Board of Education* prohibited segregation in public schools, correcting a century of injustice and unequal education experienced by generations of young African Americans. But such a necessary correction resounded well beyond its intent, triggering consequences that altered cherished institutions in black communities throughout the country. Few were affected more than the strong tradition of high school basketball, and nowhere was that transformation more graphic than in hoops-mad Kentucky.

When the high court rendered its landmark decision, more than fifty high schools competed in the Kentucky High School Athletic League (KHSAL), an association formed in 1932 by principals, coaches, and administrators of African American high schools across the commonwealth. The *Brown* decision made it clear that such schools would eventually be closed, but execution of the Court's mandate was left up to the individual states. Their only direction from the high court was that desegregation be achieved "with all deliberate speed."

In Kentucky, local school boards were given the task of determining and implementing their own plans for integration that suited local whims, politics, and inclinations. The result was a crazy quilt of compliance whereby some boards proffered integration plans quickly, while others took years to do so. For every school board that saw the new law as just and proper, others failed to be convinced that change in the world did not signal the end of the world. Therein lay the irony that treasured African American high schools survived in areas that resisted integration the longest.

In the first two years after *Brown,* a dozen KHSAL member schools closed, as half of the state's local school boards moved to comply. The black schools that remained open were allowed to apply for membership in the Kentucky High School Athletic Association (KHSAA), founded in 1917 to govern the athletic activities of the segregated white schools. That left thirty-nine African American high schools operating in Kentucky between 1958 and 1966 under a cloud of uncertainty, not knowing when their local boards would reach a decision that meant their immediate closure. Its purpose served, the KHSAL ceased operations in 1957.

Lincoln Institute in Shelby County was one of those schools. It had been founded in 1912 after the state legislature passed a law "to prohibit white and colored persons from attending the same school." Lincoln was led by a charismatic academic and theologian named Whitney M. Young. In more than three decades as the school's leader, Young overcame prejudice, funding issues, and politics to create a bastion of excellence and respect in the black community. In this book, former Lincoln Institute players, students, and teachers tell their stories of joy, regret, and resilience during a largely ignored period of transition in the nation's journey toward desegregation. Their experiences, which came in the early days of the civil rights movement, provide a unique perspective on one of America's most transformative periods.

The new black members of the KHSAA encountered a skeptical environment when the 1957–1958 school year opened. Some white crowds saw the black teams as a novelty—something they had never seen before in an era of sporadic media coverage. Curious white fans were drawn to games in which young black players showed their physical gifts while acrobatic cheerleaders performed their own unique routines on the sidelines. However, other white parents, players, and fans were not so receptive. Black teams could expect prejudiced officials, hostile fans, and opposing players who did not want to share the court with boys of a different race and, often, superior ability.

White parents were not the only ones uncomfortable with the new order. Every black school that closed released its students into the white schools, in many cases over the protests of their own parents. Many African Americans preferred the status quo and were reluctant to send their children to schools where they were not wanted and would face ridicule, racial slurs, or protests by white parents and students. To some black parents, every approved integration plan meant the end of a school that had provided generations of service, hope, and an alternative to no education at all. Black opposition to desegregation was a dissonance created when emotion meets logic, but to a population that had too few positive traditions to embrace, the loss of such a significant one was tragic.

The late 1950s were the formative years of the civil rights movement in America, when leaders such as Martin Luther King Jr. were just beginning to find their voices. Although black basketball teams were now playing white teams, their players still could not eat in most restaurants, shop freely in many establishments, or even try on shoes in white-owned shoe stores. Public restrooms were divided into "Men," "Ladies," and "Colored," and blacks had to sit in specific marked areas in movie houses and on public transportation.

Despite the challenges, the black teams acquitted themselves well during the transitional years, winning numerous district and regional titles. Winners of the "Sweet Sixteen" regional contests qualified to participate in the Kentucky High School Basketball Tournament, the most popular grassroots event in the state. Generations of young white players had shot baskets at bare hoops on the sides of barns, dreaming of playing in the state tournament. Now that dream was shared by young black players who competed for the opportunity to "go to state."

This book is enriched by tales of individual courage from men who defied comfort and custom: the coach of the segregated white high school who convinced his administrators and fans that playing black schools was the right (and necessary) thing to do; the former Lincoln Institute standout who became an Armed Forces All-Star and then had the last laugh on Kentucky coach Adolph Rupp on the Wildcats' home floor; the young tennis prodigy whose dreams were denied because he could not play at the white country club but who became the first African American to start for a champion Kentucky high school basketball team. This book is a tribute to those African American schools, players, coaches, and teachers who overcame societal obstacles in pursuit of educational opportunity during one of the most difficult periods of racial transition in our nation's history.

1

New Journey on an Old Road

Despite the examples of Little Rock and Virginia, the Deep South at this time is still not ready to accept any public school integration—token or otherwise—and likely would close schools to prevent it.
>   —Associated Press, January 10, 1960

Ten young African American men squinted into the morning sun as they walked single file out of their dormitory. Some shivered at the crisp air brought in by a cold front that would keep central Kentucky's late-winter temperatures under freezing for the day's high. Others ignored it and ambled lazily, joking and laughing until a large man in a dark pin-striped suit and neatly trimmed mustache approached. With a familiar authority, he pointed to a rusting yellow school bus that idled a few yards away and instructed them to get on board, find a vacant seat, and be quiet. Approaching from the opposite direction were eight young women, dressed alike in wide skirts and full sweaters under long coats of various hues. The large man's expression softened, and he smiled and nodded as the girls giggled nervously, one reaching up and tapping on the window to get the attention of the boys inside.[1]

The man in charge was Walter Gilliard, head basketball coach of the Lincoln Institute Tigers. A decade earlier, he had distinguished himself as a football star at Kentucky State College in Frankfort, but for the past three years, he had guided the basketball fortunes of the only boarding high school in Kentucky exclusively for African Americans. His team members, sitting on the bus in their gold satin warm-up suits and black high-topped Converse sneakers, were now engaged in a more timeless game. A few of them were practicing their offensive moves as the cheerleaders boarded the bus, while their shier teammates played defense to the girls' flirtations.. They all were restless, anxious about where they were headed, and curious about what they would see when they arrived.

The Tigers were champions of Kentucky's Eighth Region, which included all the high schools in Carroll, Gallatin, Grant, Henry, Oldham, Owen, Shelby, Spencer, and Trimble Counties, a land mass whose irregular border extended from the Ohio River southward into the Bluegrass. They had earned the opportunity to join fifteen other regional winners to compete for the Kentucky state championship. The "Sweet Sixteen" would meet at the most prominent arena in the South—Louisville's Freedom Hall—which had hosted the National Collegiate Athletic Association (NCAA) championship for the past two years. The state tournament was Kentucky's most prestigious high school athletic event, and it rivaled the Kentucky Derby as the state's most heavily attended annual sporting event.

Lincoln Institute had a mixed reputation among African Americans in the state. To the envious, Lincoln was an exclusive school for rich kids whose parents could afford to pay for an education. To its apologists, Lincoln was a dumping ground for children from other Kentucky counties that lacked the facilities to educate their own black students. To its critics, Lincoln was a last-chance destination for problem teenagers from the North and elsewhere. Each description contained an element of truth, but to its 400 students and their parents, Lincoln Institute was the most wonderful place on earth. Located twenty-two miles east of Louisville on 444 rolling green acres, Lincoln resembled a small college campus where students could learn independence while receiving an education that taught them a useful trade. It was a place where lifetime friendships could form amid a spiritual and cooperative environment.

Absent for the team's departure was the man to whom the students owed everything: Whitney Moore Young Sr., the president of Lincoln Institute. But to suggest that Young might still be in bed while his students were up and about would have been a gross misstatement of reality. In fact, to many students, faculty, and staff, it seemed that the indefatigable Dr. Young had not slept since taking over as principal of the school a quarter century earlier.

Whitney Young had been one of the first students to enroll at Lincoln Institute after its founding in 1912, precipitated by a legislative fiat demanding segregated education in the state. Young graduated from Lincoln and then fought in the Great War before following the rural postwar exodus to Detroit. But when he was asked to leave his comfortable job and take less pay to teach engineering at his alma mater, Young came home. He married his high school sweetheart, Laura, whom he had met at Lincoln, and helped her raise a son and two daughters. At the time, segregation demanded two sets of nearly every aspect of normal life. The local towns of Simpsonville and Shelbyville had separate water fountains, separate restrooms, and separate seats in the lone movie house for blacks and whites. Segregation also demanded two sets of schools.

By March 1960, the sixty-three-year-old Young and his family had endured such indignities without losing their own dignity, a trait he had instilled in his students since becoming the principal of Lincoln Institute in 1935. The economic effects of the Great Depression had compounded segregation's diminished stature of all things "Negro" and had almost forced the school to close. But with the blessings of angels both black and white, Young had somehow willed the school to survive. In accordance with Lincoln's founders, he was a disciple of Booker T. Washington's attitude that the black man's condition could be improved through self-education and hard work rather than activism. This produced an environment for Lincoln students that encouraged tolerance of their situation and gave them the resilience to march through the brambles blocking their path.

Young seldom addressed the growing turmoil occurring outside the borders of Lincoln Institute in the late 1950s, preferring that his students keep up with current events by reading newspapers in the school library or by listening to news programs on the radio. He believed the best preparation for the challenges of life was a solid foundation of study, hard work, and high moral standards. But like high school students everywhere, those at Lincoln were more concerned with the reality they knew—friends, sports, and the opposite sex—than with obscure political issues that did not affect their daily routines.

If Young had decided to send the players off with a message that morning, its content would have sounded familiar. He might have told them they were representing Lincoln Institute in their journey, but they were also representing themselves and their families. He might have told them they were representing all the African American basketball players who had been denied participation in the "white" state tournament. The vision of a barefoot country boy shooting a slick rubber ball at a barrel hoop nailed to the side of a barn fed the theme that great achievements are possible no matter who you are or where you come from. But the reality was that, until the late 1950s, those dreams were reserved only for white boys and girls.

Young typically ended every speech with a moral or an appropriate biblical verse. That day, he might have looked each student in the eye, then bowed his head in the manner of the ordained pastor he was and asked God to give these young people the faith of Job and the courage of Joshua and to protect them from harm in accordance with Psalms 121:7: "The Lord shall preserve thee from all evil: he shall preserve thy soul."

Nearly six years earlier, the Supreme Court's decision in *Brown v. Board of Education* had determined that segregated schools would no longer be tolerated anywhere in the nation. Specifically, the law attacked the only region where segregation was still widely practiced: the sentimental remnants of the old Confederacy. The celebration that followed the high court's decision in 1954 was tempered by a second ruling in 1955 in which the Court considered states' requests for relief concerning the task of desegregation. In that decision, which became known as *Brown II,* the Court delegated the task of carrying out school desegregation to the district courts and ordered that it occur "with all deliberate speed."

This dubious directive failed to establish a deadline for compliance and left desegregation to the discretion of the individual states, most of which delegated that responsibility to local school boards. School boards in nearly half of Kentucky's 120 counties complied quickly and created plans for integration, while the rest approached the issue like cats to a candle. Their indecision or reluctance was based on a combination of local politics, prejudice, and public fear. Their deliberations greatly affected the educational opportunities of young African Americans but also altered the landscape of the most visible aspect of public education. In Kentucky, that meant high school basketball.

It was Wednesday morning, March 16, 1960. Attacking windmills was not on the minds of the young Tigers as the bus pulled away from the hilltop campus on Lincoln Ridge and chugged down the one-mile access road that opened onto US Highway 60. It was a road familiar to all of them, but that day it began a journey none of them had taken before. Turning west, the bus soon crossed into Jefferson County and headed toward Louisville and the opportunity that lay before them. The participating teams were lodged at the Kentucky Hotel in the heart of downtown Louisville, and the Tigers had time for one short practice that afternoon in Freedom Hall before their game on Thursday morning. It was a great deal to pack into one day, and Coach Gilliard, seated in the front seat, glared over the driver's shoulder. He did not want to be late for any of it.

The Lincoln Institute Tigers were heading to Louisville with a 30–2 record, one of the best among the sixteen participants. They featured a combination of speed, height, and experience that complemented a fast-break offense and a pressure defense. In addition to being the first African American team to win the Eighth Region, Lincoln was the *only* African American school in a region that consisted of several consolidated high schools and a conglomeration of smaller schools from places like Bagdad, Waddy, and Eminence.

The white journalists who covered the sport and determined the favorites in the state tournament were not easily impressed. Black schools in the tournament were still a curiosity to many white journalists and spectators in 1960. It would be only the fourth state tournament in which black schools were allowed to participate, and only Lexington Dunbar in 1959 had made it as far as the semifinal round. According to the experts, the caliber of the black schools was not equal to that of the white schools, and their schedules were too easy because most played half their games against their traditional rivals—other black schools.

The Litkenhous ratings, an authoritative ranking system developed in 1934 by Louisville brothers Edward and Frank Litkenhous, listed Lincoln

Institute as number twelve among the sixteen participants. That was two slots behind Hopkinsville Attucks, winner of the Second Region and the only other African American school to make the tournament. In addition to the season-long rankings published in the *Louisville Courier-Journal,* there was another Litkenhous ranking that diminished gaudy records and weak opponents and concentrated strictly on performance in district and regional tournaments. Lincoln improved a notch on that scale, but the rankings told the Tigers they faced a formidable foe.

The top-rated teams, the ones hitting their peak at tournament time, were Louisville Flaget, winner of the Seventh Region, and Owensboro, the Third Region champion and the Tigers' opponent the following day.

If Lincoln Institute wanted to make a statement in the tournament, it could not have chosen a better opponent than Owensboro Senior High School. The Red Devils represented royalty among Kentucky high school basketball teams, participating in sixteen previous state tournaments and winning the championship in 1917 and 1949.

The 1949 team, led by Cliff Hagan, was considered the greatest in Owensboro history. Hagan had gone on to an all-American career at the University of Kentucky, and in 1960 he was starring for the St. Louis Hawks of the National Basketball Association (NBA). Graduating one year before Hagan was the Red Devils' current head coach, Bobby Watson, who had learned the game in the city's public schools before becoming a first-team all-state guard in 1948. Only five feet ten inches tall, Watson's forte was a remarkably accurate twenty-five-foot set shot that earned him a scholarship to the University of Kentucky and a starting spot on coach Adolph Rupp's 1950–1951 national championship team. Only two years out of college, Watson had been awarded his alma mater's head coaching job after longtime coach Lawrence L. McGinnis retired in 1957.

The current team was generally regarded as superior to the 1953 team (the last one to make it to the state tournament) and possibly as good as the 1949 champions. Its star was a clone of the coach. Randy Embry was a five-foot-ten-inch junior who averaged 15 points per game and would follow the distinguished line of Red Devils to the University of Kentucky. The Devils had good size, with husky six-foot-three Jan Adelman (pronounced Automan), six-foot-three David "Whip" Yewell, and six-foot-one Richard Anderson dominating the offensive and defensive boards. Owensboro had not been out-rebounded in any game during the season: Adelman had averaged 13 and Yewell 12 rebounds per game, while scoring 12.7 and 11.6 points, respectively. Anderson, who was also Owensboro's all-state quarterback, pitched in 10 points and collected nearly 8 rebounds per game.[2]

Their 22–8 record entering the tournament was deceiving because the Red Devils had lost a handful of close games early in the season as Anderson and the other football players on the team worked their way into basketball shape. As late as the first United Press International poll in February, Owensboro did not even garner an honorable mention in the state rankings. However, the Red Devils closed the regular season with three consecutive victories, including a 55–49 win over state tournament cofavorite Louisville Flaget. Then they hit their stride in the early rounds of the tournament.

Owensboro breezed through the Twelfth District tournament. Then, in the Third Region opener, the Red Devils posted a 20–2 first-quarter lead over Henderson County before coasting to a 69–39 victory behind Embry's 25 points. That game was only a preliminary to a 74–53 semifinal beatdown against another group of Red Devils from tiny Sebree High School, who had come into the game boasting an impressive 32–3 record.

More of the same could be expected when Owensboro faced district runner-up Daviess County in the finals, but the Panthers, under veteran coach Buck Sydnor, would not yield easily. Owensboro was located in Daviess County, and the city versus county rivalry was always vibrant, regardless of the teams' records. Plus, the regionals were being played on the Panthers' home floor.

Mother Nature added some intrigue to the matchup. A record foot and a half of snow had paralyzed the area, forcing Saturday's championship game to be pushed to Monday night. That was only three days before the winner would play its state tournament opener against the Lincoln Institute Tigers. The Red Devils took the delay in stride and outlasted Daviess County by a score of 69–64. Adelman scored a game-high 23 points, and he and Yewell dominated the boards, each grabbing 17 rebounds. Embry added 19 points, mostly from the outside, while Yewell contributed 16. Owensboro would be going to the state tournament for the first time since 1953, when it had lost the opening game to another Eighth Region team, Shelbyville, 64–63.[3]

Coach Walter Gilliard herded his bleary-eyed Tigers onto the bus outside the Kentucky Hotel on Thursday morning. It was the first time any of the players had slept in a hotel room, and the thick towels, soft sheets, and plush appurtenances were intoxicating. They felt like young princes in a historical novel they might have been assigned to read for a literature class. The lush accommodations, coupled with the excitement of playing the biggest basketball game of their lives in a few hours, meant that a good night's sleep was impossible.

Their bus arrived at the Kentucky Fair and Exposition Center as fans filed in to watch the 9:00 a.m. game between Symsonia of the First Region and Meade Memorial of the Fifteenth Region. Fans of the Symsonia Rough Riders wore their school's traditional red and black colors, while fans of the Meade Memorial Red Devils were distinct in their maroon and white jackets, shirts, and caps. Tickets were a bargain at only $1 for students and $2 for adults to see the biggest event that many of those standing in line would ever attend. The Lincoln bus was directed to the back loading dock of the arena, where ushers directed Gilliard and his players to their assigned locker room. The players would have about an hour to themselves, but the cheers that accompanied the ebb and flow of the game going on outside made it hard to relax. Finally, after a 69–60 Symsonia victory, Gilliard gathered his players for their final instructions.

He looked around at their faces and considered what they had overcome to get there. Some of the boys came from rural outposts, where they had been raised to get along with everyone; others came from cities, where attitudes were sharper. It had been Gilliard's task to mold them into a team, which he had done so that no single player dominated. Each of the starters had led the team in scoring more than once, and each had contributed in his own way, whether rebounding or making a key deflection or wrapping himself around the leg of the other team's best player.

If any one player stood out from the rest, it was six-foot-three sophomore forward Bill Crayton, whose long, arcing jump shot from the corner usually found its target. Big Ben Spalding, a six-foot-four senior and team leader, had battled a throat infection late in the season but had returned stronger than ever. The guards were John Watkins, a five-foot-eleven senior whose outside shooting was a ready cure for hostile zone defenses, and Clyde Mosby, a five-foot-ten junior whose long arms and quickness led Lincoln's pressing defense. But the key to the team for the past month had been Jewell Logan, a six-foot-two senior forward who had caught fire late in the season, giving the Tigers a potent scoring option.

Gilliard knew these boys were ready physically, but a coach can only prepare his players; he cannot predict how they will respond in an unfamiliar situation. In a few minutes, they would be playing in the biggest arena in the country in front of more fans than had watched all thirty-two of their games combined. Did they realize the significance of the moment? The rap on the locker room door told Gilliard he would soon find out.

Dressed in their gold uniforms with maroon numbers and trim, the players jogged down the long corridor that opened into spacious Freedom Hall. It was like emerging from a darkened cave into a foggy lowland. A layer of smoke settled over the court like wispy autumn air settling over a cold lake. Smoking was allowed in tobacco-rich Kentucky, and it seemed that every adult in the building had lit up for the occasion.

The Tigers ran onto the floor and got a modest reception from the Lincoln fans seated in an end-zone section reserved for participating schools. The cheerleaders vaulted into acrobatic flips that ended in gymnastic splits before bouncing up, clapping their hands, and encouraging the fans to stand up and cheer. As the players assembled in their routine layup line on one side and rebounding line on the other, a cheer emerged from the other end of the floor. The Owensboro Red Devils, white faces in stark contrast, trotted onto the court in their red uniforms with black numerals amid a deafening clamor from all over the arena. Not many people could be left in Owensboro, one Lincoln player said to another, for it seemed the town's entire population was present and rising in reverence to their heroes.

Bobby Watson had never seen Lincoln Institute play, but he had a good idea what his team could expect. Watson had dispatched his school's head baseball coach, Jack Hicks, to Oldham County to watch the finals of the Eighth Region tournament. Hicks came back with a scouting report that was simple but spoke volumes: "They get up and down the floor and can score points. They run and run, and we are going to have to score more than normal to beat them. Lincoln has a great team."[4]

The Tigers were true to Hicks's report as they raced to a 7–4 lead in the first minute and a half of play. Owensboro bounced back quickly and went ahead, 8–7, on Yewell's layup on the way to a 12–2 run and a 16–9 lead with 2:58 remaining in the first quarter. The Lincoln players looked frozen in place while Embry dribbled in and out of the defenders, looking for an open teammate or a shot. But just when it looked like Owensboro would make a rout of it, the Tigers stiffened. A basket by Clyde Mosby tied the score at 17 with 58 seconds left, and another by Bill Crayton tied it at 19 as the first period ended.

The hot-shooting Embry put the Red Devils in front again, 21–19, but Mosby answered with two field goals in a row that pushed Lincoln back in front, 23–21, with 7:18 remaining in the period. Big Jan Adelman's basket gave Owensboro a 26–25 lead that it expanded to a 37–31 advantage with 2:42 to go in the half. But the Tigers rallied with a 9–2 run of their own, and Mosby's jumper gave Lincoln a 40–39 edge with 1:07 remaining. Adelman connected again for Owensboro, Logan countered with two free throws for Lincoln, and Embry flipped in a fifteen-foot jumper, his 21st point of the half, to give Watson's crew a 43–42 lead at intermission.[5]

Despite the lead, Owensboro was in trouble. Forward Richard Anderson had picked up four fouls in the first half, and Adelman had three. Good sense suggested that both players should sit out the beginning of the second half, but Watson needed his big men in the lineup to offset the inside strength of Spalding and Crayton. He sent his starting five onto the floor to begin the second half.

Yewell quickly extended the Owensboro lead, 45–42, but Mosby hit two straight jump shots, and Logan's free throw put the Tigers back on top 47–45. Watson's gamble appeared doomed when Anderson picked up his fifth foul with 6:46 to go in the third quarter. The Tigers could not take advantage, however, and the Devils came back and led 51–49 on a layup by

Yewell. Crayton tied the score at 55, and Watkins intercepted an Owensboro pass under the Lincoln basket for an easy layup. The Tigers led 57–55 and extended the lead to 61–56 by the end of the third quarter. Their prospects improved even more a minute into the final period.

Adelman committed his fifth personal foul with 6:42 remaining and was finished for the game. The loss was devastating. He had scored 17 points and led the team with 12 rebounds, but with both Adelman and Anderson on the bench, the Owensboro rooters braced for the worst. Another Mosby basket put the Tigers' lead at 68–63 with 5:15 left in the game.

Clearly half the crowd at Freedom Hall sensed an upset, and their allegiance switched to the underdog Tigers. Lincoln fans were ecstatic when it looked like their team would roll into the second round. The eight cheerleaders were encouraging the crowd—both white fans and black—with their acrobatic leaps and splits, all complemented by an assortment of chants:

> Had a little pig, put him in a pen,
> He rooted for Lincoln, 'cause he knew they would win,
> Hey, hey, O Lincoln,
> Hcy, O Lincoln,
> Hey, hey, O Lincoln,
> Hey, O Lincoln,
> We Gonna Win This Game, HEY![6]

Nobody expected Lincoln Institute to be in this position—just minutes away from defeating one of the tournament favorites, and a wounded one at that. But then again, just a few years earlier, neither Lincoln Institute nor any other African American team would have had the opportunity to be here.

2

Prejudice versus Common Sense

President B. F. Allen, who heads Missouri's highest institution of learning for Negroes, says the Negro can make a contribution to progress such as no other race can make unless "he is content with being a second hand edition of the white man and strives every day to look more and more like the white man."

—Editorial, *Lexington Herald*, August 20, 1911

It was not easy to envision the center of abolition in antebellum Kentucky as a placid ridge where the foothills of the Cumberland Mountains sloped downward to meet the central plains of the Bluegrass. But it became so in 1853 when the Reverend John Gregg Fee, a thirty-nine-year-old minister and ardent abolitionist, accepted an offer to move from northern Kentucky to establish an antislavery church in an area of Madison County called the Glades. His benefactor was Cassius Marcellus Clay, a wealthy politician and fellow abolitionist, who offered the preacher a ten-acre homestead to establish the church, which attracted a congregation of like-minded citizens.[1]

Two years later, Fee established a school and church dedicated to the Christian principles of temperance and equality. He named the settlement Berea, after the biblical town whose populace had demonstrated an open-mindedness and receptiveness to the gospel.[2] The college began as a one-room schoolhouse that also served as Fee's church, and it was modeled after Oberlin College in Ohio. There was great interest in the college, as small as it was, and Governor Salmon P. Chase of Ohio, who later became President Lincoln's treasury secretary, spoke at the school's commencement ceremonies.[3]

Fee, J. A. R. Rogers, who acted as the school's principal, and other supporters drew up a constitution and pledged more than 100 acres of land for the college campus. On July 14, 1859, the constitution was affirmed and bylaws were adopted making Berea the first institution of higher learning in the South that was both interracial and coeducational. The first bylaw declared, "The object of this college shall be to furnish the facilities for thorough education to all persons of good moral character." The second bylaw was more specific: "This college shall be under an influence strictly Christian, and as such, opposed to sectarianism, slave-holding, caste, and every other wrong institution or practice." Opposition to caste meant the admission of students of all races.[4]

Fee and his followers were driven from the area during the Civil War and fled across the Ohio River to Clermont County, Ohio, just east of Cincinnati. But in 1864 he returned to Kentucky and volunteered to work at Camp Nelson, thirty-five miles northwest of Berea, where the Union army had enlisted more than 10,000 African American soldiers. Fee helped construct facilities to support freedmen and their families and to provide their wives and children with education and preaching while the men were training.[5]

In 1865 Fee and his followers returned to Berea. A year later, the school's articles of incorporation were recorded at the county seat, and in 1869 the college became a reality. Two black Union army soldiers who had learned to read became the first African Americans admitted to Berea College. This experiment in race relations was a success, and Berea cemented its reputation as a center of education for people of all races. Until the turn of the century, although black and white students at Berea freely maintained separate social lives, they engendered mutual respect in the classroom and on the athletic field. Berea had demonstrated that there was no need to draw a color line in the South or anywhere else in the Christian world.[6]

Over the last quarter of the nineteenth century, African Americans in Kentucky made remarkable progress in educating their youth. After a campaign by the Colored Teachers State Association, the Kentucky General Assembly chartered a normal school in Frankfort, appropriating $7,000 to erect two buildings and $3,000 for teachers' salaries, and the City of Frankfort donated forty acres on the east side of town on Georgetown Pike. The

State Normal School for Colored Persons opened on October 11, 1887, with John Jackson, a graduate of Berea College, as president. Two departments, literary and industrial, trained teachers for elementary schools. In 1890, after federal legislation provided for the establishment of African American land-grant colleges, State Normal added departments in agriculture and mechanics. The school's name was changed in 1902 to Kentucky State Normal and Industrial Institute for Colored Persons.[7]

The education of blacks at all levels in the latter years of the nineteenth century led to debates over not only the types of education they should receive but also their roles in the post–Civil War era. Should blacks adapt to the mores of the day and accept a second-class status? Or should they address segregation more aggressively? Both views had supporters among both races and were represented by prominent spokesmen such as Booker T. Washington and W. E. B. DuBois.

Washington, the president of Tuskegee Institute in Alabama, argued that African Americans "should first establish an economic base for their advancement." They should focus "upon the everyday practical things of life, upon something that is needed to be done, and something which they will be permitted to do in the community in which they reside." In Washington's view, vocational education was the key to black advancement. Speaking in Atlanta in 1895, Washington omitted any mention of politics and apparently endorsed segregation. In contrast, DuBois, a Harvard-trained professor at Atlanta University, believed that Washington's approach was only part of the answer. He advocated that a "talented tenth" of blacks be educated for leadership roles at the college level. Moreover, he insisted that both political and economic progress could be achieved.[8]

William J. Simmons gravitated toward Washington's viewpoint. In 1890 Simmons became president of Eckstein Norton Institute in Bullitt County, Kentucky, named for the president of the Louisville & Nashville Railroad. Backed by several wealthy white Louisvillians, his school offered training in carpentry, farming, cooking, and dressmaking. Simmons died several months into his tenure, and Charles Parrish Jr. took over in late 1890. Eckstein Norton Institute's motto—"Education of the hands, head, heart, and mind"—fit the ideals of both its white benefactors and its black founders. Central Colored High School, Louisville's only black secondary school, founded in 1873, also subscribed to that view.[9]

At least in the short run, Washington's belief system, which embodied the idea of the "self-made man," had more supporters than DuBois's approach. "I have learned that success is to be measured not so much by the position that one has reached in life as by the obstacles which he has overcome while trying to succeed," the Tuskegee president said. Most people of that era, black and white, believed in that concept, whether fact or fiction.[10]

Despite the debate among black educators, the white community cared little about the type of education given to the Negro race, so long as the races remained separate. That kept Berea College in the bull's-eye for those who abhorred "mixing" of the races. Men from elsewhere in the South observed that Kentucky could never rank as a true southern state until Berea College, with its lenient racial policy, was abolished. The Kentucky legislature did nothing to encourage Berea when it codified the segregation of schools in the state's 1891 constitution, which declared: "separate schools for white and colored children shall be maintained."[11]

Such actions sustained an atmosphere of distrust between the races that only intensified during the last decade of the nineteenth century and impeded any efforts to achieve educational reform. White racism throughout the South reached a numerical zenith in the 1890s, which recorded the greatest number of lynchings in any decade in American history. Some blacks who could afford it sought other options, such as a revival of the movement to repatriate African Americans to their ancestral land. At least three voyages delivered hundreds of black families to Liberia, drawn by promises of an escape to an all-black world with an elected black government and free land for American settlers. Unfortunately for the travelers, reality fell far short of these promises.[12]

Black activists in the North were skeptical that anything positive could happen in a country where the white man was in total control. An article published in 1903 quoted the Reverend Montrose W. Thornton, pastor of the First African Methodist Episcopal (AME) Church of Wilmington, Delaware, who called the white man "the demon of the world's races, a monster incarnate, and insofar as the Negro race is concerned seems to give no quarter. . . . I would sooner trust myself in a den of hyena than in his arms. With a court, law, and officers of law in his hands, the despised Negro can expect no mercy, justice or protection." Thornton also took issue with Booker T. Washington's perceived submissiveness, warning that Washington's "charity, insanity, advice of forgiveness, love, industry and so on will never be reciprocated by white men."[13]

Berea College had been devoted to interracial education from its inception, and in its early decades, the student body was typically more than 60 percent black. After the state constitution mandated separate schools, Berea president William Goodell Frost turned the college's focus more toward Appalachia and less toward interracial education, although it continued to serve both races. By 1902 the percentage of black students had dropped to 16 percent, which still was too many, according to one notable visitor.

In November 1903 Representative Carl Day was appalled by his visit to the Berea campus. Day was a native of Frozen Creek in Breathitt County, one of the most violent counties in the state, known for its ongoing feuds. But he was shocked at the sight of blacks and whites "living together" at Berea, and he decided to do something about it. On January 12, 1904, Day introduced House Bill 25, "An Act to Prohibit White and Colored Persons from Attending the Same School." According to Day, his legislation was intended to prevent "the contamination of the white children of Kentucky." Day further explained his rationale based on an antediluvian sense of social order that had been aggravated when President Theodore Roosevelt invited Booker T. Washington to lunch at the White House. "Coeducation of whites and Negroes leads to social equality, and social equality leads to intermarriage of the races," Day concluded. "This amalgamation will lead to the nation's downfall. We have been ridiculing Roosevelt for dining with the Negro, but coeducation is no better."[14]

Day's act made it illegal for any school to operate with both races present, and teachers and students who broke the law would be subject to fines. The bill imposed a $1,000 fine—more money than most teachers made in a year—plus a $100-a-day penalty on any instructor who continued to teach in such an institution. Students would be fined lesser amounts for attending classes. Branch schools could be established to serve each race, but even then, they had to be at least twenty-five miles away from each other.

Supported by the state superintendent of public instruction, and not opposed by Governor J. C. W. Beckham, the bill sailed through committee and passed the house by a vote of 73–5. On March 11 Day's bill was passed in the state senate by the margin of 28–5 and was signed into law by Governor Beckham. Opposing the bill were four eastern Kentucky Republicans and one mountain Democrat, none of whom would be reelected to the statehouse in 1906.[15]

A month later, on April 12, 1904, Representative Carl Day died in Lexington of pneumonia.

Berea College filed suit and engaged as counsel John G. Carlisle, a Kentuckian who had been Speaker of the US House and secretary of the treasury under President Grover Cleveland. At the circuit court level, the judge upheld the legality of the law, calling it a "blessing to Berea College." The state court of appeals, in a 1906 opinion, struck down the law's twenty-five-mile provision but allowed the rest to stand. Only Henry S. Barker, a future University of Kentucky president, stood in opposition among the judges.

In presenting the state's case before the US Supreme Court, attorney general James Breathitt not only used legal arguments but also stressed that the superiority of the Anglo-Saxon race was "innate and God-given." The conservative Court upheld the law in a 1908 decision, with two justices dissenting: William R. Day of Ohio (no relation to Carl Day) and Kentuckian John Marshall Harlan, who had also dissented in 1896 in *Plessy v. Ferguson,* which had established the doctrine of "separate but equal." Burnishing his reputation as the Great Dissenter, Harlan wrote: "Have we become so inoculated with prejudice of race that an American government . . . can make distinctions between such citizens in the matter of . . . meeting for innocent purposes because of their respective races?"[16]

The trustees at Berea College were convinced that the education of young African Americans was too important to abandon, so they voted to establish a branch institution to serve the needs of black students. It was a daring decision because public sentiment, defined as the opinion of the majority race, was not supportive and was often downright hostile. It was still a time of great racial suspicion in Kentucky, as evidenced by retaliation against Negroes for a variety of real and perceived offenses. In the decade from the turn of the century to the year the land was secured for the new institution, forty-two Negroes were lynched or murdered in Kentucky for crimes ranging from rape and murder to "improper relations" with the whites and even the fatal mistake of having a "bad reputation."[17]

After the Berea board determined to proceed with the project, the next question was where to build the school. Identifying a suitable site was a major problem, since white citizens were reluctant to have a Negro school near their homes because it was perceived as being harmful to property values. Predictably, white citizens of the original site selected—Anchorage, a suburb of Louisville in Jefferson County—objected so strongly that the Berea board dropped it from consideration. The next site selected was Simpsonville, located in Shelby County. Simpsonville had been established in 1816 and was named for a fallen hero. Captain John Simpson, a prominent lawyer from Shelbyville, had volunteered to serve in the War of 1812 and was killed at the Battle of the River Raisin in Michigan in 1813. Captain Simpson's namesake town grew, becoming the first big stagecoach stop between Shelbyville and Louisville after the stage came through in 1825.[18]

The Berea board saw many practical advantages in Simpsonville. It was only twenty-two miles east of Louisville, the center of the state's black population, but its rural location was remote enough to avoid aggravating large numbers of whites. The new Louisville and Shelbyville interurban trolley ran through the northern edge of the property near the Bloomfield branch of the Louisville & Nashville Railroad. The station at Lincoln Ridge, located at the bottom of the hill near the proposed campus, accommodated both train and trolley passengers.[19]

Access to the school by rail and trolley was fortunate, since the closest main road was little more than an unpaved buffalo trail with the unwieldy name of the Louisville-Shelbyville-Lexington Pike. As the motorcar's popularity grew, driving enthusiasts formed clubs that agitated for better roads. Many privately organized trail associations adopted existing roads and named them after famous patriots or landmarks. In 1913 the Louisville-Shelbyville-

Lexington Pike became part of the Midland Trail that ran from Washington, DC, to Los Angeles, one of the first marked transcontinental auto trails in America. Lincoln Institute was located on the Midland Trail, which became part of US Route 60 on November 11, 1926, when the new federal numbered highway system was introduced to the public.[20]

Simpsonville was not only geographically convenient for the school but also historically significant for African Americans. In January 1865 twenty-two members of Company E of the Fifth US Colored Cavalry were massacred by Confederate guerrillas just a few hundred yards from what would become the entrance to the new school. The troops, nearly all of them former slaves, had been taking a herd of 900 cattle to the Louisville slaughter-houses when a group of fifteen Confederate guerrillas ambushed the lightly armed soldiers. Their white captain was reportedly in Simpsonville, buying new boots, when the rebels attacked.

Ironically, the same soldiers had survived the October 1864 Battle of Saltville, Virginia, and its aftermath. About fifty black Union cavalrymen, wounded in the previous day's fighting, were slaughtered in their beds. Confederate Brigadier General Felix H. Robertson had bragged to another officer that they "had killed nearly all the Negroes" and was accused of participating in the massacre himself. When General Robert E. Lee learned of the atrocity, he ordered Robertson to stand trial, but blame was diverted to a subordinate, guerrilla leader Champ Ferguson, who was hanged.[21]

The Fifth Cavalry's survivors returned to Camp Nelson, where Berea College's founder, John G. Fee, was ministering to African American soldiers. After Saltville, the assignment of herding cattle surely sounded benign to the colored troops, until they too were attacked and murdered. The incident must have lingered in the memories of the older residents of Simpsonville, even as an African American school was being constructed near the site. The skirmish was largely forgotten until it was rediscovered in 2007 by a local historian.[22]

The Berea trustees launched a massive fund-raising effort with a goal of $400,00 to buy land near Simpsonville on which to build the institution. Andrew Carnegie, one of the richest men in the world, was approached for a donation, but instead of a check he gave the trustees a challenge. He would give them $200,000, but only as a matching grant after the trustees had raised the first $200,000. Berea president William Goodell Frost approached other donors, both large and small, and eventually reached his goal. "Givers of a national feeling," which included Carnegie, had pledged $350,000, while the other $50,000 had been raised from "about four thousand colored persons and about nine hundred white persons." Frost noted that the first $400,000 would be directed "for the endowment and permanent buildings," and additional funds would still be required for "furnishings and other necessary expenses."[23]

On April 26, 1909, the Berea board bought a combination of farms and other parcels from the Goodknight, Byars, Pace, and Blackaby families, totaling slightly more than 444 acres, for $44,331. The school would be called the Lincoln Institute in honor of Kentucky native Abraham Lincoln, the sixteenth president of the United States, who had emancipated the Negro.[24]

Whites in Shelby County were no more pleased by the idea of having a Negro school in their community than the citizens of Anchorage had been. Although a "colored" elementary and high school had operated in Shelbyville, whites in Shelby County were "very much aroused" by the news that a school for Negroes would be built near Simpsonville. Shortly after the purchase of property for the Lincoln Institute was revealed, white citizens in Simpsonville convened at the Masonic hall to express their outrage. They voted unanimously to use all legal means available to prevent the school from being built. A letter-writing volley ensued in the newspapers, with writers claiming that the new school would turn Shelbyville into another Brownsville, Texas, where a unit of buffalo soldiers had been falsely accused of murdering a white bartender, prompting violence between the soldiers and a mob of angry whites.[25]

The Berea trustees heard the criticism but decided to fight. President Frost enlisted citizens of Berea to write to the Shelby County newspapers, assuring their readers that the school would not degrade their community nor affect property values. He also offered to send a group of Shelbyville residents to Tuskegee Institute, at Berea's expense, to see for themselves that racial harmony could exist.[26]

Shelbyville legislator John Holland cast his lot with the resisting faction and introduced a bill that would make it mandatory for three-fourths of a county's voters to approve the location of any new school. Holland's bill passed the legislature on March 14, 1910, over the veto of Governor Augustus E. Willson. This sparked much opinion from both sides around the state. The *Hopkinsville Kentuckian* editorialized: "The Lincoln Institute has been unfortunately located in the wrong place. The white race doesn't want to surrender Shelby county." The *Lexington Herald* offered a more progressive view in an editorial headlined "A Bad Bill": "It does not seem to be within the range of possibility that the Legislature will put upon the statute books an act . . . to discourage and probably prevent the establishment of industrial and agricultural schools for white children. Surely, the Legislature will do nothing to hamper or hinder the development of the Lincoln Institute along lines modeled after Hampton and Tuskegee."[27]

The bill's legality was tested when the Columbia Trust Company, which held the donated funds for the Lincoln Institute project, asked a Louisville court what it should do with the collected money. On May 10, 1910, Judge Shackleford Miller Sr., in Jefferson chancery court, went beyond the trust company's intention and ruled that the Holland bill was unconstitutional. Miller, who would become chief justice of the Kentucky Court of Appeals, the state's highest court, declared that the legislature had exceeded its power, calling the bill "class legislation of the most pronounced character." The judge added that the requirement of local approval made it "doubtful if this school could be conducted in any desirable location in the state."[28]

The *Shelby Sentinel* celebrated the decision in an editorial two weeks later. The newspaper cited a disturbing decline in the county's Negro population, which was a dressed-up reference to the loss of the unskilled labor force required in an agricultural community. The *Sentinel* cited a school census report noting that in the previous five years, the number of Negro children in the county had declined by 346, a drop of 22.5 percent, while the population of white children over the same period had increased by 126, or 3.6 percent. The *Sentinel* suggested that improved educational facilities such as those provided by the Lincoln Institute would discourage black families from leaving the county to seek opportunities elsewhere. It urged the citizens of Shelby to "temper bigotry and prejudice from time to time with a little common and business sense. It would help to remove the millstone about our necks that is keeping us in the back-number class."[29]

The Reverend A. Eugene Thomson, a member of the Berea board, echoed the sentiment in a letter to the *Lexington Herald* in which he connected the flight of blacks from Kentucky to its weak educational system. Thomson said improved educational facilities, such as those provided by Lincoln, would stem the black exodus from Kentucky, which he claimed amounted to 23,000 in the first decade of the twentieth century, the most of any southern state.[30]

Despite objections from local residents, Shelby County had been an area of opportunity for African American families since before the Civil War. A "colony of free men" had been established at Hickory Run, just east of Simpsonville, in 1853. After the war, five lots totaling fifty-two acres had been sold to free Negroes. Subsequent subdivisions and sales of the lots occurred until the end of the nineteenth century, and the community, called Montclair, remains predominantly African American in the twenty-first century.[31]

The Berea trustees displayed great foresight by retaining the services of the Olmsted Brothers of Brookline, Massachusetts, to plan the layout of the school's buildings. Brothers John Charles and Frederick Jr. were sons of the prominent landscape architect Frederick Law Olmsted, who designed New York City's Central Park (1873), the Columbian World Exposition in Chicago (1893), and the grounds of the Biltmore estate in Asheville, North Carolina (1895). The brothers were asked to prepare a campus plan so that eventual expansion would not be impeded by poorly placed structures. The board also wanted the buildings to be a testimony to the ability of Negro architects, and they hired two: G. W. Foster, who had been employed by a prominent New York firm for twenty years, and W. V. Tandy, a graduate of Cornell. They generously returned 1 percent of their commission to Lincoln Institute as a donation.

A Louisville contractor initially won the bid to construct the Lincoln Institute, but he soon backed out, fearing violence by disgruntled whites. Lynn Gruber, a local builder who had been elected mayor of Shelbyville, expressed interest and was awarded the contract. The buildings were con-structed of brick and stone and were fitted with lights, water, heat, and sewer systems. The cost of the land and construction exceeded $250,000, which was $100,000 over budget. Another $50,000 was raised, and the remainder was borrowed. Gruber supervised the project through its completion, but he died of colitis compounded by pneumonia one month after Lincoln opened its doors.[32]

As construction progressed, racial animosity bubbled to the surface once again. Two black men, Jim West and Wade Patterson, had been jailed, accused of "detaining" a fourteen-year-old white girl. At around 2:00 a.m. on January 15, 1911, at least fifty masked men entered Shelbyville, turned off the electric power, cut the telephone wires, and proceeded to batter down the door to the jail. The jailer offered no resistance, but one of the deputies seized the keys to the cells and hid in a closet at the rear of the building. The mob spent an hour breaking the lock to the cell that held West and Patterson as well as six other blacks accused of various offenses.[33]

In addition to West and Patterson, the mob grabbed Eugene Mar-shall, who had been convicted of killing an elderly black woman. The three black men were taken to the Chesapeake & Ohio Railroad bridge over Clear Creek, the same spot where two other blacks had been hung in 1901. The mob tied ropes around the necks of the three men and threw them off the bridge, but the rope holding Patterson broke, and he fell into the water. Pat-terson frantically tried to escape, but members of the mob jumped into the water and chased him. Patterson's body was found riddled with bullets at the Seventh Street bridge, some 300 yards from the Chesapeake & Ohio bridge. Marshall strangled to death, but West, who had been left dangling, somehow managed to untie his hands and remove his head from the noose; he fell into the creek and escaped.[34]

White law officers searched for West, and the Shelby County judge offered a $200 reward for his return. However, Republican governor Will-son, an outspoken foe of lynchings, angered the white citizens of Shelby County by offering $500 for the arrest and conviction of each member of the lynch mob. Ultimately, no one collected on either reward. The Shelby County grand jury investigating the crimes refused to indict any members of the mob, and West's whereabouts remained unknown for years. West enlisted in the US Army and fought in the Great War. When his body was returned to Shelbyville for burial in 1922, he was treated as a hero by the African American community.[35]

3

A Young Man of Substance

From the very beginning of the effort to locate this institution we were confident that the community in which it was located would not only derive large benefits from its location but would in time take pride in aiding the splendid work it is founded to do, and help to make it a greater benefit to the State. We were, therefore, delighted to hear of the change of sentiment that had taken place in Shelby county even before Lincoln Institute has opened its doors for students.

—Editorial, *Lexington Herald,* July 28, 1912

Most of the opposition to Lincoln Institute had abated by September 1911, when a party of about twenty-five Negroes led by the Reverend James M. Bond traveled to Simpsonville to check the progress of the project. Born a slave in Lawrenceburg, Kentucky, during the Civil War, Bond was a worthy representative of Berea College's interests, and not only because he had assisted President Frost in fund-raising efforts. Bond's mother and his parson father had sent him to Berea College, paying his tuition fees with a calf. He graduated in May 1892 with a bachelor of science degree and then went to Oberlin Seminary, where he received his divinity degree. Reverend Bond is noteworthy in modern times as the grandfather of civil rights leader and former Georgia representative and senator Julian Bond.[1]

"A city is being built," Bond happily reported, although a small group of black intellectuals remained opposed to the industrial training philosophy the board had adopted. J. Sohmers Young, editor of the *Kentucky Standard,* a Negro weekly published in Louisville, said such training would set the Negro back and lower expectations. He appealed to his readers and told them that other subjects must be emphasized at Lincoln Institute, lest the

The agriculture students in Lincoln Institute's first class pose for a class photo in 1912. (Courtesy of Center of Excellence for the Study of Kentucky African-Americans, Kentucky State University)

Negro be educated "as hewers of wood and drawers of water" for the more favored race.[2]

But the board was persuaded by Booker T. Washington's argument that southern whites would accept the concept of industrial training for blacks more readily than education that emphasized humanities, mathematics, and science. Washington's characterization of the potential opposition made it easier for Frost and others to convince white Kentuckians of the necessity of this type of education. The board designed the courses and programs accordingly. Adherents of W. E. B. DuBois thought this approach was detrimental and kept blacks at the bottom of the economic ladder, but the Lincoln board determined that an acceptable starting point would build a foundation for other types of education.[3]

Male students were offered vocational training in agriculture, steam and maintenance engineering, business administration, and industrial arts. A full dairy was constructed, and the milking of cows and the growing of feed crops formed the basis of an education in modern agricultural tech-

A model rural home allowed female students to gain experience preparing meals, interior decorating, making clothes, and caring for a baby. Girls could also take a training course that allowed them to enroll in nursing school or find employment in a hospital. (Archives and Special Collections, University of Louisville)

niques. The Berea board, however, would not allow the raising of tobacco, Kentucky's chief crop, because students were prohibited from using tobacco. Reverend Thomson, the Berea board member who had been instrumental in efforts to open Lincoln Institute, explained that future farmers should be taught "the diversification and rotations of crops, rather than dependence on one crop, however profitable that may be."[4]

For female students, a course in home economics was essential. A model rural home was erected, where the girls could practice planning a budget, preparing meals, interior decorating, making clothes, and caring for a baby. Girls were not confined to domestic training, however; a pre-nurse training course was offered that would allow graduates to enroll in a nurses' training school or perhaps find employment in a hospital.

Reverend Thomson was appointed Lincoln Institute's first president

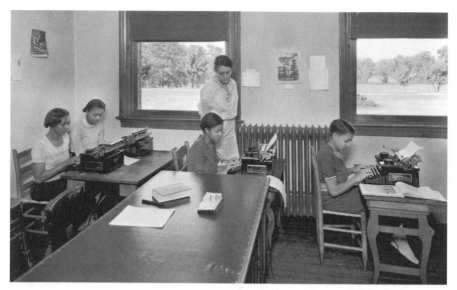

This typing class from 1932 was typical of Lincoln Institute's goal of training its students to take advantage of employment opportunities and become useful members of society. (Archives and Special Collections, University of Louisville)

In the early years, Lincoln Institute's faculty was evenly divided among black and white teachers. In this 1927 photo, Whitney Young is seated at the far left on the bottom row, two seats from A. Eugene Thomson, Lincoln's first principal and the man who hired Young. (Shelby County Public Library)

and set about hiring a faculty of dedicated teachers, white and black, who believed in the goals and aims of the institution. Seven of the first fifteen instructors came from Berea College, and another handful came from Tuskegee Institute.

Word traveled rapidly within the African American community, and hundreds of students applied to Lincoln Institute, although only eighty-five would be admitted in the first class. The charter of incorporation specified that applicants had to present certificates from responsible individuals attesting to their high moral character. The board decided against offering any form of financial aid, hoping to create a spirit of independence and self-reliance among a community of students who were willing to work. Tuition was established at $17 per month; students paid what they could and worked off the rest through on-campus jobs. In addition, all students were required to work one hour without pay to contribute to the upkeep of the school. The founders' ties to religion were evident when the board decided that the school would be religious in nature but not specific to one denomination. Students were required to attend church on Sunday and midweek prayer meetings.[5]

"While a great many details of preparation are still incomplete, along main lines the institute will be ready for business," the *Lexington Herald* reported a day before the opening on October 1, 1912. "A picked company of the finest young people from all over the state is gathering." Students and teachers were asked to report a week early to help clean the buildings and put the grounds in pristine condition. The *Herald* also noted, in what would become a recurring theme with various interpretations: "The institute is in need of at least a hundred thousand dollars with which to pay the debt which has necessarily been incurred for building and equipment, and to provide for needed enlargement."[6]

The remainder of the money could not be raised immediately, so Lincoln had to borrow it. The inability to satisfy that debt quickly led to more debt, a problem that was never entirely resolved. By 1920, the debt had grown to $83,950, according to Reverend Thomson, whose job of educating young people was nearly rivaled by the constant effort to raise money. He obtained another matching grant of $20,000 from the Carnegie Foundation in 1922,

This rare photo shows Lincoln Institute's first class of students when it opened in October 1912. Whitney Young is in the top row, and his future wife, Laura Ray, is in the third row on the left (denoted by *x*'s). (Courtesy of Center of Excellence for the Study of Kentucky African-Americans, Kentucky State University)

after raising the necessary funds to trigger the grant. Thomson's frequent letters to supporters and local newspapers carried positive news of completed courses and recent graduates, but they were always tempered with pleas for donations. Additional funds were necessary, Thomson wrote, because "our visible field of resources is about covered."[7]

Throughout the 1920s, Thomson was closely watched by a young man he had hired as a teacher in 1920: Whitney Moore Young. Born at Payne's Depot in Shelby County on September 26, 1897, to Taylor and Annie Young, he had attended Zion Public School, Mayo-Underwood School in Frankfort, and Chandler Normal School in Lexington. When Lincoln opened its doors in 1912, a white teacher at Chandler Normal, recognizing Young as a young man of substance, encouraged him to apply to this new school for colored boys and girls. Young was one of the first students to enroll, carrying a sack

Students studying agriculture could learn advanced livestock and crop growing techniques on Lincoln's model farm, which took up much of the school's 444 acres. (Archives and Special Collections, University of Louisville)

that held all his worldly belongings other than the one pair of trousers, shirt, and pair of shoes he wore.[8]

Young excelled in his studies, particularly math and the building trades, but the early years at Lincoln Institute were not always peaceful for either students or faculty. Some white neighbors still did not like the idea of having a black school in their county, and frequent threats compelled the male students to sleep with guns under their pillows just in case trouble erupted.

During his student years at Lincoln, the enterprising Young made extra money working on the institution's farm. Milking cows and feeding chickens not only helped pay his expenses; it also presented him with an unlikely advantage in the romance department. Young developed an attraction to Laura Ray, a female student from Lebanon, Kentucky, who loved fresh butter. One of the farmhand's regular duties was to churn butter for the institution's larder, and he made certain that Miss Ray got her share.

Whitney Young returned to Lincoln Institute as the engineering teacher. Here, he is shown (in the light suit) instructing students in an automotive maintenance class. (Archives and Special Collections, University of Louisville)

The courtship between Whitney and Laura became a long-distance affair in 1916, after Young became one of Lincoln's first twelve graduates. He moved to Detroit, Michigan, to work as an engineer for the Detroit United Railway. When America entered the Great War, he enlisted in the US Army and served in France for thirteen months. Young returned to Detroit after the armistice and, with a secure future ahead of him, persuaded Laura Ray to marry him. In 1920 the Youngs welcomed a baby girl they named Arnita.[9]

Later that year, Thomson contacted Young and asked him to return to Lincoln Institute as a teacher. The pay was much less than what Young was making in Detroit, but the challenge and the opportunity to return to Kentucky were compensation enough. Young resigned from Detroit United Railway and returned to Lincoln, where he headed the engineering department at a salary of $68 a month.[10]

After the Youngs' return to Kentucky, two more children followed in quick succession. Son Whitney Jr. was born on July 31, 1921, and daughter Eleanor was born on October 10, 1922. Raising a family on a teacher's pay was difficult enough for the Youngs, and it did not help that Shelby County still contained elements of racial animosity.

The Ku Klux Klan was experiencing a resurgence in the South during the 1920s, although Kentucky officials gave all indications that prejudice toward blacks, Jews, and Catholics would not be tolerated. In 1921 George Weissinger, the mayor of Louisville, responded to increased Klan activity by declaring, "As long as I am mayor of Louisville, there will be no Ku Klux Klan here." Authorities in Lexington shared his view, arresting a speaker representing the Klan in 1923 and fining him $200 for attempting to incite a riot.[11]

But the authorities could not punish every incident of racial intolerance, such as one involving the Young family when they went to Shelbyville to see a movie. Five-year-old Whitney Jr. couldn't wait to get a seat down front, and he rushed past his parents as they bought tickets. Suddenly he was grabbed by an usher, who informed him, "You know where you're supposed to be, boy? You're supposed to be in nigger heaven!" The white usher escorted the family to stairs marked "For Colored Only" and directed them to the segregated balcony, where patrons of color were required to crowd together in a tiny section filled with wooden chairs. Whitney Jr. later told the story as his first experience with discrimination.[12]

In those and later years, an occasional cross was burned within sight of Lincoln Institute, and once again, Young sometimes slept with a pistol under his pillow. But despite the war that raged outside its boundaries, Lincoln Institute was largely insulated from overt acts of discrimination or violence. It was a more subtle racism, based on "the way things have always been," that reminded African Americans they were on less than equal footing with white society. Signs above water fountains and outside restrooms designated which race could use the facilities, and on trips to Louisville, the Young family could eat meals only in the West End, the black section of town.[13]

Segregation was a fact of life. No matter how many times Laura Young disregarded "White Only" signs, her defiance failed to protect her children from other more egregious examples of American apartheid. The children were enrolled in a segregated elementary school in Simpsonville called the Lincoln Model School, a facility maintained for the town's black students. In addition to being subjected to racial slurs on their way to school, the Young children saw the white townspeople struggle to call their father Professor or Reverend, but never Mister.

Whitney and Laura Young tried to shield their children from the worst aspects of Jim Crow. They joined with other members of Kentucky's small black elite and promoted social interaction among their children. The Young family often attended social events in Louisville and reciprocated with invitations to parties at Lincoln Institute. The Young children mingled with the Wilson sisters, whose father was the principal of Louisville's Central High School. They also socialized with Alice Clement, the daughter of Rufus E. Clement, who had earned a PhD from Northwestern University and was the dean of Louisville Municipal College. Charlotte Smith, whose father was an executive in a black-owned insurance company, was another member of this small circle of friends. As long as they "knew their place" in an inhospitable environment, life for African American families in Kentucky was tolerable.[14]

4

Organizing Athletics

Here in Greater New York and New Jersey, basketball has meant more to us than baseball, for the latter sport among colored people has been so closely allied to the saloon and underground dives, whereas basketball is fostered by religious and other institutions working for the uplift of our people.
—Romeo Dougherty, *Amsterdam News,* 1921

Early American educators supported the proverb that a healthy body and a healthy mind are complementary, but from the beginning, it was basketball that bubbled the blood of students and faculty at Lincoln Institute. The sport was barely two decades old when Lincoln opened in 1912, but it had already achieved great popularity among young Americans of all races.

The *Indianapolis Freeman,* an early watchdog of racial inequity, often carried items about basketball, including a 1907 piece headlined "Colored Basketball Teams in Big Contest." It didn't matter that the games were played in New York City, more than 700 miles away; what mattered was that four teams of black players met in two games that featured a "complete disregard for the 1907–08 rules." Of particular note to the reporter was the fact that the St. Christopher Club of New York, based at St. Philip's Episcopal Church, had recruited an early ringer for the games, a "big center, Bradford, who . . . was imported the night previous from Hampton, Va., and brings with him the laurels of an all-around Southern athlete." The account reminded the modern observer that the elements of a spirited match had not changed a great deal, down to the comment that the officials "did good work, considering the crookedness of some of the players."[1]

Despite the sport's popularity, fewer than twenty black high schools in

Kentucky sponsored basketball teams that competed against one another as of the mid-1920s. Adequate athletic facilities were in short supply for black schools, reflecting anemic support in general from state and local governments. Most schools were impoverished and small, without gymnasiums, athletic fields, or equipment. At many schools, basketball was played on an outdoor court with a dirt or gravel surface. Lincoln had no gymnasium, but at least its team practiced indoors, in a large room over the power plant.[2]

Scant information on Lincoln's early teams exists. The records that survive barely mention athletics, and neither of the Shelby County newspapers, the *Shelby News* and the *Shelby Sentinel,* covered any events at Lincoln Institute until the late 1950s. Lincoln basketball or football games were mentioned by the press only if their opponents were teams from around Lexington, which the *Herald* covered in a section titled "Colored News Notes." Although only a handful of schools could support football teams, the first published report of a Lincoln Institute athletic event was a three-line note in the February 28, 1921, edition of the *Lexington Herald,* which informed readers that "Chancellor Normal football defeated Lincoln Institute here Saturday by a score of 7 to 0."[3]

Growth in interscholastic sports at African American schools came with the conversion of black high schools from two-year to four-year programs in the late 1920s. By then, more than fifty such schools in Kentucky were engaged in sports competition. This increase in numbers paralleled the growth in support for the education of blacks, which resulted in the founding of many new high schools, higher enrollments, and improved facilities. Considerable support came from northern philanthropists such as Julius Rosenwald, the head of Sears, Roebuck. Rosenwald contributed to the construction of 5,300 schools, shops, and teachers' homes in southern states during the 1920s. His funding formula demanded that local blacks contribute 17 percent of the cost, and he persuaded local white officials to provide 64 percent from public funds. At least five Kentucky high schools serving an African American population were named after the famed philanthropist.[4]

As Louis Stout wrote in his seminal book on the history of black high school basketball in Kentucky, "Despite ever-increasing hardships, athletic programs began to grow and flourish. Communities throughout Kentucky took enormous pride in the athletic accomplishments of their local teams. Better coaches were brought in, which translated into better athletics, better teams and more excitement."[5]

It was during this burst of opportunity that African American high schools began to organize for competition, creating regional leagues. The structure emulated the formation of the Kentucky High School Athletic Association in 1917 for segregated white schools. In 1922 principals of African American high schools in central Kentucky formed the Blue Grass Athletic League, whose inaugural weekend featured games between Lexington Russell High School and Versailles Simmons, Frankfort Mayo-Underwood versus Lawrenceburg, and Winchester Oliver versus Richmond High School.[6]

Lincoln Institute joined the association, which also included Nicholasville Rosenwald, Paris Western, and Lexington Dunbar. Many other schools across the commonwealth organized district and regional committees to devise regulations on athlete participation and game rules, primarily for football and basketball. Each state section governed schools in its area, and the differing rules and varying levels of enforcement produced inconsistency and competitive inequities. The desire to standardize rules and equalize competition demanded a broader, statewide structure.[7]

Northern states and some border states were far more advanced by that time, having organized much earlier than Kentucky. Black prominence in Chicago high school athletics dates back to the turn of the twentieth century. In 1901 the first Cook County League basketball champion, Hyde Park, featured an outstanding black athlete, Sam Ranson, who also led his teams to football and baseball titles. In 1906 black educators in the District of Columbia formed the Inter-Scholastic Athletic Association of the Middle States to bring together African American schools. The league's founder, Edwin Bancroft Henderson, believed the broader organization would provide training and opportunity for black high school students, allowing them to break down barriers of segregation through their athletic achievements. In 1910 Henderson expanded his idea and formed the Public Schools Athletic League in Washington, modeled after a similarly named association in New York.[8]

With the advent of World War I, Chicago and many other northern cit-

The Lexington Dunbar Bearcats won the Bluegrass League basketball title in 1932–1933 and 1933–1934. Coach F. L. Baker is standing on the top row at the left. (Courtesy of Kentucky High School Athletic Association)

ies experienced a great migration of blacks from the rural, segregated South to take advantage of job opportunities opened up by the war boom. Phillips High School dominated the Chicago school league and commonly played white teams, although racial tension and outbreaks were frequent. Prior to the playoffs in 1925, league authorities forced the school to withdraw its team from competition, and Phillips became one of the first high school barnstorming teams. Armstrong High School of Washington, DC, traveled to Chicago to play Phillips in a game that drew 4,500 fans to the Eighth Regiment Armory. The crowd included the integrated elite of Chicago society and business, seated in the fifty-five box seats.[9]

The Phillips football team also played white schools during the season, but it was prohibited from participating in postseason tournaments. So the school turned to black opponents in nearby states, which created another tradition. In 1925 Phillips began a Thanksgiving Day rivalry against Louisville Central; the following year it returned to play Central on Thanksgiving and Owensboro Western two days later.

Missouri and Kansas were border states with a history of segregated schools, but they were comparatively more enlightened in terms of race relations. Black schools in those states received sufficient support from the governing agencies and even competed against white high school teams on occasion. In 1918 the Mississippi Valley Interscholastic Athletic Association was founded in the metropolitan St. Louis area to provide athletic competition among segregated schools. Black schools in Illinois and Indiana, the only northern states where school segregation was legal, formed separate state organizations in 1919 and 1920, respectively. Another major athletic association of black high schools arose in 1925 with the West Virginia Colored High School Athletic Union. The league was launched with a basketball tournament that drew eleven of the state's twenty-four black high schools; participation increased to seventeen schools by 1927 and twenty-two by 1930.[10]

Whitney Young was instrumental in efforts to organize Kentucky's African American schools into a statewide association. In 1929 Young joined Henry Arthur Kean, the football coach at Louisville Central, in proposing the Kentucky Colored State High School Athletic Association to the Kentucky Negro Educational Association (KNEA).[11] The association's members, who were primarily school principals and teachers, fully endorsed the value of athletic competition. In an article that appeared in the April 1931 issue of the KNEA's journal, H. S. Wilson of Louisville (who was not further identified) wrote that athletics was "a savior of young boys, who would drop out of school if athletics did not exist." Wilson painted athletics as a necessary aspect of education, avowing that "no better means could have been devised to stimulate education among the youth, and with their development along cultural and athletic lines, a better citizenry will be in the making and hence a better means of attacking world problems sanely."[12]

Their initial effort to organize athletics did not generate sufficient support, but Young and Kean persuaded the KNEA to establish two coach-

Whitney Young (left, wearing a sweater) was Lincoln's football coach before he became its principal. His 1930 team ran up 198 points against 87 for its opponents and defeated such rivals as Lexington Dunbar and Danville Bate. (Courtesy of Bernard Minnis Sr.)

ing schools, one in Frankfort and one in Paducah, to improve the quality of coaching in boys' and girls' basketball and boys' football. As the KNEA's vice president for athletics, Kean was given the task of operating the schools, but he admitted the idea had come "from the fertile mind of Whitney Young at Lincoln Institute."[13]

Young had the ear of the state's coaches, having served as Lincoln Institute's de facto athletic director and coach of the football and basketball teams from the late 1920s through 1931. His reputation as a coach was summarized in an article that praised Lincoln's 1930 team, which "ran up 198 points against 87 [points] of their opponents" and defeated such schools as Lexington Dunbar and Danville. "Although all of this certainly reflects

Lincoln also sponsored a track team in its early years. This is the 1931 team. Standing in the back row from left to right: William Stone, Dewey Allen, Charles Payne, James Griffin, Eugene Thomas, and James Miles. Middle row: Clay Grey and John Douglas. Front row: Edward Foster, John Dupree Jr., and Clifford Whiteside. (Shelby County Public Library)

favorably upon the brand of coaching Young is noted for," the article noted, "much credit, he states, should be given to the outstanding play of Sharp, left half; Guy, fullback; Miles, quarterback; Trigg, left tackle and Thomas, right half." The article also reflected Young's persistence in promoting athletics. "All schools should make a special effort to have better equipped players, and thereby give more encouragement to players and add color to the game," Young advised.[14]

In 1931 another organizing effort was undertaken by T. Max Bond of Louisville, editor of the KNEA's *Athletic Voice*. Bond had helped form regional associations in western Kentucky and the upper Cumberland region and now proposed to join all these loosely organized groups under the banner of the Kentucky Negro Athletic Association. The stated purpose of the new organization would be to coordinate football and basketball and to promote intersectional games, but it would not affect the integrity of the existing associations. Others, including Young and Kean, believed the best approach was one organization with the power to establish rules, enforce discipline, improve coaching skills, and create and administer championships.[15]

The efforts of Young, Kean, and others bore fruit in 1932 when leading African American educators in the state formed the Kentucky High School Athletic League (KHSAL). The stated purpose of the league, in accordance with Young's sentiments, was "to encourage clean athletic participation and to stimulate the expansion of health and physical education in the black high schools throughout Kentucky." A chief executive officer ran the league's day-to-day operations, and a Board of Control, consisting of coaches and school principals, would determine rules and regulations for eligibility and competition.

Kean, who had recently left Louisville Central to become the head coach at Kentucky State Industrial College, was elected KHSAL's first executive secretary. A former artillery officer in World War I, Kean was a logical choice for the position. He was a tireless advocate for athletics and was familiar with the task from his own attempts to organize African American sports statewide. Kean, then thirty-eight years old, was five years older than his brother, William L. "Bill" Kean, who had come to Central High School in 1922 as a health and physical education teacher and coach.[16]

Henry Kean immediately advised the KHSAL member schools that the rules would be enforced. The schools had to pledge to forgo the loose regulations established by their sectional arrangements and abide by the rules and regulations of the Board of Control. Such strict governance created problems for some schools. Attracting paying customers to the football field or the basketball court was a major means of financial security for some schools, so it was not unusual for them to seek an advantage. Violations were common, particularly with regard to eligibility or age.[17]

The initial guidelines prohibited a player from participating in more than four state tournaments, although this limit was later revised to eight semesters after enrolling in grade nine. In the early days, students could participate in athletics until they reached age twenty, but this was later changed to nineteen. Some schools, unaccustomed to such strict regulations, made

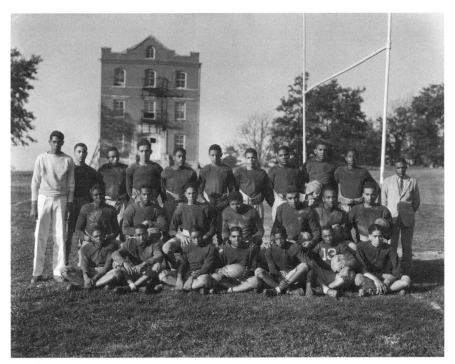

Whitney Young had given up coaching when this picture of Lincoln's 1932 football team was taken, but he was a driving force in organizing African American schools into a statewide league that year. (Archives and Special Collections, University of Louisville)

the mistake of challenging Kean. One offender was Madisonville Rosenwald, which had two players who exceeded the twenty-year age limit. Kean suspended the school from the league indefinitely, sending a message to other would-be violators.

The only state championship sponsored by the KHSAL was the annual boys' basketball tournament, although the league also regulated competition in football and track and field. The state was divided into five geographic regions for basketball: West of US 41, East of US 41, Central, Blue Grass, and Mountain-Eastern. T. Max Bond, acting president of the league, directed the first tournament in 1932 at the Kentucky State Industrial College in Frankfort. It was not surprising that the first championship was won by Louisville Central, the primary option for African American students in the state's largest city. Central had the support of the black community and its pick of athletes, which enabled Bill Kean to create a sports dynasty in basketball and football. Central became the envy of every other black school in the state and the fiercest rival of its neighbors at Lincoln Institute.[18]

5

The Faith Plan

Race prejudice in the United States is such that most Negroes cannot receive proper education in white institutions. A separate Negro school, where children are treated like human beings, trained by teachers of their own race, who know what it means to be black . . . is infinitely better than making our boys and girls doormats to be spit and trampled upon and lied to by ignorant social climbers, whose sole claim to superiority is ability to kick "niggers" when they are down.

—W. E. B. DuBois

By May 1935, Whitney Young had relinquished his coaching duties to LaMont H. Lawson, and an issue of greater importance drew his attention. Lincoln Institute's enrollment had decreased to seventy as the Great Depression reduced the number of black families who were financially able to send their children to school. Dr. A. E. Thomson had resigned in 1927 to return to the pulpit, and Lincoln had four presidents during the next eight years, creating a lack of dedicated leadership. The board sought alternatives and even voted to change the school to a junior college, but that experiment was abandoned after three years. The school was foundering in debt, and the board saw no alternative but to close Lincoln's doors. Letters were sent out to all school employees thanking them for their services and offering every assistance in helping them find new employment.[1]

At this critical juncture, Whitney Young and J. Mansir Tydings, a white financial expert from Louisville and Lincoln's business manager, believed they had a solution. The unlikely duo persuaded the board's executive committee to allow them to operate the school under an innovative, yet dangerous, plan that would free the board from all financial responsibility. The two

J. Mansir Tydings and Whitney Young stand before the student body in 1937.
Tydings, a Louisville financial expert, was Lincoln's secretary-treasurer. He and Young
worked diligently on the Faith Plan and in the effort to have the state take over the
school. (Archives and Special Collections, University of Louisville)

men devised the "Faith Plan," an intense effort to recruit new students while
paying teachers prorated salaries and promising to make them whole when
the institution regained a sound financial footing. The board agreed to let
Young and Tydings operate the school for one year, and all the employees
signed on. They divided the staff into pairs and sent them all over the state to
recruit students. The canvass resulted in 125 new applicants, which enabled
Lincoln to trim its debt to $10,000.

The recruiting campaign required hard work and dedication, but
two weeks later came an unexpected assist that Young considered purely
providential. John Henry Hughes, a prominent African American busi-
nessman from Lexington, died and left the school $10,000 cash and a
trust fund of almost $100,000. The gift wiped out Lincoln's outstanding

debt and provided hope for the future. The financial crisis was over—at least for now.[2]

Young's actions so impressed the board members that they named him principal of the school, the first African American to hold that position. With Young's leadership and Tydings's financial skills, Lincoln burnished its reputation as a center of learning for African American students. This reputation was enhanced in 1936 when it became a teacher training center for Kentucky State Industrial College, the predominantly African American school in Frankfort.

Lincoln Institute's improved financial position allowed Young to assemble an able faculty that was the equal of white schools. He continued the policy of subtle integration by hiring a few white teachers who, like their black colleagues, worked closely with the students. In 1937 he brought in several new black teachers, most of whom were graduates of black colleges. Joseph A. Carroll, a graduate of Kentucky State, taught agriculture and later chemistry and biology, and Kathleen A. McClain, an alumna of Louisville Municipal College with an MA from Indiana University, taught mathematics. Anna Howard Russell, another Kentucky State graduate with an MA from Atlanta University, became the dean of women, and Medora F. Hayes, who held a BS from Tennessee Agricultural and Industrial State College, served as librarian and taught commercial courses.[3]

Young carefully screened applicants because he wanted teachers who bought into the concept of Lincoln as a family. He wanted teachers who enjoyed teaching, who liked the interaction with students, and who would participate in student activities. To foster that feeling of camaraderie, Young often invited the teachers to his house at the edge of campus for a barbecue and croquet on his front lawn. This attitude of togetherness, of knowing that everybody cared, extended to all staff members. Young once remarked to his daughter Eleanor: "The janitor is just as important, the cook is just as important as anybody else on this campus."[4] Lincoln Institute was a family of students, teachers, and staff, all of whom cared for one another and felt a responsibility toward the school.

In this environment, the students appeared to enjoy their educational experience in the prewar years. Students could join a wide range of clubs and play myriad intramural sports. Varsity athletics was becoming increasingly important, and many of the boys participated in basketball, baseball, or foot-ball.[5] These activities fostered a sense of community, and school spirit was an attractive commodity. In 1933 Willie Belle Williams, a music student, wrote "Dear Old Lincoln," which became the official school song:

> Here's to our dear old Lincoln,
> So loyal and so true,
> A school above all other schools,
> We can depend on you,
> Rah! Rah! Rah!
> You'll hold first place in all our hearts,
> In all our mem'ries too,
> Where'er we go, the heights we reach,
> Will be because of you.[6]

Students wrote and edited a periodical called the *Lincoln Log,* which covered campus news, student activities, and sporting events. Under the heading "Student School Spirit," the 1936–1937 edition reported fund-rais-ing activities that collected $15 to purchase dishes for the boarding hall, $24 to send the school's outstanding basketball team to the Southern Tourna-ment, $50 to build a section of concrete walk for the campus, and $30 to purchase 100 new hymnals for the institute's church. The *Log* also reported that, as a farewell gift, the class of 1937 gave a section of sidewalk in front of Berea Hall, the main building on campus.[7]

The devastating Ohio River floods that inundated parts of Louisville in January and February 1937 also rallied the Lincoln students. They raised $75 for the "flood sufferers" and provided temporary housing to "130 Negro flood refugees from Louisville, furnished food, warmth and shelter for a six weeks period." Another entry in the *Log* provided a glimpse of campus life, particularly the students' ability to work at jobs around the school to help pay for their education:

> Last Wednesday at prayer meeting, a Senior arose to say goodbye to his
> friends at Lincoln Institute. He told of how he had been at Lincoln for

The 1937 flood that devastated parts of downtown Louisville prompted Lincoln students to collect money for those left homeless and to house many of them in the school's dormitories. (Archives and Special Collections, University of Louisville)

four years and never paid one cent toward his maintenance in all that time, but had worked his way through school. In his senior year alone, he had taken the Poultry project on the student Farm and raised from 300 baby chicks 134 cockerels which he sold as fryers, and his hens produced 800 dozen eggs which he sold on the campus. Before the school year was over he had earned enough to pay all of his expenses and turned over to another boy 103 hens which are still laying eggs.[8]

The Tigers basketball team under coach LaMont H. Lawson became a state power in the early years of the Kentucky High School Athletic League (KHSAL), winning back-to-back state championships in 1937 and 1938. Typically, both the *Shelby Sentinel* and the *Shelby News* ignored these Lincoln titles, although front-page stories detailed results from the Kentucky

Dr. Young and his wife Laura fostered a family atmosphere by inviting students and faculty members to their home on campus for get-togethers or games of croquet on the lawn. (Courtesy of Center of Excellence for the Study of Kentucky African-Americans, Kentucky State University)

High School Athletic Association tournament in both years, despite the absence of Shelbyville High School, or any of the county's eight schools, in that tournament.[9]

The *Lexington Herald* covered the 1937 KHSAL district tournament, but well after the fact, and probably only because it had been played at Lexington Dunbar High School. The story noted that "trophies were awarded Lincoln, Dunbar and Paris for first, second and third" and that the top two finishers, Lincoln and Dunbar, were eligible for the state tournament, which opened the following Thursday at Kentucky State College in Frankfort.[10]

The *State Journal* of Frankfort memorialized "the sixth annual tournament of the Kentucky High School (Negro) Athletic League" with a short article on March 10, 1937. The story gave the scores of the first two rounds of the sixteen-team tournament, including Lincoln's victories—a 33–17 romp over Henderson Douglass, and a 37–18 thrashing of Winchester Oliver. Lincoln's opponent in the finals, Danville Bate, had taken a similar road to the title game, rolling over Bowling Green High Street, 46–35, in the opener before dispatching local favorite Frankfort Mayo-Underwood, 35–31, in the quarterfinals.[11]

The *Louisville Courier-Journal* picked up a wire story on the two sessions of the final day, reporting that Lincoln defeated district runner-up Dunbar by a score of 25–20, while Danville Bate whipped Harrodsburg 28–18. The Lincoln Tigers left no doubt as to their supremacy, defeating Danville Bate 33–16 for the title.[12]

The *Lincoln Log* took great pride in the achievement, which included the team's right to participate in the national Negro tournament at Tuskegee, Alabama (an annual event that began in 1935 and lasted until 1941, when travel restrictions during World War II intervened). The *Log* featured a photograph of the team, showing the five starters seated in uniform (including their horizontal striped kneesocks), arms crossed on their knees. Behind them stood four others in warm-up jackets, another wearing an "L" sweater, and Coach Lawson in suit and tie. The group was surrounded by trophies, apparently won during their championship season. The *Log* reported:

A sound body is a prerequisite to a sound mind. Through athletics Lincoln Institute seeks to provide that prerequisite. Last year, our basket ball team went to the semifinals in the State Tournament. This year they won the State Tournament as well as the Bluegrass Regional Tournament. In March a fund was raised by local and Louisville merchants to send the boys to the Southern Tournament at Tuskegee, Alabama. The boys won third place, being defeated in the semifinals by the Avery, South Carolina, team which won the championship. Out of 25 games played during the season, Lincoln Institute won 22.[13]

Even more illuminating was an editorial comment that described the hurdles Lincoln Institute and other African American schools of the day had to overcome to achieve their place: "The work of the team is more surprising

Seniors in the class of 1937 gather around the flagpole at their graduation ceremony. (Archives and Special Collections, University of Louisville)

when you consider that Lincoln Institute is without a gymnasium and all the practicing was done in a room over the Power Plant. With 250 boys and girls living throughout the winter at Lincoln Institute, there is quite a problem in providing recreation for them. Some day we are going to find a friend who will give us the $25,000 needed to build and equip a gymnasium."[14]

Lincoln repeated its state championship the following year "before a crowd that filled all available space in the Kentucky State Industrial College gymnasium," according to the *Frankfort State Journal*. This time, Frankfort Mayo-Underwood was the victim, falling to the experienced Tigers 27–21 in the championship game. As the *State Journal* reported: "The game was nip-and-tuck until late in the final quarter, but in the final few minutes Lincoln, led by forward John Henry 'Jackie' Love and guard George Beauchamp, forged ahead and won going away. For the Frankfort team, Coleman and Parker were outstanding, although a stout defense by Lincoln held the big center somewhat in check." The All-Tournament team was led by Love and Beauchamp, while Aaron Lewis, another Lincoln forward, was voted to the second team. Whitney Young Jr. and Earnest Stone of Ballard County were the only seniors on the team.[15]

Coach Lawson continued his tradition of high-quality basketball in the early years of World War II. The Tigers advanced to the KHSAL championship game in 1941, losing to Frankfort Mayo-Underwood. The next year the team finished with an astounding 40–4 record behind a fast-break offense and a sticky man-to-man defense but did not make it to the finals.[16]

6

"Janitorial Engineering"

Of the 25 classes that had graduated by 1940, Lincoln produced three college deans, one college president, 76 teachers, three preachers, six lawyers, 26 businessmen, 21 farmers, three doctors, four dentists, 14 engineers, 58 trained domestics, 10 government employees, 10 carpenters, five nurses and 11 insurance agents. In addition, Lincoln produced the only African-American postmaster in the state, who happened to be Young's wife, Laura, who was appointed postmaster of the Lincoln Ridge post office by President Franklin D. Roosevelt in 1940.

—*New History of Shelby County, Kentucky*

In 1940 the chief assets of Lincoln Institute were reported as 19 buildings, a dairy herd of 35 Jersey and Holstein cows, and a vocational high school department with 13 teachers and 295 students. Lincoln could look at its physical assets and its list of graduates and conclude that its educational mission, so far, had been a success.[1]

But a problem existed throughout the state that would have a dramatic effect on Lincoln Institute. Young black boys and girls in Kentucky were not attending high school. Before World War II, less than half of Kentucky's 120 counties supported high schools for black students, whose education therefore ended after elementary school. The Kentucky General Assembly had passed a law in 1934 requiring each public school district in the state to maintain a separate school for blacks. However, available cash and the inclination to move rapidly were in short supply in many districts, effectively gelding the law.

In 1938 another bill presented the districts with an attractive option. Representative Charles W. Anderson, an attorney from Louisville and the first African American in the state legislature, proposed that each county that lacked separate accommodations could send the black students in their districts to an accredited high school in another county or district and pay tuition. After much debate and some resistance, the bill passed the legislature and solidified Lincoln's position as the state's only boarding high school for African American students. The law solved a thorny problem for local school districts and worked to Lincoln's benefit, as it began to acquire more students from across the state.[2]

World War II gave Young another opportunity to expand vocational horizons for his students. In 1942 Lincoln Institute was designated one of fourteen locations in Kentucky for US Signal Corps trainees. The pace of modern war increased the demand for radio technicians, and trainees learned how to operate, overhaul, maintain, and repair radio equipment. According to administrators of the program, candidates for training needed no previous electrical or radio experience, although "fundamentals of spatial relationships, arithmetic, simple mechanics and physics" would be helpful background courses.[3]

Despite state law requiring the education of African Americans and Young's enterprising use of the campus, Lincoln's enrollment declined during the war years, resulting in a corresponding dip in revenue. Facing another financial crisis, Young and Tydings considered drastic measures to ensure the school's long-term viability. They came up with the idea to transfer Lincoln to the state, since the institution enrolled students from around the commonwealth.

In 1943 Tydings made the proposal, declaring that the "problem of educating Negroes from counties unable to provide for their education" had become a state problem. In the past, such counties had paid $145 of the $206 per capita cost of training students. Under his proposal, the appropriation would be made to the State Board of Education instead of directly to the school. The proposal was tabled until the end of the war, when Representative Harry F. Walters, a Democrat from Shelbyville, sponsored legislation to transfer Lincoln Institute to the State Board of Education. The bill specified that Lincoln would continue its work as a high school for African American boys and girls and as a teacher-training laboratory for Kentucky State Col-

The Lincoln Institute faculty in 1952 reflected Whitney M. Young's insistence on hiring teachers who liked to teach and were comfortable around their students. Front row, from left: Alexander Pinkney, dean of men; Kathleen Carroll, dean of education; Whitney Young; his wife, Laura Ray Young, postmistress; Joseph Carroll, vice president and professor of agriculture; and Helen Pinkney, inventory clerk. (Courtesy of Bernard Minnis Sr.)

lege. It was a major step forward for Lincoln, providing $100,000 to restore a dormitory that had burned and raising the school's annual state funding from $45,000 to $75,000. The bill also formally designated Lincoln as an adjunct of Kentucky State, whose board would administer the school. The respected Walters shepherded the bill through the legislature, and Governor Simeon Willis presided at the formal transfer ceremony on March 26, 1947.[4]

Whitney Young had guided his alma mater through difficult times, and his efforts began to draw attention from his peers. In 1945 he was named assistant state supervisor and coordinator of Negro education, a position that enabled him to travel across the state to determine the problems of educating African American students and to recommend solutions. In announcing Young's new assignment, the *Kentucky Negro Educational Association Journal* published his statement about Lincoln Institute's progress and his hope that Lincoln would become the "State High School" for African Americans.[5]

Still, Young had to use his extensive gifts of obfuscation and legerdemain when dealing with the State Office of Public Instruction. Its board rejected Young's proposal to add electrical engineering to Lincoln's industrial training track, which focused on carpentry and the building trades. Undaunted, Young and department head Albert Minnis Sr. changed the name of the program to "janitorial engineering," which the board approved without objection. Thus, Lincoln began teaching electrical engineering, but under a banner with which white legislators were more comfortable.[6]

Whitney Young had overcome traditional and societal hurdles, enhancing his own reputation as both an educator and a spokesman for racial equality. In recognition of his achievements, in 1948 Young was elected president of the Kentucky Negro Educational Association (KNEA). An even greater honor came a year later when Young's long service to Lincoln Institute was rewarded and he was named its first African American president. That same year, he was asked to give the keynote address at the KNEA's 1949 convention. "It is the inescapable duty of the county, state and federal government to protect the rights and liberties of all people," he told the assembly. He deplored a public school system that excluded an individual because of his color in a democracy where all men were forced to pay taxes. "No individual should be denied the right to vote, and he should not be denied free and equal educational advantages."[7]

Young knew his subject well. His own son, Whitney Jr., had graduated from Lincoln in 1937 at age fifteen as the valedictorian of his class. He went on to earn a pre-med degree from Kentucky State Industrial College. Whitney Jr. enlisted in the US Army in 1941 and was sent to the Massachusetts Institute of Technology, where he studied electrical engineering before being promoted to first sergeant in the 369th Regiment Anti-Aircraft Artillery Group, an all-black unit under white officers. He received an honorable discharge, but despite his credentials, he was denied admission to the University of Kentucky, which was still segregated. Young drew from his son's experience when he told KNEA members that the association's

Dr. Whitney Young (front row, second from left) sits with other past presidents of the Kentucky Negro Educational Association in this 1949 photo. (Courtesy of Center of Excellence for the Study of Kentucky African-Americans, Kentucky State University)

outstanding accomplishment of the previous year had been its assistance in the Lyman Johnson case. Johnson, a black teacher at Central High School, had won a decision in federal court that allowed him to enter the University of Kentucky Graduate School, thereby breaking the school's policy of segregation.

It was after his experiences in the segregated military and his rejection by the University of Kentucky that Whitney Jr. determined to make race relations his life's work. He graduated from the University of Minnesota in 1947 and helped organize a chapter of the Congress of Racial Equality before becoming director of industrial relations at the Urban League in St. Paul, Minnesota. Whitney Jr. later moved to Omaha, Nebraska, where he became executive secretary of the Omaha Urban League and an instructor at Creighton University and the University of Nebraska.[8]

Whitney Young Jr. enlisted in the US Army in 1941 and was sent to the Massachusetts Institute of Technology, where he studied electrical engineering. He was promoted to first sergeant in the 369th Regiment Anti-Aircraft Artillery Group, an all-black unit under white officers. (Courtesy of Center of Excellence for the Study of Kentucky African-Americans, Kentucky State University)

Young Sr. was also a strong influence on his daughters, both of whom graduated from Lincoln and went on to obtain degrees at Kentucky State College. Arnita graduated from Lincoln in 1939 and earned a degree in home economics in 1943 and a graduate degree in social work from Atlanta University. During World War II, she joined the American Red Cross and served as a recreation director for soldiers stationed in Germany. On her return, she became a social worker with the Red Cross. A Tuskegee airman whose unit was stationed at Godman Field at Fort Knox even taught her to fly.[9] Young was skeptical of the young airman's attentions toward the attractive Arnita, whom one Lincoln graduate described as the spitting image of singer Lena Horne. Once, while courting Arnita, the airman was assigned to fly his bomber to Fort Knox, but he diverted his flight plan to take the aircraft over Lincoln Ridge. "You could see the teeth in the pilot's smile," said one witness as the plane buzzed the campus to impress Arnita.[10]

Whitney and Laura Young's children—Arnita *(left)*, Eleanor *(below)*, and Whitney Jr *(below left)*—all went on to distinguish themselves in the fields of education and civil rights. (Courtesy of Center of Excellence for the Study of Kentucky African-Americans, Kentucky State University)

Eleanor graduated from Lincoln in 1940 and then attended Kentucky State, where she worked in the library to help pay her expenses. After graduating in 1944, she accepted a scholarship from Atlanta University to pursue a degree in library science. She took a job in the library at Florida A&M College but returned home to Lincoln Ridge in 1953, when her father informed her that he needed a full-time librarian to keep Lincoln's accreditation.[11]

In the early 1950s Young continued to proclaim Lincoln as the solution to the rising dropout rate among young blacks in Kentucky. "It is much more expensive for the State to try to rehabilitate drop-outs than it is to provide the proper counseling and guidance in the earlier years," he explained. "A State high school such as Lincoln Institute can serve as a preventive rather than a cure for delinquency and crime."[12]

Lincoln's role in serving the African American population of Kentucky was also emphasized in a report by the state's Legislative Research Commission:

> Kentucky requires "equal but separate" schools for Negroes. The major practical problem in providing equal but separate opportunities for Negroes lies in the geographical distribution of our Negro population. For a long time to come, Lincoln Institute may have to provide a high school education for many of Kentucky's students. Population distribution and segregation laws make this approach necessary. No one knows how many qualified Negroes of high school age are deprived of an education because they live in an area that does not maintain facilities for one reason or another or are unable to attend Lincoln Institute.[13]

Young quoted a report titled "Negro Education in Kentucky" that said approximately 1,000 students in seventy "sub-marginal" counties were not receiving an education and needed the services that Lincoln provided. "The future of Lincoln Institute is bright," he wrote, noting that the school was at full capacity and a waiting list of seventy students existed. "Those of our friends who have stood by us when the going was tough and the resources limited deserve the gratitude of all the Negro people of the state, who for more than twenty years have fought, preached and prayed for a square deal for the Rural Negro Child."[14]

Young's opinion of his institution was well supported in Frankfort. Sam B. Taylor, director of supervision in the Kentucky Department of Education, commended Lincoln Institute and its leadership in a letter urging the state legislature to support Lincoln Institute "generously." Wrote Taylor: "The high rating of the school does not lie altogether in the strength of its faculty, regardless of how important this item is to the school. It has one of the ablest administrators to be found in any school in the State. The curriculum and course of study is one of the widest and richest offered in any school. In addition to the academic subject including the languages, sciences, mathematics and the humanities, it offers four vocations to prepare its students for life's work."[15]

Young's appreciation of continuing education was not limited to his students. After being named principal at Lincoln, he earned a bachelor's degree from Louisville Municipal College in 1938 and a master's degree from Fisk University in 1944. Although his practical experience no doubt qualified him for an advanced degree, he never took the time to pursue one. That was resolved in 1955 when he was presented with an honorary doctorate from Monrovia College in Liberia. He was referred to as "Dr. Young" for the rest of his life.[16]

Lincoln Institute's financial situation stabilized after it was added to the state system, but the white public schools in Shelby County were facing a crisis. Overcrowding and low academic ratings demanded change in this rural area that supported eight schools, grades one through twelve, in addition to Shelbyville's independent schools.

As early as July 1948, the Shelby County school board had proposed building a new consolidated high school to house students in grades nine through twelve from Simpsonville, Bagdad, Waddy, Glenyrie, Cropper, Mount Eden, Henry Clay, and Finchville. Under the proposal, the new high school would be built one mile west of Shelbyville at the junction of Finchville Road and US 60; it would accommodate approximately 450 high school students then enrolled in the eight high schools. Grades one through eight would remain at their old locations. The cost of the new high school was estimated at $650,000.[17]

But a group of forty-five taxpayers filed suit in circuit court to stop the proposal. According to a spokesman for the group, they opposed construction because of the high cost of material and labor. The plaintiffs' petition also declared that the county board could not adequately support the school system and also retire the proposed bonded indebtedness for the new school. Although the plan factored in an increase in school taxes, a recent raise in the school tax rate from $1.25 to $1.50 per $100 assessed valuation had generated only an additional $43,000 annually.

The following March, while the political battle continued to rage, the State Board of Education informed the county school board that unless a resolution was reached quickly, six of the schools—Cropper, Glenyrie, Henry Clay, Finchville, Mount Eden, and Waddy—would lose their accreditation. The state gave the county board ninety days to bring the high schools up to standard. To emphasize the serious nature of this demand, the state board ordered that nine other high schools across Kentucky be dropped from the list of accredited schools. The Shelby County board responded with a proposal to merge with the Shelbyville independent school district, but the city board apparently had no interest in doing so.[18]

Six weeks before the deadline, the Shelby County school board informed the state that it would reduce the number of high schools from eight to three, consolidating Glenyrie and Finchville with Simpsonville, Henry Clay and Mount Eden with Waddy, and Cropper with Bagdad. The state board accepted the move, although county school superintendent George Giles predicted "a lot of unpleasantness will follow." The mergers took place in time for the 1950–1951 academic year.[19]

Young must have watched the proceedings with bemused satisfaction. Because of their color, none of his students were permitted to attend any of the eight county schools, yet the high school they were "forced" to attend was the only one in Shelby County that received an "A" rating by the Kentucky Department of Education or that had been accredited by the

Southern Association of Colleges and Schools since at least the 1936–1937 school year.[20]

If Shelby County needed a model for resolving its educational crisis, it need look no further than neighboring Anderson County. An August 1949 *Lexington Herald* article reported the good news for that county's 1,700 students: A new building program was progressing apace, and its latest feature was the merger of Lawrenceburg city schools with those in Anderson County. The schools would operate as one system in the 1949–1950 school year. Plans for a new high school in Lawrenceburg had been completed, and it would be known as Anderson High.[21]

The new school would accommodate students who had formerly attended Lawrenceburg City High School and Kavanaugh High School. The new building, featuring ten spacious classrooms and a brightly lit cafeteria, would be erected on the site of the old City High building. Until the new school was complete, students would attend classes at Kavanaugh, while the City High gymnasium would be used as an auditorium and for sports events.

Western Anderson High School, the only other high school in the county, was also part of the improvement plan. Its existing gymnasium would be renovated, and its auditorium would be enlarged to accommodate eight new classrooms and a cafeteria. These improvements were part of a plan that included the previous merger of four grade schools at Alton, Ninevah, Herndon, and Hampton into the Alton Consolidated School; another consolidated grade school would be built at Glensboro.

The superintendent of schools, Emma Lee Ward, proudly reported that all building plans were completed and had been turned over to the school board. She also confirmed that there would be no major changes in the curriculum this term, although county students who did not have a music instructor and city students who could not take classes in home economics or agriculture would now have access to all courses offered.

Readers of the *Lexington Herald* article could not help but conclude that such an ambitious building program and such attention to its young people placed Lawrenceburg and Anderson County at the forefront of education in Kentucky. The images of bright, happy youngsters danced between every line, assuring improved educational opportunities. That the building program and the listed benefits were intended only for the white children of Anderson County was not mentioned until the eleventh paragraph of the thirteen-paragraph story. This became obvious with the information that "all colored high school students will attend Lincoln Institute in Shelby County. William Coleman will serve as principal of the Colored Graded School here."[22]

John Norman Cunningham attended the Colored Graded School in Lawrenceburg, Kentucky, along with his brothers, sisters, and cousins. He enjoyed a carefree childhood, spending his summers and free time playing with the neighborhood children, both black and white. The children of Lawrenceburg were color-blind when it came to playing baseball or football on the town's vacant lots or shooting basketballs into barrel hoops nailed on the sides of buildings. Kids got along because nobody told them they couldn't.

Lawrenceburg was a community where people had grown up together and knew one another; they were mostly intent on the common goals of working hard, feeding and clothing their families, and attending church. It was a laissez-faire atmosphere that did not invite change or conflict. Animosity was a word in the dictionary, not a feeling triggered by color. But segregation was different. Segregation could exist without the burning of crosses or the shouting of slurs, as the African American citizens of Lawrenceburg knew.

Johnny Cunningham never experienced any acute racial problems growing up, so long as he knew which doors he could enter and which ones he could not. The Lyric was the only movie theater in Lawrenceburg, but Johnny learned early that if he wanted to see *Treasure Island* or *Rio Grande* with John Wayne, he could not use the front door on Main Street. He and other people of color walked around to the back door, where an elderly black man sat taking tickets at the Negro entrance to the theater. Johnny and his friends paid their money and were directed down a dark corridor, with only the light of an open door ahead to guide them. Rows and rows of cushioned seats beckoned, but *their* seats were located at the front of the theater on several rows of hard wooden boards.

The differences became more apparent when school started in the fall. Johnny Cunningham and his friends might have played freely with the white kids all summer long, but come September, the white boys and girls caught the new bus owned by the county system and were dropped off in front of Anderson High School on Main Street. Across the street from the school, the black kids stood around, waiting for their rides. With no educational accommodations for them in Anderson County, black students had the choice of attending Simmons High School, located ten miles away in Versailles, or Lincoln Institute, located more than thirty miles away in Simpsonville.

As Cunningham recalled: "A white fellow who I played ball with told me later, he said, 'John, we saw you every day in the summer, but we always wondered where y'all went when school started. But then we knew that when summer came, you'd show back up again.' That's just how it was."[23]

The boys who had played together all summer waved to one another across the street, and then the white boys went inside the building. Johnny and his friends turned away, feeling sorry—but not for themselves. They felt sorry for those poor white boys who had to attend Anderson High, while they had the opportunity to go to Lincoln Institute.

John Cunningham arrived at Lincoln Institute as a freshman in September 1951. He was fueled by the excitement of attending the same school where so many of his family members had gone. Because such a large number of students from Lawrenceburg attended Lincoln, the school sent a bus to town twice a year—the day before school began in the fall, and the day school adjourned for the summer.

The bus from Lawrenceburg traveled down US 60, through Shelbyville, and on past Simpsonville to the gates of Lincoln Institute. Those who had heard the story would inform the new students that they were passing through the "Blue Gate" and leaving their childhood behind. The gate was actually red brick, but the symbolism hit every new student who was sad, or "blue," at the prospect of leaving home for the first time. Four years later, they would pass through the "Blue Gate" again, but then it would signify their sadness at saying good-bye to friends.

The bus rolled down the one-mile lane and crossed the tracks of the

Berea Hall, situated prominently at the center of Lincoln's campus, served as the administration building and a primary classroom. (Courtesy of Daniel Thomas)

Louisville & Nashville Railroad where the passenger trains stopped at Lincoln Ridge station. Crossing the creek at the bottom of the valley, the bus chugged up the hill and gave the students their first look at their home for the next four years. The school was visible from a distance. The single tower of Berea Hall, the administration building, loomed high on the hill like a stately cathedral. Surrounding Berea Hall was a farrago of buildings, lush green fields, orchards, and growing crops. What the new students could not see were the educational opportunities and the new friends and memories waiting to be made.

The campus layout, designed by the Olmsted brothers, was like the face of a clock. Berea Hall was at its center, surrounded by an inner circle and an outer circle. In the inner circle at eight o'clock was Eckstein Norton Hall, the girls' dormitory; behind it on the outer circle and extending to ten o'clock was a model farm to facilitate the teaching of agriculture classes and farm-related projects for the male students. At eleven o'clock on the outer circle was an apple orchard that produced 1,200 bushels per year; extending from there to twelve o'clock was the reservoir that supplied all the water for the campus. Staying on the outer circle, from twelve to two o'clock was the institute's farm, which included forty head of Jersey and Holstein milking cows, a dairy, and herds of sheep and beef cattle. At two o'clock sat a garden that produced nearly 1,000 bushels of vegetables for the kitchen. At three o'clock was the athletic field, and at four o'clock sat Belknap Hall, the boys' dormitory.

On the inner circle at nine o'clock, adjacent to Berea Hall, was Hughes Hall, which held the basketball gymnasium, a music room, an economics classroom, and a caretaker's apartment. At twelve o'clock on the inner circle was the Embry Building, which housed the heat, light, and water plant; to the west at three o'clock sat the Industrial Building, which housed vocational and trade programs.

The campus and its precise layout were viewed in various ways by the new students, depending largely on where they had come from. The boarding students from rural towns like Lawrenceburg and the "day" students bused in from surrounding communities saw Lincoln Institute as just another cluster of structures around a dairy farm, not unlike their own hometowns. Other boarders from more "exotic" venues such as Indianapolis, Cincinnati, and Cleveland thought they had been dropped on some distant planet, cut off from civilization as they knew it.

The Lincoln administration took steps to ease the transition, down to the smallest of details. For instance, to ensure that the new students brought everything they needed for dormitory living, the Student Guide provided a comprehensive list:

Each student will bring four sheets, each measuring 60 x 84 inches; one pillow and two pillow slips, 22 x 32 inches; and the blankets he will require for cold weather; also a washable bed spread or quilt, two would be preferable. Shower cap and shower shoes, mattress cover (90 x 40 inches), and gym shoes. One white uniform for girls taking home economics. All linen should be plainly marked in indelible ink with the owners' name. The basement of each dormitory is equipped with laundry tubs. Each student must provide his own towel, soap, comb, hair and tooth brushes. Umbrellas, rain coats and rain shoes should be a part of the equipment of each student, and also a small pocket-size dictionary.[24]

However, no measure of proper planning could alleviate the anxiety and fear of a fourteen- or fifteen-year-old living away from home for the first time. Out from under the protective eyes of parents or grandparents and removed from their comfortable routines, new students were entering the unknown. "I cried when I got to the Blue Gate," one former student recalled. "I had to start doing things for myself that I knew about but I didn't want to do. I didn't want to wash out a pair of socks at night so I could wear them to school the next day. I'd been taken care of all my life, and now I had to take care of myself."[25]

7

"Inherited Tendencies"

Despite all the postwar enthusiasm for family life, there was increasing recognition that the family now exercised less influence on young people than other societal institutions, such as schools. As the baby boom pulled the population's center of gravity downward and mothers were increasingly working outside the home, the school seemed to be replacing the family as the institution that would mold the values of young people.

—Donna L. Franklin

By the time John Cunningham arrived, Lincoln Institute was well established in terms of academics, athletics, and expectations of its students. The ease of adapting to their new surroundings depended on the new students' ability to not only handle a rigorous academic schedule but also adhere to Dr. Young's strict code of conduct. Rules were clearly set out, and students were expected to follow them. If not, discipline was swift and often harsh.

The Student Guide, given to each student upon arrival, was explicit in its requirements. Each student was expected to conduct himself or herself as "a gentleman or lady." Gambling, drinking, smoking on campus, and "swearing" were positively forbidden. All students were expected to attend church, Sunday school, regular chapel exercises, and Wednesday "vespers." Lights in the students' rooms had to be turned off at 10:30 p.m. and remain off until 5:30 a.m. Violation of the "lights out" rule was punishable by a fine of fifty cents for each offense. All student mail was subject to inspection by the dean. Any request to leave campus had to be accompanied by a note from a parent.

Most students spent their first few days making new friends, some of whom had come from as far away as Cuba and Honduras. All complexions were represented, and two students with the same name might be distinguished by "Black John" and "Brown John." Lighter-complexioned students were described as "bright skinned." Lincoln also introduced a new age of personal hygiene for students from rural settings who still had outhouses at home. Lincoln was the first time many of them had seen, or used, an indoor bathroom.[1]

Hazing of new students was not allowed, but freshmen were logical targets for harassment. One of the favorite traditions at Lincoln was for an upperclassman to approach a freshman and demand that he buy a "Lincoln penny" for a quarter or more. The intimidated freshman readily turned over his quarter, only to discover that the "Lincoln penny" was a regular copper one-cent piece with Abraham Lincoln's likeness on it. That was the extent of freshman initiation, and the victims were cheered by the knowledge that they could do the same thing to the incoming freshmen next year and get their money back.

Students from northern states, where racial tolerance was more widely practiced, had to adapt to the new hurdles of southern living. Judith Taylor came from Cleveland, where the schools were integrated and black customers could trade at the same stores, eat at the same lunch counters, and sit in the same movie seats as white patrons. But during her first year at Lincoln, she and some schoolmates were surprised when they traveled to St. Matthews, a suburb of Louisville, and stopped to eat at the popular White Castle restaurant. "I had to go around to the back of the White Castle to buy a hamburger," Judith recalled. "I had never faced that in Cleveland. I hadn't been around whites enough to tell me I couldn't do something." When it came to education, however, she believed Lincoln had an advantage over her northern school. "We had white teachers and a few black teachers in Cleveland," she said, "but I think I did better in school [at Lincoln] because I was encouraged to do well by someone who looked like me, who told me that I could do well. I excelled because of it." When Judith and her friends wanted a diversion, they would sneak down to the campus farm, wait for a cow to mosey close to the fence, and then jump on its back for a ride. They weren't supposed to do it, but it was a way to pass the time.[2]

About one-quarter of Lincoln's enrollment consisted of "day" students from the surrounding communities in Shelby County who traveled back and forth to Lincoln every day. One of them was William Mack. His father was a sharecropper, managing a white owner's farm in return for a weekly salary of about $25 and a share of the tobacco crop. Mack and his father rose at 5:00 a.m., picked up kerosene lanterns, and went to the dairy barn to milk the cows. The milking was finished by 6:30 a.m., giving Mack enough time to clean up before catching the school bus. The bus was an older model provided by the school board and was warmed (or not) by a balky kerosene heater. Sometimes the bus broke down, and Mack would have to hitch a ride to school. At 3:00 p.m. the process was reversed, and Mack arrived home in time for the afternoon milking. Sons of dairy farmers knew from an early age that cows had to be milked twice a day, seven days a week, regardless of weather, conflicts, or the milker's disposition.[3]

Some new students found it most difficult to adjust to Lincoln's Sunday meal policy. The kitchen served a hot breakfast and a hot lunch on Sunday, but students received only a sandwich in a paper bag for dinner. The more enterprising students solved that problem by crafting makeshift hot plates with a piece of tin foil and an iron. Hot baloney sandwiches and pork and beans warmed in this manner became a Sunday staple, as were Dr. Young's lengthy sermons.

Sunday afternoon was free time, when female students were expected to write letters to their parents and male students could play cards or walk down to the Blue Gate and back. Fraternizing with the opposite sex outside of sanctioned events was strictly forbidden. The line of demarcation was a fireplug placed halfway between the boys' and girls' dormitories. Any student who ventured past the fireplug in the direction of the wrong dormitory would be punished.

Once a new student was settled, he or she could look forward to a full schedule of courses based on Booker T. Washington's theory of a practical education, along with touches of W. E. B. DuBois's idea that young African Americans needed to learn the arts and sciences. Young's own philosophy of education combined the two disciplines. He wanted his teachers to take an approach not unlike that of a sculptor to a glob of unformed clay: certain extraneous elements had to be cut away and smoothed so the form could be shaped to fit the desired model.

The Lincoln Institute cafeteria provided three meals a day during the week for students and faculty, but Sunday supper was usually a sandwich in a paper bag. (Archives and Special Collections, University of Louisville)

Freshmen were required to take English composition, elementary algebra, world history, physical education, and health science. Electives included "everyday science" and a course in a vocation of the student's choosing among agriculture, engineering, building trades, and home economics. Students on the agriculture track could choose animal husbandry, dairying, field crops, or gardening. "Janitorial engineering" students could elect to study elementary electricity, elementary plumbing, heating systems, building maintenance, or radio. Students interested in the building trades could choose general building practice, cabinet making, building maintenance, or drawing (architecture). Home economic students were schooled in cooking, sewing, child care, and homemaking.

Completion of the basic requirements in each area led to advancement each year. For example, freshman English composition was followed by advanced composition for sophomores, English literature for juniors, and American literature for seniors. The freshman math and science component led to advanced algebra for sophomores, plane geometry for juniors, and chemistry for seniors. Other subjects such as biology, American government, and economics were also available, and students could take electives in music or French. Every subject was taught in the same context—application of the acquired knowledge to the student's real-life existence.

Dr. Young explained his view of Lincoln's mission in the 1952 Student Guide in an article titled "Philosophy":

We conceive education to be a democratic way of life. The things we have to do by choice or otherwise and the way we do them constitute our educational program. The vital question confronting each teacher and principal is "How may I provide the proper setting to stimulate the youth entrusted to my care?" When he comes to school, he has certain inherited tendencies, a physiological frame work and other tangible assets as a basis for our work. The teacher's job is to curb some of these tendencies, stimulate others, capitalize on the tangible assets, and provide the opportunity for full aesthetic development of the frame work involving each of the sense organs.

The spirit of cooperation, mutual helpfulness, interracial goodwill, cooperative planning as regards staff, students, communities and boards have priority in the building of Lincoln Institute. English, science, mathematics, social sciences, guidance, health and vocations are not taught as dry subject matter but in relation to real and abstract life situations. Students are encouraged to inject real life problems as they exist in the community into class discussions, problem solving in classroom, laboratory, dormitory boarding hall, on the campus and in the shop. These constitute the basic concept of curriculum building at Lincoln Institute. To us the student is not preparing to live; he is living. He is not working for a diploma on some day in June, but for knowledge with or without the commendation of his fellow students and teachers now. This makes education dynamic, effective and interesting.[4]

Dr. Young's philosophy stipulated that part of the teacher's job was to curb some of the students' "inherited tendencies." All teachers and administrative officers had full authority to enforce the rules and regulations at any time and place. Students who refused to cooperate with the dean in the matter of "boisterousness" in the dormitories or elsewhere on campus would be asked to withdraw.[5]

Lincoln's punishment for various infractions was definitely from another generation and would not be tolerated in later years, but it achieved the desired result. Mary Taylor from Ekron, Kentucky, near Fort Knox, had grown up with brothers and was not afraid to answer an insult with a hard right to the chin. On her first day at Lincoln, she and another girl got into a fight, and their punishment was to scrub gum off the floor on their hands and knees. Another time after a basketball game, a girl "three times my size" stepped on the heel of Mary's shoe, and she responded with a haymaker to the jaw. "I got to know Dr. Young very well," she said years later. "I scrubbed a lot of gum off the floor."[6]

For serious transgressions, punishment often came down to a simple choice: get sent to Dr. Young or take a paddling. Hickory-switch discipline was alive at Lincoln, and it was far preferable to the ultimate punishment for violating the rules: expulsion, or being "sent home" in the Lincoln vernacular. That was the final option for Dr. Young, who knew that many of his students' problems could be traced to their home lives and the environments in which they were raised. A serious infraction required a meeting with the principal, but when Dr. Young told the offending student, "I'm thinking of sending you . . . ," the student would likely interrupt: "Please, please do anything to me but just don't send me home." Young would often relent and let the student off with a warning: "If you ever do that again, you're going to get sent home."

Dr. Young also made certain that discipline was enforced when his students left campus for an approved activity such as an athletic event. He made his expectations clear in a letter to one staff member who was chaperoning students to off-campus basketball games in 1953: "You will cooperate with the deans in setting up regulations to govern the conduct of our students at the games. Along with the other chaperones you will have complete responsibility for the enforcement of the regulations. All cases of misconduct should be reported immediately to the dean of women or the dean of men. It is understood that for this service you will be given free lunches in the boarding department."[7]

Teachers were not looking to punish every infraction, no matter how serious. When several boys were discovered with liquor, Joseph A. Carroll, the biology teacher, confiscated the bottle but did not tell Dr. Young. For the rest of the school year, he never let the offenders forget the incident, frequently teasing them with the reminder, "Your punishment is not knowing what I'm going to do." He never turned them in.

For young black boys and girls growing up in the racially sensitive 1950s, Lincoln Institute was a learning laboratory for life's lessons. President Young taught dignity, self-reliance, discipline, respect for self and others, and practical skills that would prepare his students to become useful members of an often hostile society.

One former student recalled feeling inferior when she first came to Lincoln, believing that because she was black, she wasn't as good as whites. At age ten she had participated in a program at a white church, reading a passage aloud and hearing a white voice say, "Oh, she can read?" "It eats at you, but at Lincoln Institute the teachers kept telling you that you were worthy, and I finally got a sense of self. I got out of feeling that I wasn't good enough. That was much more important than the reading, writing, and arithmetic we learned."[8]

"Dr. Young was always trying to show students their purpose in life," said Jennie Williams, who taught French and English at Lincoln from 1946 to 1960. "'I'm going to send you to Timbuktu,' he would say in mock frustration for sloppy dress or behavior. If you go to church, dress up and go. Always look like you belong. He preached that whatever you do, keep your dignity."[9]

John Cunningham was not worried about academics when he arrived at Lincoln. After all, good grades were a tradition in his family. His aunt Maddie Cunningham had even been valedictorian at Lincoln several years earlier. But after his first series of tests, young John got an early wake-up call and realized that the courses at Lincoln were not going to be the breeze he expected. During the first grading period, he missed the first honor roll of his life. What subject nailed him? "Congregatin' them verbs didn't make sense then, and they still don't make much sense today," he said, laughing, years later. "Math I could handle, but when I started congregatin' them verbs, I said 'shit' I ain't going to use that when I get out of here!" His Aunt Maddie, who by then was an administrator in the Lincoln office, disagreed. She sat him down and told him to his face: "Cunninghams don't miss the honor roll, and boy, you'd better get it in gear!" John never missed another honor roll at Lincoln Institute. After that initial scare, he discovered that the formula for making good grades was to get his homework done as soon as he left the classroom. It was like a basketball game, but one in which he was in total control. "No gallivanting around," he explained. "Get the lessons while they were fresh. I was a Cunningham. They expected me to produce academically."[10]

Good grades were essential if a young man wanted to play basketball, which was a passion John shared with several others who had enrolled at Lincoln in 1951. He found a common bond with a rangy mountain boy from Hazard, Kentucky, named Robert Combs, and they became best friends. At six foot two, John had always been the tallest boy in his class, but Combs towered over him at six foot six. Neither boy was afraid of hard work. Combs had grown up around the coal mines of eastern Kentucky, and Cunningham had spent most summers on his grandfather's farm near Salvisa in nearby Mercer County.

Most boarding students worked in the cafeteria, in the dormitories, or on the farm. After a stint in the cafeteria, Cunningham asked for a new job. The pay of $8 a month was acceptable, but nobody would sit next to him on Fridays because he smelled like fish—the traditional meal served on meatless Fridays.

Cunningham and Combs volunteered for the backbreaking work of hauling coal. The buildings at Lincoln were warmed by coal furnaces, and the coal was delivered by rail to the Lincoln Ridge station. Flatcars filled with coal would be dropped on a side track, signaling Cunningham and Combs to get to work. They drove the school's truck down the hill, loaded the coal onto the truck, and then hauled it back to the various buildings on campus. They climbed on top of the load and tossed shovelfuls of dusty black coal into the basements through open ground-floor windows. When one basement bin was full, they moved on to the next building and repeated the process until the flatcar was empty and all the basements were filled. For every flatcar they unloaded, the boys split $60, which was good money at the time.

As the school year progressed into late autumn, earning money took a backseat to basketball. Lincoln's head coach was Herbert Garner, but the players spent most of their conditioning time with assistant coach Walter Broadus, who was also the head football coach. Broadus, who commuted to the campus every day from Louisville, had a unique approach to conditioning that took advantage of the team's height. He believed that any player over six feet tall should be able to dunk the basketball, so he trained his team with weights to increase that advantage. He had each player pick up the equivalent of 150 pounds and put it on his back while standing with a two-by-four under his heels. Regular squats with the weights and the boards increased leg strength and jumping ability. Broadus also took advantage of the campus's hilltop location. Berea Hall was one mile from US 60, and he required the players to run down the hill to the Blue Gate and back before practice every day.

Cunningham had all he needed at Lincoln—basketball, meals, and a bed—so he never went home on weekends. Having his aunt on staff helped, because he always had family close by. Many of his fellow boarders, however, headed home on Friday afternoons. It was a time when hitchhiking was common and skepticism and fear were the exception, so seeing young men and women thumbing for rides on US 60 became a normal Friday afternoon routine for regular travelers of that route. The students often caught rides with the same people, white or black, each week. Workers returning to Shelbyville, Frankfort, or Lawrenceburg from their jobs at General Electric's massive Appliance Park or the Ford plant in Louisville had no fear of picking up young hitchhikers in front of the Blue Gate and helping them get home.

Some students who stayed on campus found rides into Shelbyville on the weekends. A black nightclub operated there, and alcohol was readily available to those who knew where to find bootleggers. Students were cautious, however, because they had heard stories of white harassment of African Americans who walked on Main Street after hours. Drugstores in Shelbyville sold ice cream to black customers, but they were not allowed to sit on the stools and eat it at the counters. Black workers helped build the municipal swimming pool, but once it was opened, they were not allowed to use it.

For the students who did not go home on weekends, church was mandatory on Sunday. The students sat in rows of folding chairs arranged on the floor of the gymnasium in preparation for a sermon from Dr. Young or a guest speaker. While the students listened, the deans silently counted heads. Anyone missing from services would be the subject of an immediate search.

Despite the rule, John Cunningham occasionally slept in on Sunday mornings, especially after a Saturday night game. He knew that once the teachers discovered he was missing from church, they would knock on his door, so he devised a hiding place in his dormitory room. A high storage shelf ran along the top of the clothes closet, just big enough to accommodate a boy who stood six feet two inches tall. He climbed up onto the shelf and sat with his back to one wall and his legs stretched out to the other wall. One day, Cunningham's ingenious scheme seemed to be in jeopardy when a teacher came into his room, looked under the bed, and then checked the closet. The teacher looked inside and moved the hanging clothes around but never looked up at the shelf. When the teacher left, Cunningham quietly stepped down and went back to bed.

If he were ever caught breaking a rule he considered inconvenient, Cunningham figured his reputation as a basketball player would get him out of any punishment. That belief was tested the night he decided to shoot baskets in the gym in defiance of the strict 9:00 p.m. curfew. It was already 10:00 when Cunningham entered the gym. Three dim lights glowed inside as he pushed shot after shot through the basket until, suddenly, a voice behind him interrupted his routine.

"John Cunningham, what are you doing here?" said Julia Wilkinson, the dean of men. She had been walking across campus when she noticed the lights in the gymnasium. "You are not supposed to be out on campus after nine o'clock, and here it is past ten. I am going to turn you in to Dr. Young, and you are going home tomorrow for breaking the rules. I will see to that!"

Cunningham was scared to death that she would follow through with her threat, and he did not sleep much that night. He was torn between the thought that the dean had simply overreacted and was taking her authority a bit too far and the fear that she meant what she said. The dean's son, Jimmy Wilkinson, was also on the basketball team, and Cunningham thought she might be jealous that he was a better player than Jimmy, who was a year younger.

The next morning, Cunningham rose, dressed, and went to his first class, hoping all had been forgiven or forgotten. But he was not so lucky. He was sitting in class when a note was delivered to the teacher, who informed him that Dr. Young wanted to see him immediately. Young did not socialize with the students, but when he walked around campus, he always acknowledged every boy and girl with a polite nod or perhaps dispensed some fatherly advice or wisdom. Students gravitated to the president because of his warmth, but also because of the confidence he exuded when he strolled across campus. They all knew Dr. Young had their best interests at heart. But every student also dreaded seeing "the picture of Lincoln"—the picture of the sixteenth president that hung on the wall behind Young's desk. If you saw the picture, it was because you had been summoned to Young's office. Another dreaded sight was Dr. Young's brown suit. The scuttlebutt among the students was that you didn't want to be around Dr. Young when he was wearing his brown suit because he always seemed to be in a bad mood when he wore it.

The picture of Lincoln was the first thing Cunningham saw when he was ushered into the president's office that morning. "John Cunningham from Lawrenceburg, Kentucky," Dr. Young said as the young man meekly took a seat in front of the huge desk. He unfolded his long legs and noticed with relief that Dr. Young's suit was blue. Young asked him if Maddie Cunningham who worked in the office was his sister, and the boy replied that she was his aunt. But the pleasantries ended right there. "What were you doing in the gymnasium at ten o'clock at night?" Young asked pointedly, staring straight into the boy's eyes.

Cunningham stammered and answered, "Truthfully . . ."

"That is all I want," said Young.

"Well, I had a shot I was working on that I was trying to get perfected. It's a one-handed push shot from long range, and I'm getting to where I can hit about eight out of ten."

Young looked interested but didn't divulge that he had coached basketball in Lincoln's early days. "How does the team look this year?" he asked.

"I think we'll go all the way."

"All the way to what?"

"I think we can win the state tournament."

"Really?"

"Yes, sir. We are on track to do it."

Shifting gears to his favorite subject relieved some of the tension in the room as the older man asked a few more questions about the basketball team and the younger man supplied the answers to his satisfaction.

"Well," Young said, hesitating just enough to prolong the uncertainty of the moment, "you keep working on that shot, but try not to be out after nine o'clock. Go on back to class."

Later, when Cunningham returned to the dormitory, Mrs. Wilkinson saw him and chided: "Well, I guess you'll be going home this afternoon."

"No, ma'am, I don't think so," Cunningham responded.

"Well, what did Dr. Young say?" she asked indignantly.

"He told me to go on back to class, and that's what I did."

"Well, you must have had something awfully good to tell him."

"No ma'am," Cunningham responded. "I just told him the truth, natural, like I'm talking to you now."

"Well, I doubt that," she said as she spun and walked away.

_8_

"Inherently Unequal"

The anti-American, anti-democratic façade of segregation and discrimination is slowly crumbling under the force of our persistent struggle. Let us maintain a relentless pressure until the rotten structure in its entirety comes tumbling down around those who would perpetuate a sordid chapter of American history.

—Dr. Ralph Bunche to the 1950 graduating class
of Kentucky State College

Entering the 1950s, members of the Kentucky High School Athletic League identified two major areas of concern within their association that required immediate attention and one external concern that could undermine its very existence.

The first internal issue involved schools that sponsored football teams and wanted to enhance the state football championship. High costs prevented most KHSAL members from fielding football teams, but among those schools that did, there were no standard regulations governing the rules of play. It was not until April 11, 1946, that officials of the Kentucky Negro Educational Association and the KHSAL met to discuss the enforcement of football eligibility and playing rules. They adopted a redistricting plan for football that created a championship format by dividing the state into two regions with eight to ten schools in each.[1]

The second internal issue that continued to trouble league members was the inconsistency of officiating. Until 1951, officials who worked league events were not required to participate in ongoing education, pass competency tests, or be approved by the KHSAL. Home teams hired the officials, often with little regard for their experience, temperament, or knowledge of

The Kentucky High School Athletic Association's Board of Control did not shy away from admitting former KHSAL schools. From left: Cecil A. Thornton, K. G. Gillaspie, Robert Forsythe, W. B. Jones, Russell Williamson, commissioner Ted Sanford, Louis Litchfield, W. H. Crowdus, and Jack Dawson. (Courtesy of *Lexington Herald-Leader,* University of Kentucky Special Collections)

the rules. The need to upgrade the quality of officials through training and mandatory clinics became more apparent as the league took a stronger stand on this issue relative to basketball and football. Central High's coach William Kean, a Board of Control member, suggested that the board contact KHSAA commissioner Theodore A. "Ted" Sanford and ask permission for KHSAL referees to attend clinics directed by the KHSAA. Further, the board asked the KHSAA to recognize and certify black officials who attended and passed the KHSAA clinic. Sanford agreed to these requests, perhaps in part because he correctly gauged the winds of change blowing across the land and the issue that most troubled KHSAL members.[2]

Talk of desegregation trumped all other issues for KHSAL members. It dominated discussions among basketball coaches in the black schools and raised a litany of unanswered questions: What will it mean? When will it happen? Will black schools have to play white schools? Will black students be forced to attend white schools? Will black schools be closed immediately?

Can black and white players coexist on the same team? These questions were new and frightening in places where segregation was the only law people had ever known. It did not occur or even matter that such questions had been resolved in most states and would soon be resolved in Kentucky and its southern neighbors. But nobody knew to what degree, at what cost, and, perhaps most importantly, when.

The questions were less frightening to some KHSAL member schools that had already played white teams, although such games were neither publicized nor encouraged. Louisville Catholic was one of the first all-black schools in Kentucky to take on an all-white school in basketball when the Crusaders played—and defeated—a good team from Louisville St. Xavier during the 1952–1953 season. "St. X" was one of the oldest and most respected high schools in the state and one of its traditional athletic powerhouses. Interestingly, several years later, Catholic High guard Eddie Hill, a slick ball handler who scored an average of 14 points per game, would become the first black player invited to enroll at St. Xavier.[3]

Meanwhile, all the questions and uncertainty would be accelerated by a tidal wave that inundated the black schools, carried them along, and dropped them into a world where segregation was replaced by a new order whose objectives were noble but whose implementation would be painful.[4]

Public education in the first half of the twentieth century operated on a "separate but equal" basis established in 1892. A mixed-race man named Homer Plessy was arrested for refusing to give up his seat to a white man on a train near New Orleans, as he was required to do by Louisiana law. Plessy sued, contending that the law separating blacks from whites on trains violated the equal protection clause of the Fourteenth Amendment to the US Constitution. By 1896, his case had made it all the way to the US Supreme Court, which ruled against Plessy by a vote of 8–1.[5]

In his majority opinion, Justice Henry Billings Brown wrote: "The object of the [Fourteenth] amendment was undoubtedly to enforce the equality of the two races before the law, but in the nature of things it could not have been intended to abolish distinctions based upon color, or to endorse social, as distinguished from political, equality. . . . If one race be inferior to the other socially, the Constitution of the United States cannot put them upon the same plane." Interestingly, the lone dissenting vote came from a former Kentucky slaveholder named John Marshall Harlan, who, in his nineteenth year on the Court, interpreted the Fourteenth Amendment another way: "Our Constitution is color-blind, and neither knows nor tolerates classes among citizens." Harlan called the law a "badge of servitude" that degraded Negroes and claimed the majority ruling would become as infamous as the high court's 1857 ruling in the *Dred Scott* case, which had declared that Negroes, whether enslaved or free, could not be citizens and therefore had no standing to sue in federal court.[6]

The *Plessy* decision stood as legal precedent for more than half a century as the Supreme Court continued to uphold the legality of Jim Crow laws and other forms of racial discrimination in subsequent cases. With such a legal history reinforcing attitudes on both sides, most blacks tended to act cautiously into the late 1940s. The vast majority of black soldiers who fought during World War II abided segregation in the military because there was little they could do about it. When black soldiers returned to the South in 1945, they knew they would encounter the same unyielding system of segregation and discrimination they had endured prior to the war unless they worked to change it. Whitney Young Jr. also endured the unequal treatment, but he joined a cadre of black leaders in the late 1940s who began to look toward change.[7]

One of the men who dominated the strategies employed to promote change in southern race relations was Thurgood Marshall, a Baltimore attorney with the National Association for the Advancement of Colored People (NAACP). Most black leaders had acted carefully, relying on legal campaigns that were unavoidably slow, but by the late 1940s, Marshall was thinking seriously about confronting segregation head-on. Many other black leaders in local NAACP branches resisted such tactics, unable to imagine that the white-dominated courts would support any significant transformation in racial traditions or attitudes.

Others wondered what school desegregation would really mean in practice. Black teachers worried that desegregation would force the closure of African American schools, costing them their jobs. The NAACP, they said, should contest inequality, not segregation. It should push to ensure the "equal" part of "separate but equal." Not until 1950, after much debate within the NAACP, did Marshall dare to demand the figurative lynching of Jim Crow in the schools.

In June 1950 Marshall took the fateful step of challenging the constitutionality of racially segregated public schools. In October the NAACP board publicly supported Marshall, dropping its emphasis on achieving equality within a segregated education system. Henceforth, according to the board's resolution, "pleading in all education cases . . . should be aimed at obtaining education on a non-segregated basis and . . . no relief other than that will be acceptable."[8]

Marshall argued against segregation on behalf of the NAACP Legal Defense and Education Fund. The case that came to be known as *Brown v. Board of Education* was actually five separate cases involving segregation in the public schools in four states and the District of Columbia: *Brown v. Board of Education of Topeka* in Kansas, *Briggs v. Elliot* from South Carolina, *Davis v. Board of Education of Prince Edward County* in Virginia, *Boiling v. Sharpe* from the District of Columbia, and *Gebhart v. Belton* from Delaware. Although the facts of these cases were different, the main issue in each was the constitutionality of state-sponsored segregation in the public schools.

Despite acknowledging some of the plaintiffs' claims, a three-judge panel of the US District Court that heard the cases ruled in favor of the school boards. The plaintiffs appealed to the US Supreme Court, and in 1952 the Court consolidated all five cases under the name *Brown v. Board of Education*. Marshall argued before the Court, pegging his case on the contention that separate school systems for blacks and whites were inherently unequal, which violated the equal protection clause of the Fourteenth Amendment. Furthermore, he argued that segregated school systems had a tendency to make black children feel inferior to white children; thus, such a system should not be legally permissible.

The justices of the Supreme Court were deeply divided over the issues and were unable to reach a consensus by the end of the Court's 1952–1953 term in June 1953. Chief Justice Fred Vinson of Kentucky decided to rehear the case in December. However, the sixty-three-year-old Vinson died sud-

denly of a heart attack on September 8 and was replaced by Governor Earl
Warren of California. After the case was reheard in 1953, Warren was able
to achieve what his predecessor had not: he persuaded all the justices to support a unanimous decision. On May 14, 1954, Warren delivered the opinion
of the Court: "We conclude that in the field of public education the doctrine
of 'separate but equal' has no place," Warren stated. "Separate educational
facilities are inherently unequal."[9]

The decision generated a mixed but generally calm response among Kentucky's white population, but anxiety rippled through the state's public
school systems and associated athletic organizations.[10] KHSAL members
realized that the decision would have a lasting effect on their schools and
their league, and the KHSAA, governing the white schools, came to the
same conclusion. Three months after the decision, the KHSAA discussed
desegregation at its annual convention at Kenlake Hotel on Kentucky Lake.
According to the association's minutes, on Friday morning, August 6, the
association's Board of Control had "a lengthy discussion concerning various
implications of the recent Supreme Court ruling on segregation." The discussion was reduced to one paragraph in the minutes, which suggested there was
no need for a quick decision by the white schools: "Since Negro children will
not be integrated in the schools during the school year 1954–55, by order of
the State Board of Education, it was the opinion of members of the Board
that a Negro high school, organized as such, is not eligible for membership
in the KHSAA at this time."[11]

Schools in Shelbyville and Shelby County, however, faced more immediate problems. A month after the Court's decision was announced, the
Shelby County board of education formed a Citizens Committee to study
the problems of overcrowding and the poor performance of its students. The
committee included a representative from each of the eight local districts to
address such issues as inadequate facilities to accommodate increased enrollment, transportation, and "a more adequate curriculum."[12]

A report disseminated in 1948 had cited the "impoverished condition"
of the academic program in the county's high schools. A study conducted
by Griffenhagen Company, an educational consulting firm from Chicago,

pointed out the need to improve the curriculum, particularly science and language courses. At the time of the study, not one of the county's eight high schools was accredited by the Southern Association of Colleges and Secondary Schools. Only Lincoln Institute achieved a "class A" rating by the Kentucky State Department of Education.

The Shelbyville school board addressed similar issues in an August 1954 meeting with Wendell Butler, the state superintendent of public instruction. Butler advocated moving forward with a planned building program, and he advised that Shelbyville High School and the three county high schools at Simpsonville, Bagdad, and Waddy, which had survived consolidation of the eight high schools in 1949, consider further consolidation. At the first meeting after the *Brown* decision, the board tabled the building program until issues involving desegregation and consolidation had been clarified.[13]

In November the NAACP requested a meeting with the Shelbyville city school board to discuss desegregation plans for the district. At the meeting, held on January 26, 1955, the board expressed a willingness to cooperate with the NAACP in drafting a desegregation plan. However, agreeing to help create a plan is a long way from actually devising a plan. The board said that owing to overcrowded conditions at the white schools, particularly Simpsonville, which would house the largest number of black students, any attempt at immediate integration was impossible. Without suggesting a timetable, the board pledged to "effectuate total desegregation as soon as possible." But, the board cautioned, "to force it (integration) would imperil opportunities for blacks and whites and impair relations between races and deter an ultimate orderly desegregation program."[14] This cautious approach was supported by the state, which instructed the board to await further developments from the Supreme Court.

Meanwhile, at Lincoln Institute, Dr. Whitney M. Young Sr. knew what the future held for his cherished institution. It was about that time that he began to share another, more personal view with his faculty members and students. "Segregation created Lincoln Institute," he told them. "Integration will destroy it."[15]

The Supreme Court decision had little immediate effect at Lincoln Ridge. Another subject of critical importance took priority and aroused the passion of

Lincoln Institute's students in the early months of 1955: the Lincoln Tigers were holding their own in the Kentucky High School Athletic League, and John Cunningham's predictions of a state championship appeared to be realistic.

The gangly freshmen of 1951–1952 had grown into men by the time the 1954–1955 season started. The team was blessed with enormous size for a high school team. Cunningham, a guard, was six foot two, and center Robert Combs, his best friend, was six foot six. Forwards Jimmy Wilkinson, son of the dean of men, and Joe Holmes from Louisville were six-five and six-four, respectively. Alongside Cunningham at guard was six-foot-tall Shirley Atkins from Indianapolis; backing them up was another boy from Lawrenceburg, Amos "Fruity" McKee III, who was also a valuable contributor to Lincoln's KHSAL champion football team in 1953 and 1954.

Wilkinson was a year younger, but the rest of the team had been together for four years. They had started out on the junior varsity team and one-by-one were promoted to the varsity. Along the way, they had learned one another's skills and preferences. Combs and Wilkinson controlled the boards in almost every game, while Holmes was a prolific scorer within fifteen feet of the basket. At guard, Atkins ran the team on offense and was a good press defender, but Cunningham was the captain and the soul of the team.

By then, the team's effervescent captain had adopted the nickname "Slam Bam" Cunningham. When defenses sagged on Holmes, Cunningham wanted the ball. Cocking his right leg like a spring, Cunningham would push up a one-handed set shot from long range that more often than not split the nets. "When Cunningham cocks that leg," said a fellow student, "it's going in!" It was the same shot that Cunningham had risked expulsion from Dr. Young to perfect.[16]

The Tigers set the tone for every game as soon as they walked onto the floor. Every starter and a few reserves turned the layup line into an exhibition of slam dunks, windmills, and over-the-shoulder dunks. Their height and athleticism were on full display as the Lincoln players stuffed ball after ball in full view of their often awed opponents. At the opening tip, Lincoln launched into a full-court press on defense and went the other way with a fast-breaking offense. "From the time they tossed the ball up," Cunningham remembered, "we were in their jock, and we stayed there."

Lincoln even employed an early-day platoon system. Once the starting five had run up a comfortable lead, coach Herbert Garner would take them out and put in five fresh players. At such a pace, the other team was usually wilting by the third quarter. But a curious quirk of construction might have contributed to Lincoln's ability to tire out the other team. For reasons lost to history, the floor in the gymnasium at Hughes Hall measured ninety feet long by fifty feet wide, instead of the more common high school lengths of between seventy and eighty-four feet. The players believed the extra distance was a factor in wearing down their opponents, which may or may not have been true. But it was likely a psychological advantage because the Tigers believed it.[17]

On the road, Lincoln played teams from all corners of Kentucky. From Paducah to Pikeville, from Hopkinsville to Harlan, the Tigers' road show was on the move. The team traveled by bus on shorter trips, but when they had multiple games at more distant locations, Coach Garner and assistant Walter Broadus drove the players in their cars, with five boys piled into each vehicle.

Lincoln scheduled three or four "tours" each season during which the Tigers would play two or three teams before returning home. A trip to western Kentucky might include games with Hopkinsville Attucks one night and Bowling Green High Street the next. Trips to eastern Kentucky might take them to Ashland Booker T. Washington one night and Maysville Fee the next.[18] The Tigers' receptions were often less than hospitable. "They all hated us," John Cunningham recalled years later. "They thought we were privileged, wealthy people going to a private boarding school. 'Where are you getting all that money?' they asked us. They thought we were something special. Of course, we acted like we were special because we were proud of our team and proud of Lincoln Institute."

Accommodations were usually arranged by the home team, since most hotels in small towns did not allow black guests. Lincoln's players normally stayed with the families of the players on the opposing teams. Before they arrived, the coaches cautioned the players to exercise good judgment and be on their best behavior. But that was often difficult after a tough game. The level of hospitality often depended on the final score.

The Tigers did not win every game during the regular season that year. They lost to Columbia Colored School in their first game with white officials. Race did not matter when it came to "home cooking" (favoritism toward the home team), and nearly every call went against the Tigers in the first half. After assessing the situation, Garner decided not to send his starters back into the game after halftime.

Lincoln also lost to Lexington Dunbar, 72–67 in overtime, as the Bearcats avenged an earlier loss at Lincoln.[19] But Lincoln's true nemesis that year was once again the Louisville Central Yellowjackets, who won both games during the regular season. The Tigers hoped the 1955 KHSAL tournament would give them a chance for redemption.

From the KHSAL's inception in 1932, its basketball tournament structure offered sixteen teams an opportunity to participate in the state tournament. However, in April 1949 the Board of Control changed the format to a series of district tournaments, with winners and runners-up advancing to eight sectional games.[20] The eight sectional winners advanced to the state tournament. The alignment of schools for basketball was as follows:

Region I: Hickman Riverview, Paducah Lincoln, Mayfield Dunbar, Murray Douglass, Princeton Dotson, and Hopkinsville Attucks.

Region II: Morganfield Dunbar, Henderson Douglass, Providence Rosenwald, Madisonville Rosenwald, Earlington Million, and Owensboro Western.

Region III: Drakesboro Community, Elkton Todd County Training, Russellville Knob City, Franklin Lincoln, Glasgow Bunche, Bowling Green High Street, and Horse Cave.

Region IV: Elizabethtown Bond-Washington, Bardstown Training, Harrodsburg West Side, Danville Bate, Campbellsville Durham, Columbia Colored, and Lebanon Rosenwald.

Region V: Louisville Central, Louisville Catholic, Lincoln Institute, Frankfort Mayo-Underwood, Versailles Simmons, Lexington Dunbar, and Lexington Douglass.

Region VI: Covington William L. Grant, Cynthiana Banneker,

Georgetown Ed Davis, Paris Western, Mount Sterling DuBois, Maysville Fee, and Ashland Booker T. Washington.

Region VII: Nicholasville Rosenwald, Winchester Oliver, Richmond, Lancaster Mason, Stanford Lincoln, Somerset Dunbar, and Barbourville.

Region VIII: Harlan Rosenwald, Benham Colored, Hazard Liberty Street, Wheelwright, Lynch Colored, Jenkins Dunham, Pikeville Perry Cline, and Middlesboro Lincoln.[21]

This format was used until a new plan was approved at a board meeting on April 22, 1954, for dividing the state's eight regions into districts and East and West sections to determine the eight tournament finalists. The new plan, which took effect in the 1954–1955 basketball season, provided that the four semifinal participants in each sectional would advance to the finals, regardless of who won. That, in effect, allowed multiple members of former Region V, which included Louisville Central, Lincoln Institute, and the Lexington schools, a shot at the finals.[22]

Lincoln Institute had such a shot in the 1955 state tournament. Although Lincoln lost in the West sectional semifinal to Central and in the third-place consolation game to Henderson Douglass, it advanced to the state finals held in Bell Gymnasium at Kentucky State College. In the first round, Lincoln drew the Lexington Douglass Demons, the defending league champions led by six-foot-five center Amos Burdette, who averaged 29 points a game. Although two previous matches between the schools had been canceled after snow and ice storms closed many roads, Coach Garner had seen Burdette often enough to devise a strategy to stop him. He ordered Lincoln's tall front line to stay in a zone close to the basket while his quick guards, Cunningham and Atkins, were in charge of harassing the all-state center.

"When the ball was on Atkins's side of the floor," Cunningham explained, "I would back up into Burdette's arms, crowding him. When the ball was on my side of the floor, I'd go out and get my man, and Atkins would back up into his arms. That frustrated him, and he started pushing us to get us out of his way, and he picked up some early fouls."

Burdette, plagued with four fouls in the first half, was held scoreless in the second quarter when Lincoln grabbed a 36–28 halftime lead. Burdette sat out most of the third quarter, and the Tigers extended their lead to 62–45 on the way to an 81–70 victory. Burdette was held to 15 points, slightly more than half his average. Meanwhile, Atkins and Holmes paced Lincoln with 18 points each, while Wilkinson added 16 and Cunningham 14.[23]

The state tournament format was grueling. The first semifinal game would be played at Bell Gymnasium at 1:00 p.m., with the second following immediately. The winners would move on, literally about thirty miles, to Lexington Dunbar's new gymnasium, where the championship game would start at 9:00 p.m.

In the first semifinal game, Lincoln took an early lead and then had to hold off Hopkinsville Attucks to achieve a 68–62 victory. Holmes led Lincoln with 24 points and was ably supported by Cunningham and McKee, who scored 12 points each. In the other semifinal game, heavily favored Louisville Central embarrassed Henderson Douglass, 74–33. After racing to an 18–7 first-quarter lead, coach Bill Kean sat out his all-state trio of six-foot-four center John "Pie" Liveious and guards James Beck and Edgar Smallwood, to make sure they were rested for the title game.[24]

The championship game was expected to be just one more Central coronation. There was no debate in the African American community over which school was superior; Central surpassed Lincoln in every conceivable category. The Yellowjackets were the Yankees, the Celtics, and the Cleveland Browns of black high school basketball in Kentucky, at the apex of Louisville's African American social order. Central's players considered Lincoln a country school filled with farmers, hairdressers, and delinquents who symbolized a submissive past that already was disappearing in the cities.

The Yellowjackets had long dominated the KHSAL, winning more titles than any other school. They had already earned five and appeared to be headed for a sixth against Lincoln. Central had won twenty-nine games during the season, losing only to a Tennessee team. Central had beaten Lincoln twice during the regular season and again in the West sectional game by a score of 88–75. Fortunately for Lincoln, the new tournament format gave the Tigers one more chance.

Lincoln's starters got no rest during the difficult semifinal game against

Attucks earlier in the day, while Central's players relaxed during most of their semifinal walkover of Henderson. The Tigers, however, were determined to write another ending, as the football team had done the previous fall. In October 1954 Lincoln's football team had beaten Central for the first time since 1921 on their way to the KHSAL football championship. The Lincoln players knew that Central's domination of them on the basketball court that season was partly to avenge what the city school considered a major embarrassment on the football field. But the Tigers were tough, resilient, and experienced, and they believed it was time to show everyone that a Lincoln Institute championship was not an aberration.

Cunningham gathered his teammates before the tip, reminding them of everything they had been through the past four years. They had been humiliated by Central all season long and were considered second rate compared with the more established city school, but they had one final game in their high school careers to change that perception. Cunningham put his right hand out in front of him, palm down, and one by one his teammates placed theirs on top. Five boys dedicated to a common goal triggered their mission with a simultaneous shout: "Ready, let's go!"

Central's players soon realized that this game would be nothing like their easy win earlier in the day. The Tigers came out running on offense, pressing on defense, and playing the Yellowjackets close. Still, Central held a 24–21 lead at the end of the first quarter and was ahead 35–34 at the half. Garner did his best to rest his starters when he could, sending in Fruity McKee, Bobby Jones, and Clarence Hall.[25]

Cunningham's one-hand push shots kept Lincoln close, but Central lengthened its lead to 54–50 at the end of the third quarter. Lincoln's leading scorer, Joe Holmes, had been held to 14 points so far, but when the teams walked onto the floor for the final quarter, Cunningham whispered in Holmes's ear: "We've got 'em right where we want 'em!" The joke must have inspired Holmes, who went on a fourth-quarter rampage. The six-foot-four jumping jack countered every Central basket and then some with a series of jump shots and put-backs until his two free throws gave Lincoln a 65–64 lead with three minutes to go.

The 1955 Lincoln Institute Tigers won their third KHSAL title. Flanked by coaches Walter Broadus, left, and Herbert Garner, right, the starters included Shirley Atkins (6) in the front row and Jimmy Wilkinson (12), Joe Holmes (10), Robert Combs (9), and John Cunningham (8) in the back row. (Courtesy of John N. Cunningham)

Cunningham scored his 21st point on a long one-handed push shot, but James Beck matched it with a basket for Central. Holmes scored another bucket, which was countered by one from Smallwood. The parry and thrust continued until eight seconds remained and Lincoln was ahead 72–70. Beck was fouled while shooting and stepped to the line, hoping to tie the game. The all-state player missed his first shot but hit the second, cutting the margin to 72–71.

Atkins tossed the ball in bounds to Cunningham, who was surrounded by three Central defenders. But this meant that somebody was open, and he saw Holmes free under the Central basket. Holmes caught the pass and was fouled as the buzzer sounded, but it didn't matter. The Tigers had done it! Holmes sank one of two meaningless free throws, his 12th point of the quarter and 26th of the game. Lincoln Institute had won its third KHSAL championship.

9

"With All Deliberate Speed"

The Supreme Court decision does not mean that all Negro schools should be closed. To do this would be just as foolish as to say that no Negro doctor, lawyer, newspaper or business man should have the patronage of Negro people.

—Dr. Whitney M. Young Sr.

Two months after "Slam Bam" Cunningham and the Lincoln Tigers won Kentucky's "colored" state tournament, the Supreme Court announced its second ruling in *Brown v. Board of Education.* However, in many minds, this ruling did little but confuse the process. On May 31, 1955, the Court directed that public schools would be desegregated "with all deliberate speed." This oxymoronic phrase gave succor to local school boards that had been unenthusiastic about the original order and now seemed to have as much time as they needed to comply.

After initial opposition to its 1954 ruling, especially in the South, the Supreme Court requested input from the states before issuing instructions on how to implement that ruling. The attorney generals of all states with laws permitting segregation in the public schools were asked to submit desegregation plans. Still more hearings produced the Court's declaration that became known as *Brown II.*[1]

Although the language "with all deliberate speed" was blamed for slowing the desegregation process in many states, officials elsewhere were encouraged. Morton Walker, the Louisville school board's white president, later said that, after the Supreme Court's initial decision in *Brown,* the board had been concerned about moving too fast or too slow. The Court's second ruling provided more details. Even then, the board did not want to be pressured into immediate integration, so Walker announced that the Louisville schools would integrate in the fall of 1956, and the superintendent agreed.[2]

Louisville's liberal approach to desegregation reflected a similar change in Kentucky's all-star high school basketball series with neighboring Indiana. This annual battle between the two hoops-crazy states had started in 1939 and was played at the largest venue available: Butler University's 15,000-seat field house. Home-court advantage agreed with the Hoosiers, who won fifteen of the first sixteen matches. But there was another reason for Indiana's dominance. From the first game, which starred future Major League Baseball player George Crowe, Indiana had allowed black players to participate. Kentucky, in contrast, had been lily white all those years.[3]

The organizers never publicly banned black players, but some Bluegrass backers believed that Western Kentucky State College coach Ed Diddle selected players for the all-star team based on who he was recruiting for his own segregated program. If a player was not considering (or being considered by) the Hilltoppers, Diddle left him off the team—or so the theory went. In any case, Kentucky set out to wipe away the past in 1955.

For the first time, the all-stars from Kentucky would be chosen through a complicated selection process. The head coach and game sponsors would select the first two players, and then a panel from the news media would select the rest of the team. The voting would take several weeks and would not be completed until June 10, a week before the first game in the new two-game format. The first two players chosen were "Mr. Basketball" Kenny Kuhn, a phenomenal three-sport star from Louisville Male High School, and John "Pie" Liveious of Louisville Central. The color line had been broken.

The six-foot-four Liveious had earned all-state and even all-nation honors after Central won the national Negro tournament in Nashville. Both the champion and the runner-up for the KHSAL title had been invited to the national tournament, and the Yellowjackets had prevailed after Lincoln was beaten in the other bracket. Liveious's teammate James Beck was also selected to the all-star team, along with Johnny Cox of the KHSAA state champion Hazard, Terry Randall of Adair County, Donnis Butcher of Meade Memorial, Larry McDonald of Burkesville, Ed Huffman of Newport, Joe Viviano of St. Xavier, Bobby Austin of Paducah Tilghman, and Julian Steffen of St. Henry's in Boone County.

The team convened on June 11 at Western Kentucky State College in Bowling Green, and Diddle put the players through a week of two-a-day practices before driving to Indianapolis two days before the game. Dressed in new red uniforms, the Kentucky squad shocked the 13,264 fans in the Butler field house by jumping out to a 16–4 lead behind the play of Kuhn and Cox (a future University of Kentucky star). Liveious dominated the game inside with several key rebounds as the Kentucky stars expanded their lead to 26–10. But, in a flashback of previous games, the all-stars from Indiana stormed back to win 94–86. Kuhn was brilliant in defeat, winning game honors with 25 points; Liveious contributed 12 points and as many rebounds.

The next game, before a sellout crowd of 6,500 at the Louisville armory, was almost a reversal of the first match. The Hoosiers charged out to an early 9–4 lead before Kentucky regrouped and moved ahead 14–13. Indiana trailed until the start of the third quarter, when the Hoosiers took a 41–39 lead. Then Cox, Kuhn, and Liveious took over. Cox scored three quick baskets, and Kentucky pushed its lead to 58–47 with less than six minutes left. Once again, Indiana rallied and tied the score at 74 with thirty-one seconds remaining. Kentucky failed to get a shot off, and the game went into overtime.

In the extra period, baskets by Liveious, Cox, and Butcher gave Kentucky an 81–74 lead, and the team withstood a Hoosier rally to claim its first win (86–82) since 1945. Cox, the darling of University of Kentucky fans in the arena, finished the game with 21 points, but Liveious was even better. The former Central star was named the game's "Star of Stars," with 27 points and 17 rebounds.

John Cunningham did not see the game. After graduating in May, the former Lincoln Institute star was offered a basketball scholarship to Central State College in Wilberforce, Ohio, located between Cincinnati and Columbus. One of the Marauders' coaches drove him and two other recruits north to show them around the campus. They saw the basketball gym and the dormitory where the student-athletes lived, and that is when Cunningham, for the first and maybe last time in his life, got cold feet. "These dudes on the basketball team had fancy lockers and all these fancy clothes hanging up in them," Cunningham recalled. "I said, 'Shit, this ain't for me. I can't compete with these guys.' My dad wasn't making big money, and I left the next day and came back home." In January, Johnny "Slam Bam" Cunningham joined the US Air Force.

In the fall of 1955, some Kentucky school districts made quick decisions in response to the Supreme Court rulings. Lafayette High School in Lexington admitted its first female African American student, and several black students entered the Griffin School in Wayne County without incident. The process was advanced when the Kentucky Court of Appeals followed the dictates of *Brown* and ruled that the Day Law was unconstitutional in *Willis v. Walker,* a case involving the Columbia school system in Adair County. On the opening day of school in 1955, Columbia's superintendent and board of education ordered the principals of both the elementary school and the high school to eject all Negro children who had previously registered. However, the white children were allowed to remain. The court ruled, "It is clear from the record that the only reason these plaintiffs and those for whom they plead were denied was because they were Negroes." Desegregation had begun in Kentucky.[4]

Although Lincoln Institute, as a state school, was not under the supervision of the local school boards, any decisions made by the Shelbyville and Shelby County boards with regard to desegregation would directly affect Lincoln. If the boards approved an integration plan, day students at Lincoln might choose to attend the integrated public schools at no cost to their families. By the summer of 1955, any consideration of integration was complicated by increased overcrowding at the white schools. In August a committee of three blacks and three whites was established to recommend an integration plan to the board. The board decided not to accept black pupils into the white schools until the committee had completed its study.[5]

This postponement seemed to reflect a general shift in the board's attitude. The minutes of the August 25 board meeting stated, "Public relations seemed such that it was unwise to start integration this school year."[6] The board's inaction was reinforced when one of its members reported on an integration workshop held in Louisville, which concluded that although segregation had been declared unconstitutional, integration was not yet mandatory.

In the early months of 1956, George Giles, superintendent of the Shelby County schools, reached out to Whitney Young and asked him to survey the county's black families with students at Lincoln Institute. The results, which were released in April 1956, were unanimous: black families wanted no part of integration, preferring to have their children remain at Lincoln.[7]

In August the Shelbyville school board released a plan formulated by the integration committee and referred to as the "gradual integration plan." Under this proposal, black students in first through seventh grades would be given the option of attending either the colored graded school at Eleventh and High Streets or the white schools. Variations of this plan were proffered in 1957 and 1958, but it would be nearly a decade before black students in Shelby County would attend an integrated high school.[8]

The large contingent of Lincoln students from Lawrenceburg found themselves at a crossroads when the Anderson County school board voted to integrate its schools. Sometime during the 1955–1956 school year, Dr. Young called all the Lawrenceburg boarders into the gymnasium and informed them that any African American students who lived in Lawrenceburg had the option of attending Anderson County schools during the 1956–1957 school year. Young loved his students, but he also loved Lincoln Institute. He candidly added the kernel that if students withdrew from Lincoln en masse, it would be the beginning of the end for the school.[9]

Attending that meeting was Pearl Washington Allen, whose mother had been contacted by Emma Lee Ward, the superintendent of the Anderson County schools, and asked why her daughter did not want to attend Anderson High School. "My mother told [Ward] that she would talk to me, but it would be my decision," Mrs. Allen said. "My mother added that she would rather I stay at Lincoln. We sat out on the front porch, and she asked me if I wanted to go to Anderson High. I told her I do not want to go to school there. I am going back to Lincoln because that's where I belong."[10]

Other Lincoln students had similar options. In the fall of 1955 Veltra Moran, from East Burnstadt in Laurel County, was one of the first black students enrolled at a white public school located five miles away in London, Kentucky. Each day, white protesters picketed the school and shouted slurs at the black students whenever they entered or left. After two weeks of such harassment, Veltra told her mother she was not going back. Because there was no African American school in the county, the school board paid her tuition to attend Lincoln Institute.[11]

Although integration was now a fact of life, how it would be imposed, administered, or enforced was unknown. It was obvious that parts of the South would continue to resist the federal law, but it was less obvious how racially moderate states and local school districts would respond. Even in those areas where cooperation without violence was likely, the fear existed that forced integration would mean the automatic closure of all black schools. Dr. Young responded to such fear in the November 1955 issue of the *Tower Gazette,* the Lincoln Institute periodical:

> The Supreme Court decision does not mean that all Negro schools should be closed. To do this would be just as foolish as to say that no Negro doctor, lawyer, newspaper or business man should have the patronage of Negro people. Every accredited Negro school, including our state schools, should be maintained as part of the regular public school system and expanded. Some of the promoters of desegregation unwittingly have taken the position of liquidating all Negro schools. Nothing could be more disastrous to the Negro people in the small communities. Our larger cities will have little to worry about. Their future has been taken care of by districting. Unless desegregation can be made a two-way street, we are all headed for real trouble.[12]

Dr. Young's viewpoint was understandable, because his institution was thriving. Enrollment had reached an all-time high of 553 during the 1954–1955 school year and rose to 581 the following year. Lincoln Institute held an "A" rating by the Kentucky Department of Education and was accredited by the Southern Association of Colleges and Secondary Schools. Its faculty consisted of sixteen teachers who held master's degrees from leading universities.[13]

Dr. Young portrayed Lincoln as "one of the best investments which could possibly be made in the interest of the State, Counties and Independent Districts." Students from sixty-five Kentucky counties and independent school districts attended Lincoln during the 1955–1956 school year. Any student who lived in a county where there was no black high school paid an annual fee of $40.50, which included room and board, tuition, lab fees, an athletic fee, laundry, insurance, and medical services. Commuting students paid only $10 for the year. In either case, the Shelby County and Shelbyville school boards paid $11 per month for each student who attended Lincoln. Its participation in the federal lunch program enabled Lincoln to feed the approximately 100 day students who attended, in addition to the boarding students.[14]

According to Young, "One of the great problems in the education of the Negro people of our state is how to give them competence and skill in the trades." Yet, he wrote, "Lincoln has done an outstanding job in several vocational fields, including Home Economics, Building Trades, Industrial Arts, Janitorial Engineering and Commerce. All the vocational courses with the exception of Commerce are under the Federal Smith-Hughes program."[15]

The Smith-Hughes National Vocational Education Act of 1917 provided federal funds to promote vocational agriculture and to train people "who have entered upon or who are preparing to enter upon the work of the farm." As such, it was the basis for both the promotion of vocational education and its isolation from the rest of the curriculum in most school settings. The funds available for teacher training under the act were apportioned on the basis of 75 percent for the University of Kentucky for the training of white teachers and 25 percent for the Kentucky Normal and Industrial Institute (later Kentucky State College) for the training of black teachers.[16]

Thus, Dr. Young concluded, "Lincoln is in a better position to give scientific training in agriculture than any other high school in the state. We are now operating a 350-acre farm, a large 'A' class dairy, a project farm for agricultural students, experimental plots for the University of Kentucky Agricultural Extension Department and the state 4-H Club organization."[17]

To answer the moral calling Dr. Young had envisioned from the start, Lincoln also served as a training school for the Carver School of Missions and the Southern Baptist Theological Seminary. Students from both institutions spent considerable time on the Lincoln campus, training for domestic and foreign missionary work. Lincoln also shared its resources with other schools and communities in surrounding counties. In 1955 Lincoln's faculty volunteered to help out in communities with meager resources, teaching in seventeen schools in six counties.

Young's message in the *Tower Gazette* was accompanied by a letter from Frank L. Stanley Sr., the respected editor and publisher of the *Louisville Defender,* the state's largest African American newspaper, praising Lincoln's work in the Negro schools of nearby Eminence, Kentucky. "The work which they have done in the past has had a remarkable effect on the young people of Eminence," Stanley wrote:

> The courses that can be obtained at Lincoln Institute is in itself a great attribute in its favor. The outstanding work of this school has had a great bearing on the educational standards of Kentucky. We hope that it will continue doing the great job it is doing.
>
> Insofar as Lincoln Institute is concerned, I think it has a bright future. I believe that it can continue to live and thrive by accepting students not only from Kentucky but from outside of the state who wish to come to a 'private' school. Therefore, it may be well that an investment at this time in dormitory facilities to alleviate the overcrowded condition will enhance Lincoln Institute's opportunity for growth.[18]

10

At the Highest Level

This is a time when we must evidence calm dignity and wise restraint.
Emotions must not run wild. If we become victimized with violent intents,
we will have walked in vain and our 12 months of glorious dignity will be
transformed into an event of gloomy catastrophe.

—Martin Luther King Jr., announcing the end of
the Montgomery bus boycott

On December 2, 1955, Mrs. Rosa Parks, a seamstress and former secretary to
the president of the NAACP, was arrested in Montgomery for refusing to give
up her seat on a segregated bus to a white passenger. Martin Luther King Jr.,
then pastor of the Dexter Avenue Baptist Church, to which Parks belonged,
called a meeting at his church in response to the incident. King told the large
crowd that the only way to respond was to boycott the bus company. The
boycott began three days later, on December 5, and lasted for more than a
year, when the US Supreme Court struck down the Alabama laws allowing
segregated public transportation and issued federal injunctions. The charismatic young preacher was arrested thirty times for his efforts to break down
racial barriers and was catapulted to national prominence as the de facto
leader of the civil rights movement.[1]

Principals and coaches from African American high schools in Kentucky
sought to end another boycott of sorts when they began peppering the Kentucky High School Athletic Association with questions regarding membership. The fact that a federal law had been passed that would eventually force
the end of all-white and all-black schools roused emotions on both sides.
Many coaches and administrators of both races were, in effect, feeling their

111

way down a long, dark corridor, looking desperately for a glimmer of light to guide them.[2]

The minutes of the KHSAA Board of Control's annual meeting at Kentucky Lake in July 1955 acknowledged "a discussion of segregation problems" as the board waded through its legal obligations. "It was the opinion of all members of the Board," the minutes noted, "that the Commissioner should continue to rule that Negro schools organized as such are not eligible for membership in the KHSAA, but schools in districts which integrate are thereafter eligible for membership."[3]

The KHSAA could not expect any help or direction from its national organization, which comprised high school associations from every state. Commissioner Ted Sanford had just returned from the annual convention of the National Federation of High School Athletics, held June 26–30 at York Harbor, Maine. Remarkably, desegregation was not included on that organization's agenda or in any of the conference's breakout sessions. One agenda item was headed "legislative action and court cases," but the impending transition for southern schools was not an official subject of discussion. Although the attendees included high school officials from Kentucky, Alabama, Mississippi, Louisiana, Georgia, Arkansas, Maryland, Indiana, North Carolina, and South Carolina—states facing the tumultuous repercussions of compulsory desegregation—the national board likely saw it as a regional matter that did not affect the majority of its members.[4]

Especially anxious were the KHSAL elite who wished to play at the highest levels of high school basketball while keeping a cautious eye on their local school boards. Among those schools that clearly qualified for membership under the KHSAA's policy was Louisville Central.

After the *Brown II* decision was announced, Morton Walker, president of the Louisville school board, concluded that there was insufficient time to make any drastic changes before the fall 1955 semester, but he and superintendent Omer Carmichael promised that Louisville city schools would desegregate in September 1956. Looking over their shoulders was the local NAACP branch, which pressed the board that summer and announced in July that it had twenty parents ready to act as plaintiffs if a lawsuit became necessary.[5]

In November 1955 Carmichael presented his plan for integrating the city schools to the Louisville board of education. The plan called for a city-wide redistricting of all schools without regard to race, based only the capacity of the buildings. Students would attend the school located in their residential zones; if there were two existing schools, parents could choose between them. As the proposal developed, the board decided to allow open enrollment in the high schools, meaning that students could choose to attend any school.

After Carmichael announced his plan, Central's coach Bill Kean and principal Atwood S. Wilson sent a letter to the KHSAA, requesting membership. "The Commissioner read a letter which he had received from Prin. Atwood S. Wilson and Coach W. L. Kean of the Central High School (Negro), Louisville, applying for membership in the KHSAA," the association's minutes noted. Sanford then read his reply to Wilson and Kean, which was consistent with board policy: "Since the public schools of Louisville will be desegregated, beginning next September, I agree with you that it would seem that no public school could be classed either as a 'white' or a 'Negro' school only. I assume, of course, that you are referring to schools in a deseg-regated district. If the plans mentioned for the Louisville schools are con-summated, I have every reason to believe that your school will be admitted to the Kentucky High School Athletic Association at the beginning of the 1956–57 school year."[6]

The Shelby County and Shelbyville school boards were still mulling over the timing of integration, but their decisions did not affect Lincoln's eligibility for the KHSAA. As a state school under the auspices of Kentucky State College, Lincoln was not bound by the local school board's timetable. Kentucky State's Board of Regents had forestalled the issue in September 1955, when it voted that Lincoln Institute was open to any student, regardless of race, who "could measure up to the requirements of the institution."[7] This meant that Lincoln Institute was no longer a segregated institution, which opened the way for it to join Central in applying for KHSAA membership.

The Lincoln Institute Tigers, the defending KHSAL champions, faced a rebuilding year in 1955–1956. The team had only one returning starter, Jimmy Wilkinson; however, guard Bobby Jones from Louisville more than

Walter Gilliard *(left)* was head coach at William Grant High School in Covington before he returned to Lincoln Institute. His 1953–1954 team finished with a 17–9 record but did not make the KHSAL state tournament. (Courtesy of the Walter Gilliard family)

stepped into the scoring void left by the graduation of John Cunningham and Joe Holmes. With Wilkinson controlling the boards and Jones frequently putting up 30 or more points from the outside, coach Herbert Garner's Tigers held their own with teams such as Lexington Dunbar and its stars Julius Berry and Robert Burbage. Lincoln did not have the depth of Louisville Central (the eventual 1956 champion) or Lexington Douglass (the runner-up), but the Tigers finished the season with a respectable 15–7 record.

Lincoln received a double dose of bad news after the season ended when head football coach and assistant basketball coach Walter Broadus departed for a coaching job in Mississippi. The players had great affection for Broadus and had spent hours participating in his training and conditioning program. That influence was confirmed when Bobby Jones, Lincoln's best returning player, announced that he would be following Broadus to his new school. The basketball cupboard was further depleted by the graduation of Wilkinson, who might have been an even better writer than rebounder, winning a

Walter Gilliard was a leader on the playing field and in campus organizations at Kentucky State. Here is a clean-shaven Gilliard (top row, far right) with his Alpha Phi Alpha fraternity brothers. (Courtesy of the Walter Gilliard family)

Shelby County student essay contest with a paper titled "How Forest Conservation Can Benefit My Community."[8] Wilkinson would continue his athletic career at integrated Bellarmine College in Louisville.

With Broadus's departure, Dr. Young asked Garner to perform double duty as head football coach, probably after consulting with his new athletic director. Earlier that year, Young had hired twenty-nine-year-old Walter Gilliard as athletic director and physical education teacher at an annual salary of $3,960.[9] Gilliard was no stranger to Lincoln Ridge. He had come to Lincoln in 1950 as an assistant football coach after an outstanding career as a quarterback at Kentucky State College. He left in 1952 to coach at his alma mater, Covington Grant, and to obtain a master's degree in education at the University of Kentucky.

Gilliard was born in Anderson, South Carolina, but after a relative touted employment opportunities in the Cincinnati area, Walter's father, Samuel Quincy Gilliard, moved the family to Covington, Kentucky. Walter thrived in his new home, growing to an imposing six foot three and developing a rugged build. He excelled in all sports at Grant. World War II interrupted thoughts of college, and in October 1943 he enlisted in the US Coast Guard. After twenty-eight months in service, Walter was discharged on February 26, 1946, and soon enrolled at Kentucky State College on the GI Bill.[10]

Gilliard's first major task as Lincoln's athletic director was to follow the lead of Louisville Central and enter the new world of integrated high school athletics. On April 18, 1956, Gilliard wrote to KHSAA president Sanford requesting a formal application for membership. Sanford replied promptly in a letter to Dr. Young, asking whether the school was a "desegregated school at the present time" and whether the application was for the upcoming 1956–1957 school year. Sanford sent along a copy of the KHSAA book of rules and regulations, noting that "the principal and the principal alone, is held completely responsible by the KHSAA for seeing to it that his teams comply with Association regulations."[11]

Dr. Young responded, confirming that Lincoln was "not a segregated institution" and was, indeed, applying for the 1956–1957 school year. He also asked whether it was permissible, during the transitional period, to continue to schedule games with Lincoln's traditional rivals, the KHSAL schools that had not yet joined the KHSAA. Sanford replied on April 25 that Lincoln's application would be accepted and that he would forward a membership form immediately. He also informed Young that Lincoln could continue to schedule games with KHSAL members, so long as they were not eligible for KHSAA membership because their local boards had not yet integrated.[12]

Lincoln Institute thus became one of the first four black schools admitted into the Kentucky High School Athletic Association, joining Lexington

Dunbar and the two finalists for the most recent KHSAL tournament, Louisville Central and Lexington Douglass.[13]

In Kentucky, the first two years after *Brown* were filled with much confusion, a smattering of compliance, and a great deal of apprehension. Desegregation across Kentucky was a product of local whim and politics, which hampered a quick transition from a segregated public school system to one of inclusion. The Kentucky Department of Education reported that of the 3,714 white schools under state auspices, only 85 elementary and secondary schools integrated during the 1955–1956 school year. That number increased the following year to 232 schools. By then, only 8,114 black students were enrolled in schools that accommodated 125,665 white students. The department acknowledged that 543,469 white students and 36,328 black students still attended schools that operated in a segregated manner.[14]

Some local boards had moved quickly to implement integration, but these decisions often meant the immediate closure of African American high schools. After the 1955–1956 school year, Pikeville Perry Cline and Georgetown Ed Davis shut their doors forever; the next year brought the closure of Cynthiana Banneker, Harrodsburg West Side, Hazard Liberty Street, and Winchester Oliver. Bond-Washington in Elizabethtown also graduated its last senior class in 1956, and its high school students were integrated into Elizabethtown High School the following year.

But the grim underbelly of desegregation was manifest during the 1956–1957 school year. As historian and Shelbyville native Bill Ellis notes: "In September, 1956, the good will, good sense, limits of government and intentions of both integrationists and segregationists were tested." Crucial tests of the governor's will and Kentuckians' inclination to follow the Supreme Court's ruling came at Sturgis in Union County, Henderson in Henderson County, Madisonville in Hopkins County, and the Clay city schools in Webster County.[15]

The entire Larue County school system desegregated successfully without incident, but things did not go so smoothly elsewhere. On September 4, 1956, a cross was burned on the grounds of Lexington Lafayette High School, which had admitted its first black student the year before. That same day, nine black students from Dunbar High School in Morganfield were confronted by a mob of whites when they tried to enroll in the previously all-white Sturgis High School. At first, it appeared that the locals would prevail, but then Governor A. B. "Happy" Chandler (who had been the commissioner of Major League Baseball when Jackie Robinson became the first African American to play in the major leagues in 1947) ordered Kentucky National Guard units to mobilize and enter Sturgis over the weekend. Only a small number of white students showed up on Monday, September 10, as National Guardsmen escorted seven black students into the school. Sturgis mayor J. B. Holeman stated that his constituents had not faced facts and would have to do so sooner or later. However, it was not until the next year that tempers cooled and black students peaceably attended Sturgis High School.

In Clay, Mayor Herman Z. Clark became combative, claiming that only Kentucky law applied in his town, not that dictated by the Supreme Court. He exulted: "There will be no integration here this year, next year, or ever."[16] The governor also sent troops into Clay, only eleven miles from Sturgis, after crowds blocked nine black students from enrolling and prohibited newspapermen from entering the town. M-47 tanks were deployed, and soldiers patrolled the streets with fixed bayonets. White demonstrators and students were liberal in their use of abusive language and racial slurs as they denounced the attempt to integrate the schools. Adjutant General J. J. B. Williams, commanding the National Guard troops, took two black children by the hands and escorted them into the Clay school.

Problems were exacerbated in some white communities in western Kentucky when White Citizens Council members from both inside and outside the state protested and were supported by the local newspapers. The tense situations in both Clay and Sturgis drew national and even international attention. For example, one English reporter complained to Governor Chandler about his rough treatment by irate whites.

Meanwhile, Kentucky attorney general J. M. Ferguson ruled that the *Brown* decision did not apply to Sturgis because the law gave school officials, "not parents or students, the right to decide when and where integration would take place." Since the school boards had made no plans to integrate these schools, Ferguson reasoned, blacks should not be admitted.

However, he also acknowledged that if black parents sued, they could prove that the school boards were not acting in good faith and adopting plans "with all deliberate speed," as ordered by the Supreme Court. In the end, both the Sturgis and Clay school boards voted to keep blacks out of their schools, and black parents decided to give up the fight, at least in the short term. White teachers and students returned to the Clay and Sturgis schools. Within a few days, the National Guard and a contingent of state police were sent home.[17]

The Hopkins County schools also rejected integration, and a boycott of the Henderson schools encouraged by the White Citizens Council was ruled illegal by the attorney general's office. When segregationists in Henderson County voiced their disapproval of the integration of black children before any formal plan had been offered, assistant attorney general Robert Matthews of Shelbyville ruled that a board "has no legal right . . . to abandon these plans" and go back to a segregated system.[18]

As a counterpoint to these efforts to resist federal law, the Louisville board of education enacted its desegregation plan. Superintendent Omer Carmichael and the school board ignored criticism from the Louisville NAACP, which Carmichael called "radical and often pushy." He had much more respect for criticism from the black population, to whom he appealed, stating, "It is very important for everything to be well in place before proceeding." Carmichael believed that immediate integration would never garner sufficient support and that a reasoned, well-planned approach would achieve the purpose of peaceful integration.[19]

Carmichael's plan consisted of several parts, including redistricting to allow students to attend the schools that were closest to their homes. "Freedom of choice" was also an important part of his plan. Due to the housing situation in Louisville, many whites found themselves living in close proximity to blacks. Freedom of choice meant that blacks could attend mixed schools and whites could attend segregated schools if they wished.

The moderate plan implemented by Carmichael and the Louisville board of education was praised by educators and politicians across the nation. Carmichael was invited to the White House by President Eisenhower in recognition of his role in the peaceful integration of the Louisville public schools. It appeared that Kentucky had secured its place at the forefront of the civil rights movement.

The irony was that very little integration actually occurred in the early years. Only a small number of blacks enrolled in white schools, and no whites attended black schools. Furthermore, it appeared that the few blacks who attended Louisville's white schools had been chosen because of certain attributes. The black students who enrolled at Male High School, for example, had very high intelligence test scores. Also, many of the first black students at white schools were outstanding athletes, a pattern that became common in many schools.[20]

Athletics was rarely, if ever, mentioned as an incentive for desegregation, but local teams were often the inadvertent beneficiaries. Desegregation would force a seminal change in Kentucky high school athletics immediately and forever. Star players who had carried KHSAL schools to prominence in the small and largely unknown pond of black basketball were now available to the white teams that played in an ocean of fan fanaticism, media attention, and color-blind adulation.

Indeed, whites in Kentucky appeared to be much more receptive to integration if formerly all-white schools obtained some gifted black basketball players who could step right into their starting lineups. That instant transfusion of talent occurred for at least three high school teams in Cynthiana, Hazard, and Maysville, all of which, coincidentally, were known as the Bulldogs.

During the 1956–1957 school year, Cynthiana High School underwent a radical transformation when coach James Cinnamon obtained seven former Banneker players. The best of them was Louis Stout, a slender six-foot-four soloist on the court who had also sung in the Banneker choir. Stout earned all-state honorable mention in his junior year but would dominate during the 1957–1958 season, averaging 31 points and 24 rebounds per game. Cynthiana would fall in the 1958 state tournament to Clark County, but Stout would go on to play basketball at Regis College in Denver, coached by another Cynthiana native and former Kentucky high school coach named Joe B. Hall.[21]

When Hazard High School coach Goebel Ritter ended the 1955–1956 season with the worst record of his career, 7 wins and 20 losses, he could take some consolation in the knowledge that help was on the way. When Liberty Street High School closed in 1956 and its students were integrated into Hazard High School, Ritter must have thought Christmas had come early to the mountains. The Bulldogs received immediate help from three former Liberty Dragons—Don Smith, Linville Wright, and Bobby Baker. Wright would become a solid starter, and Baker would provide help off the bench, but Smith was the prize.

Smith was one of eleven children whose father had been killed in a coal mining accident in 1949. His mother, Myrtle, never remarried, dedicating herself to supporting her children through odd jobs during lean times. When Smith entered Hazard in the fall of 1956, he had little trepidation because, as he explained years later, "We didn't have a choice. We had to pack up and go, because we had to go to school. But we thought Hazard High School was nice. I never had a problem at Hazard." Making the transition to the white school in town was easy because the Hazard students welcomed the Liberty students, many of whom they had known all their lives.[22]

Smith entered Hazard High as a skinny, six-foot-three, 160-pound junior who was a scoring machine. With Smith averaging 20 points per game, the Bulldogs bounced back with a 22–9 record and won the Fourteenth Region championship in 1957. Hazard won its state tournament opener, beating Clay County 50–47, before losing to Pikeville by a score of 68–52. But Smith, Wright, and Baker made history as the first African American players to participate in the KHSAA state tournament. The following season the Bulldogs went 29–5 and again won the regional championship before falling to Daviess County, 71–68, in the semifinal game. That year, Smith was named to the all-state tournament team and the all-state first team before accepting a basketball scholarship to Jackson State.

The best of all the transferred players in the early days of integration might have been Bobby "Toothpick" Jones, a wiry six-foot-three scorer who transferred from Maysville Fee to Maysville High School for his senior year in 1956. Jones had played on the Fee team since the seventh grade, but his breakout game had come as a freshman, when his 24 points kept Fee close in an eventual 60–51 loss to powerful Lexington Dunbar.[23]

In his first few games for Maysville High School, Jones helped the team jump out to a 9–0 record, to the delight of Bulldog fans. "Maysvillians, all of whom take their basketball seriously, find themselves in their greatest frenzy since 1947," wrote one effusive reporter, referencing Maysville's only state championship. "The excitement is because the Bulldogs of Coach Woodie Crum in the first nine games . . . have taken all opponents both at home and abroad with comparative ease. Although it is Christmas time, the fans do not fail to keep an eye on the Bulldogs. The chatter between the young folks and adults alike is equal between the Bulldogs and Santa Claus." The writer added: "Six-three Bobby Jones, who came to Maysville High from Maysville Fee High, is the team's top point maker and rebounder."[24]

Jones and five-foot-nine playmaker Allen Smith led Maysville to a number-one ranking in the state, but in January, sophomore Jack Guy transferred to Nicholas County. The Blue Jackets featured six-foot-nine Ned Jennings, a future University of Kentucky star, and the addition of Guy made the difference in Nicholas's 62–60 victory over Maysville in the Tenth Region final. Jones was duly recognized, however, becoming the first African American elected to the all-state first team before accepting a scholarship to the University of Dayton.[25]

During the 1956–1957 academic year, six more African American schools joined the KHSAA: Louisville Catholic, Mayfield Dunbar, Owensboro Western, Danville Bate, Ashland Booker T. Washington, and Covington Grant.[26] Of the teams playing in their first KHSAA tournament in 1957, Lexington Douglass, Lexington Dunbar, Danville Bate, Louisville Central, Louisville Catholic, and Ashland Booker T. Washington all lost in district play. The lone bright spot was Covington Grant, which became the first African American school in Kentucky to win a KHSAA district tournament and participate in a regional. The Warriors acquitted themselves well in the Ninth Region tournament, defeating Erlanger Lloyd before falling to Dixie Heights, the team they had beaten for the district title.

Lincoln Institute and Mayfield Dunbar chose not to participate in the

KHSAA tournament as first-year members. Lincoln's reasoning was understandable, considering Garner's need to rebuild his team. However, athletic director Gilliard might have had other priorities. He and Dr. Young's youngest daughter Eleanor, the Lincoln librarian, had developed a mutual attraction and were soon married.

KHSAL schools that were denied immediate membership in 1956 began to pressure the KHSAA, claiming that its eligibility policy was restrictive and discriminated against the majority of African American high schools. Members of the KHSAA Board of Control listened and began to consider alternatives. At the KHSAA's annual meeting, held during the 1957 state tournament, board member W. B. Jones of Somerset, where schools had not yet been integrated, made a motion that, beginning with the 1957–1958 school year, "any approved or accredited two-year, three-year or four-year high schools shall be considered eligible for membership in the KHSAA." The proposal was approved unanimously.[27]

Nothing remained to impede KHSAL members from joining the KHSAA. It no longer mattered whether their local school boards had voted to desegregate or were addressing the issue "with all deliberate speed." The consequence of this exodus was clear: desegregation was the order of the day, and league members realized that what had begun in 1932 to give black student-athletes in Kentucky an opportunity to participate in organized athletics had served its purpose and would soon come to an end. The KHSAL's last state tournament was played in 1957 at the Mayo Gym in Frankfort, where Hopkinsville Attucks defeated Paris Western for the state title. After the tournament, the KHSAL Board of Control voted to cease operations.[28]

It could be considered poetic that the KHSAL's demise came the same year that one of its strongest supporters also passed from the scene. Bill Kean had come to Louisville's Central High School in 1922 after graduating from Howard University, where the five-foot-seven, 140-pounder had been a Negro all-America quarterback. His football teams at Central won 80 percent of their games and produced such stars as Lenny Lyles, who would break the color barrier at the University of Louisville in 1954 before having a long career in the NFL, primarily with the Baltimore Colts.

Kean's Yellowjackets were equally proficient on the hardwood, dominating the KHSAL during his tenure. His offenses featured a controlled fast break, and his defenses included a relentless 1-2-1-1 full-court trapping press that broke down the opponents' offenses. Of the twenty-six KHSAL championship games, Central won five tournaments and finished as the runner-up in five others. Kean had the distinct advantage of coaching at the predominant public African American high school in the state's largest city. He could pick and choose his players, whose only high school options were Central, Louisville Catholic, and Lincoln Institute.

Unfortunately, white audiences had few opportunities to watch Kean's teams. His only season competing in the KHSAA as a head coach came in 1957–1958, when failing health forced him to turn over most of the coaching responsibilities to his assistants. Still, the Yellowjackets had little trouble with opponents of either color, posting a 24–2 record before losing the district tournament opener 61–59 in overtime to the eventual state champion, St. Xavier. Kean died on April 29, six weeks after the 1958 tournament.[29]

Other KHSAL teams distinguished themselves at different times during the league's existence. Maysville Fee finished second in the first two tournaments in 1932 and 1933 but never won the title. Frankfort Mayo-Underwood won titles in 1933 and 1941 (over Lincoln Institute) and finished second in 1934 and 1938 (to Lincoln). Madisonville Rosenwald won the 1936 championship, one year after finishing second to Beaver Dam Bruce— that team's only appearance in a title game. Other teams that won in their only appearance in the finals were Winchester Oliver in 1934 and Harrodsburg West Side in 1939.

Richmond High School won three titles, in 1940, 1942, and 1943, before closing in 1947. Horse Cave won the last war-era tournaments in 1944 and 1945; it was undefeated in both years and won a remarkable sixty-five games in a row. Madisonville Rosenwald won its second title in 1946 after losing to Horse Cave in 1945. Lexington Dunbar played for the championship six times but won only twice, in 1948 and 1950. Hopkinsville Attucks won the 1947 tournament, in addition to winning the final KHSAL tournament in 1957.

As Louis Stout noted, the importance of the KHSAL cannot be overstated, despite its relatively brief history. "It brought order out of chaos, and in so doing, provided a level playing field for all black athletes and black schools," he wrote. "Had the KHSAL not come into existence, it is impossible to imagine how athletics in black schools could have succeeded. The KHSAL's success did not just happen by accident or without tremendous sacrifice by hundreds of individuals. It succeeded because it was blessed with great leaders who understood the need for solidarity and uniformity. From that shared belief, black student-athletes were given the opportunity to compete and often to excel."[30]

It is a conundrum of progress that traditions established and nurtured in the flames of injustice fall victim to the virtues of fairness and propriety. The KHSAL schools were underfunded and were denied the privileges enjoyed by white schools. But their leaders, coaches, and players planted a weather-beaten acorn, nurtured it, and watched it grow into a tree of opportunity, excellence, and dignity. When it fell to a righteous axe, its seeds found fertile soil and sprouted a new generation of players whose achievements stood as an unspoken tribute to the past. Integration came with a price, including the loss of those cherished schools that belonged to the KHSAL.

The surviving schools had a limited opportunity to pay tribute to their KHSAL heritage. They did not know how much time would pass before African American high school basketball became nothing but a fond memory. Until then, the black schools that survived could prove to a new and larger audience that their teams were at least the equal of any that had played before. Their window of opportunity was closing, but until it slammed shut on the hard sill of full integration, African American programs still had a chance to compete.

Former champions Maysville Fee and Horse Cave joined Louisville Catholic and Russellville Knob City in closing their doors in 1957, but thirty additional former KHSAL members submitted applications to the KHSAA and were approved for the 1957–1958 academic year. With the nine schools that had been accepted into membership the previous year, a total of thirty-nine African American schools were now eligible to participate in district tournaments in March 1958.[31]

11

In Front of the Parade

Nineteen Senators and 77 members of the House of Representatives, all from the eleven states of the Old Confederacy, have signed the "Southern Manifesto," a resolution condemning the 1954 Supreme Court decision in *Brown v. Board of Education.* The manifesto accused the Court of jeopardizing the social justice of white people and "their habits, traditions, and way of life" and claimed that the *Brown* ruling would "destroy the amicable relations between the white and Negro races that have been created through 90 years of patient effort by the good people of both races."
—Associated Press, March 12, 1956

Lincoln Institute's basketball team suffered through a disappointing 1956–1957 season, finishing with a 10–13 record while being embarrassed by both their Lexington rivals. Douglass rolled over the Tigers by scores of 101–52 and 115–66, and Dunbar defeated them 76–46. None of coach Herbert Garner's starters could match up with Douglass's Paul Price, John Henry Burdette, and the Bell brothers—George and Henry—or Dunbar's Julius Berry and Vertner Taylor. Lincoln's prospects appeared to be no better for the 1957–1958 season, so Eleanor Young Gilliard suggested to her father that it might be time for a change.

Eleanor's influence had grown since her return to Lincoln, and it was common knowledge among the faculty, staff, and students that her authority on campus matters was exceeded only by her father's. The exact conversation between the parties is unknown, but the record shows that in the spring of 1957 Garner resigned and Young named his athletic director (and son-in-law) Walter Gilliard to replace him as head basketball coach.[1] Gilliard's promotion was not unreasonable. He had served as head coach at Covington Grant after the respected Paul Redden left in 1952 to coach at Knoxville College. Gilliard had led his 1952–1953 team to a 20–8 record, and his 1953–1954 team had finished with a respectable 17–9 season.

After his discharge from the US Coast Guard, Gilliard had enrolled at Kentucky State, where he was exposed to a number of prominent African American coaches who likely helped mold his own coaching philosophy. His first football coach with the Thorobreds was Bill Willis, an all-American defensive lineman who had helped lead Ohio State to an undefeated season. A professional football career was unlikely when Willis graduated in the spring of 1945. No African American had played in the National Football League since 1933 because of a "gentlemen's agreement" entered into after segregationist George Preston Marshall joined the league as owner of the Boston Redskins. In his physical prime, but with no prospect of playing professionally, Willis took the job as head football coach at Kentucky State College in the fall of 1945.[2]

Willis's heart was "not really in coaching," he later admitted, and after one year in Frankfort he contacted his former coach at Ohio State, Paul Brown, who was coaching a team in the newly formed All-America Football Conference (AAFC). Brown signed the former Buckeye, and Willis became one of the best defensive linemen in professional football. The Cleveland Browns won each of the AAFC's four championship games, and Willis made the league's all-star team each year. The AAFC dissolved in 1949, but the Browns extended their string of success in the National Football League, and Willis continued to excel before retiring prior to the 1954 season. No record exists of Coach Willis's interaction with his Kentucky State players, but for at least for one year, freshman quarterback Walter Gilliard was exposed to an African American player-coach who in 1977 would be elected to the Pro Football Hall of Fame.

Gilliard did not play basketball at Kentucky State, but his knowledge of the game was sharpened from a distance. Head basketball coach J. G. Fletcher had an impressive coaching pedigree and a history of success in the KHSAL. A graduate of Hampton Institute and Cornell University, Fletcher had won varsity basketball letters at Hampton and had been a star center on the 1929 Central Intercollegiate Athletic Association (CIAA) championship team. He served as an assistant basketball coach at Hampton and then spent seven years at Richmond (Kentucky) High School, where he coached the Ramblers to three KHSAL championships during the war years. Fletcher was appointed head basketball coach and associate professor of English at Kentucky State College in July 1946, one year before Richmond High School shut its doors.[3]

Meanwhile, Gilliard would become an all-America quarterback worthy of election to the Kentucky State University Hall of Fame in 1993. He was also a leader off the football field, serving as an officer of Alpha Phi Alpha fraternity. But as a new assistant high school basketball coach, Gilliard would find his inspiration from a Kansas native who had learned the game at the feet of the master. John McLendon picked up the intricacies of basketball from the sport's inventor, Dr. James Naismith, who was then the athletic director at the University of Kansas. McLendon was not permitted to play college basketball, as Kansas's varsity team was not integrated until 1951, but he was a willing student.[4]

After a brief period as a high school coach, McLendon became head coach at North Carolina College for Negroes, where he led the Eagles to eight CIAA championships from 1941 to 1952. McLendon's teams were credited with speeding up the game from the slow, deliberate tempo of its early years to the faster pace that would later dominate. McLendon was also a progressive who fought segregation and injustice throughout his life. While at North Carolina College, he even arranged a game with the best team at Duke University, which happened to be from the medical school. He scheduled the game for a Sunday morning, when the police were in church and the campus was silent, and his Eagles won the "secret" game by a score of 88–44.[5]

Despite McLendon's success, North Carolina College's new president, responding to state budget cuts, elected to de-emphasize athletics. McLendon moved to Hampton Institute in 1952, and in 1954 he was hired by Henry A. Kean, the athletic director at Tennessee A&I (later Tennessee State) and former director of the KHSAL. It was at Tennessee State that McLendon would gain the recognition he had long deserved, leading his Tigers to three championships between 1954 and 1959 in the integrated National Association of Intercollegiate Athletics (NAIA) tournament.[6]

Gilliard knew it would take time to build a team that could run and press like McLendon's Tennessee State Tigers, but the 1957–1958 season proved difficult for a reason that went far beyond coaching. It was the first year Lincoln Institute and other African American schools that were new members of the KHSAA could schedule games with white teams. Gilliard soon learned that having the ability to play white teams and actually doing it were two different things. The Lincoln coach called the local schools in Shelby County first; he talked with some of the coaches and left messages for others. Some coaches told him their schedules were full, while others candidly admitted their reluctance to be the first to schedule a game with a black school. Their fans, they said, had not warmed to the idea of integration. However, one coach had no reservations about playing a black school and actually welcomed the opportunity. Arnold Thurman, the new head coach at Bagdad High School, had played with African American teammates at Berea College, Lincoln Institute's founding institution.[7]

Thurman grew up on a farm near Eminence in Henry County and was comfortable with his black neighbors. One of his best friends growing up was a black boy, and the two were inseparable, playing in the fields or shooting baskets at a rusty rim hanging from the barn. When Thurman worked at harvesting tobacco on humid, ninety-degree August days, it did not matter what color his fellow workers were. As each of them cut and spiked six stalks on a five-foot tobacco stick, the gum from the leaves covered their arms like glue. Then they loaded the sticks onto a wagon and hauled them to a three-story barn, where they hung the sticks to cure. Color did not matter to those who worked in the tobacco patch. They were all miserable together.

Thurman arrived at Berea College in 1951 to play basketball and baseball and to run track, but he also learned that others did not share his liberal view of race relations. Thurman became friends with the black students who lived on the same floor of his dormitory, and when the basketball team went on the road, he volunteered to room with Berea's star center, six-foot-five Irvine Shanks, an African American from Richmond, Kentucky. On road trips with the team, Berea's head coach Clarence H. "Monarchy" Wyatt

Arnold Thurman was a young coach at Bagdad High School when he convinced the principal and the team's fans that playing Lincoln Institute was not only the right thing to do; it was essential. (Courtesy of the Arnold Thurman family)

would go into a restaurant by himself and then come back out and tell his players, "They can't serve us here. They're closing up." It did not take long for the players to figure out that the restaurant's hours often depended on the color of the would-be patrons. While on a road trip to play Wittenberg College in Springfield, Ohio, Thurman suggested to Shanks that they go into a drugstore for some ice cream. Thurman went into the store and sat down on a stool, but Shanks knew he could not sit down with his teammate because of his color. Thurman never forgot that.

After the Supreme Court rulings in the *Brown* case, Thurman saw the future and was not frightened by it. Bagdad was his first head coaching job, and he had not won a single game, let alone enjoyed the success that would earn him the support of fans and players. None of that mattered. Thurman courageously launched a subtle campaign to prepare his administrators, Bagdad's fans, and his own players to accept the reality that the end of segregation meant the end of all-white basketball.

Bagdad was a typical rural Kentucky farming town, where the residents' priorities were no more complicated than church, dairy production, and a healthy tobacco crop. Other than a Civil War skirmish fought nearby on December 12, 1861, Bagdad enjoyed the peace that comes with uneventful anonymity.[8] Indeed, when Thurman began suggesting that Bagdad should play Lincoln Institute, the typical response was: why? Thurman replied that sooner or later, they would have no choice. The law was changing, and they would be forced to play the colored school. But he saved his best argument for last: if the Bagdad Tigers wanted a chance to go to the state tournament, they would have to beat all comers, including Lincoln Institute. Thurman recalled years later: "I told them I didn't have any problem with that. Do you? And they reluctantly said, 'Well, naw, we don't have a problem with that.'" If a parade was heading through Bagdad, Thurman told his supporters, then it's best to get in front of it. And if it helps your favorite basketball team, all the better.

Thurman and Gilliard agreed that their teams would play on November 22, 1957, the first game of the new basketball season.

Gilliard was not certain what kind of team he would have for his first season, but help was on the way. Transfer senior Ralph Willingham was a six-foot-four center from the far western Carlisle County hamlet of Bardwell, just five miles from the Mississippi River. Gilliard also liked a cat-quick junior guard from Jefferson County named Henry McAtee, who, though only five foot six, was athletic enough to dunk the basketball. But a promising group of sophomores gave Gilliard the core he needed to mold a team after John McLendon's at Tennessee State. Their names were John Watkins, Ben Spalding, Jewell Logan, and Daniel Thomas.

Watkins grew up in relative stability, the son of the Reverend and Mrs. J. M. Watkins of Bloomfield in Nelson County, forty-two miles south of Louisville. As befits the son of a preacher, Watkins had a calm demeanor, and his only goals at Lincoln were to study, learn, and graduate with honors. Although Gilliard would never be satisfied with his lackluster defensive effort, the five-foot-eleven Watkins was fearless when he had the ball. He would pull up and shoot, regardless of the distance, and he was not afraid to run over a defender who stood between him and the basket.[9]

Spalding grew up only sixteen miles from Watkins in Springfield, Kentucky, a small farming community in heavily Catholic Washington County. Spalding attended Holy Rosary Catholic Church and learned to play basketball on the church's playground. The basketball court consisted of a dirt floor and a basket that was, in reality, an open rim on top of a pole. It did not have a backboard, so Spalding and friends Everett Cooper, Roscoe Spalding, and Alphonso Coleman sharpened their shooting eyes by aiming directly at the rim.[10]

Spalding was taller than the others and pretended he was Bill Russell, the six-foot-nine African American center who had led the University of San Francisco to consecutive National Collegiate Athletic Association (NCAA) titles in 1955 and 1956 before landing with the Boston Celtics. Spalding and his teammates were the best players on the playground, but Big Ben was smart enough to know there weren't many opportunities for young black basketball players in Springfield. When Spalding and his friends got to the eighth grade at St. Catherine's School, they boldly approached Mr. Osborne, the superintendent of all-white Springfield High School, and told him they wanted to attend Springfield High and play basketball for the Panthers. They had grown up playing with the white boys on the Holy Rosary playground during the summer, and there was little doubt that Spalding and his friends were better. The superintendent was sympathetic but admitted he was helpless. Springfield was not yet integrated, and he could not enroll black students without causing trouble in the community.

For Spalding, the logical option was nine miles away in Lebanon, where the Rosenwald Foundation had built a school. He was the youngest of eight children, and all his brothers and sisters had attended that school. But Ben's mother saw something special in her youngest and wanted him to get a better education. She asked her sister, an elementary school teacher, for advice. "Why, Ben belongs at Lincoln Institute," she responded. So they applied to the local school board, which by law was required to pay Ben's tuition to Lincoln.

Jewell Logan and Daniel Thomas took more direct roads to Lincoln. Like Johnny "Slam Bam" Cunningham, Logan and Thomas grew up in Lawrenceburg and had gone to the African American elementary school there. Anderson High School in Lawrenceburg was not yet integrated, so Logan and others had the option of taking a commuter bus to Versailles Simmons High School or attending Lincoln Institute. The Anderson County board of education paid their tuition to Lincoln, but the students still needed money for clothes and other expenses during the school year. The boys found jobs around town, primarily working in the tobacco patches or pitching hay bales. They would load the bales, which could weigh up to eighty pounds, neatly stack them onto wagons, and then haul them to barns and rick them in the hayloft, to be used to feed livestock during the winter. The boys were usually paid an hourly rate, but certain jobs, such as cutting tobacco, could pay up to $7 a day. The boys did not decline any jobs that were available, regardless of pay.

Daniel Thomas made $1.25 an hour for tending a man's garden and cutting his lawn, which was good money, but it was only one day a week. Other jobs paid less, such as the merchant who offered ten cents an hour to deliver handbills around town. When Thomas's mother found out what he was being paid, she demanded that he quit the job or get a whipping. Other jobs depended on the whim of the employer. When one man told Thomas he had to let him go because he wasn't keeping up, the boy begged to keep the job because he needed the money for clothes to go to school.[11]

Thomas's mother, who worked as a domestic for a white family, could not help much with expenses. The family treated Daniel's mother well, and the white children in her care loved her so much they called her "Momma"—at least until the lady of the house heard the reference and snapped at the children, "She is not your momma." It was a societal irony that did not dawn on Daniel until years later at the white father's funeral, where one of those children, then grown, remarked, "You know what, Danny, that must have been really something. You left home at fourteen and your momma took care of us while we were here at home." Daniel smiled sadly at the memory of the way life was in a bygone day.

On Monday mornings during the school year, Logan, Thomas, and their friend Victor Brown would stand on Main Street in Lawrenceburg, across from Anderson High School, and put out their thumbs, hoping to catch a ride to Lincoln Ridge, thirty-five miles away. At about the same time, the white kids would be getting off the buses that dropped them at Anderson High. The white students would wave at the hitchhikers, whom they knew from summer basketball and baseball games, where race was not an impediment. Like John Cunningham and others before them, Logan, Thomas, and Brown waved back, confident that their school had a better reputation than Anderson High or most other white schools.[12]

At Lincoln Institute, Logan, Thomas, and Brown shared a dormitory room with two other local boys; they called it the "Lawrenceburg room." Basketball and their studies took up most of their weekends during the season, but when sports did not interfere, the boys would walk out to US 60 on Friday afternoons and hitchhike back to Lawrenceburg, where they had part-time jobs. They never had a problem getting a ride, and they were often picked up by the same people each week, many of whom worked in Louisville and took the same route home every day. Not all rides were as welcomed as others, however. One man from Lawrenceburg would pick them up in his 1953 Chevrolet sedan. The man was frugal with his gasoline and used every trick he knew to conserve fuel, including chugging slowly up one hill, shifting out of gear into neutral, and coasting down the next hill. The boys moaned when they saw that '53 Chevy stop to pick them up because they knew it was going to be a long ride back to Lawrenceburg.

The integration of Kentucky's public schools progressed modestly in the 1957–1958 school year. In its annual report on school attendance, the Department of Education reported that when classes commenced, 10,397 Negroes and 133,132 whites were enrolled in 263 integrated schools in 94 districts. The state had a total of 630,400 students in public schools, including an estimated 40,000 African Americans. These figures represented slight increases from the year before, when about 8,000 Negro students had attended school with 120,000 whites.[13]

The numbers were skewed, however, by Louisville's progressive approach. In that city, 7,647 blacks attended classes with 28,147 whites. The reality was that nearly 70 percent of the state's blacks in integrated schools were in Louisville and Jefferson County, indicating there was much work left to be done under the state's policy of gradual compliance. Thankfully, there was no recurrence of the violence that had taken place the previous year at Sturgis. This was not the case in other states, particularly in the South.

Easily, the nation's most heated confrontation over school desegregation erupted at Little Rock, Arkansas, in September 1957. In some ways, this was an unexpected venue for violence. Until then, Arkansas had been more moderate on racial issues than other states in the Deep South, and in 1948 it had desegregated its state university.[14]

Ten Arkansas school districts had announced in 1955 that they would gradually comply with the *Brown* decision. One of these was Little Rock, which had desegregated its parks, buses, and hospitals and had approved a token plan to admit six black girls and three black boys to Central High School in 1957. Arkansas governor Orval Faubus was a product of the largely white Ozark hill country. He had been elected in 1954 as a progressive advocate of economic development, and in 1955 leaders of the segregationist Citizens Council had dubbed him "Awful" Faubus. Challenged by a staunch advocate of segregation in 1956, he had taken a relatively moderate stance on racial issues and won reelection.

However, Faubus operated behind the scenes to rally Arkansas senators and representatives in support of the "Southern Manifesto," a document signed in March 1956 by ninety-nine Democrats and two Republicans from states of the old Confederacy to protest the racial integration of public places. By 1957, Faubus was looking for an issue to help him win a third term. He thereby announced that desegregation of Central High School in Little Rock could not be managed without violence. To avert trouble, which Faubus alone foresaw, he called out the National Guard, which surrounded Central High on September 3, the first day of school. No mob materialized, and the soldiers had nothing to do, but Faubus had whipped up racist feelings. White community leaders, who had devised a plan to isolate desegregation within the largely working-class neighborhoods in the Central High School district, did virtually nothing in the struggles that followed to counteract Faubus's stance. The next day, when the nine black students sought to enter the school, they faced crowds of irate whites, and troops barred them from the building.

President Eisenhower summoned Faubus to his vacation home in Newport, Rhode Island, in an attempt to reach a settlement. Faubus pledged to accept the courts' decisions on integration and hoped federal authorities would show "understanding and patience" by acknowledging the complexity of this issue in the South.[15] On September 20 a federal district judge enjoined Faubus from preventing the black students' attendance at Central High. The governor ordered the troops to withdraw, leaving the nine black students at the mercy of a howling, spitting mob. On September 23 violent whites attacked blacks as well as "Yankee" reporters and photographers. Local police were clearly sympathetic to the mob and did little to stop the violence.

The standoffs during these three weeks captured national and international attention. Television, by now a fixture in millions of American homes, showed many of the ugly scenes. Integrationists demanded that Eisenhower intervene on behalf of the embattled black students, but he hesitated, hoping that local authorities could resolve the crisis. When that did not occur, the president ordered regular army troops and federalized Arkansas National Guardsmen to the city.[16]

Southern politicians were outraged at the intervention of federal troops, whom Senator Richard Russell of Georgia compared to "Hitler's storm troopers." Some of the white students at Central High cursed, pushed, kicked, and spat on their black classmates. Segregationists set fires, instigated bomb scares, and threatened to kill the school superintendent (one such attempt was made but failed). Other extremists fired bullets into the Little Rock home of Daisy Bates, president of the Arkansas branch of the NAACP.

Eisenhower refused to consider federal prosecution of the alleged instigators of violence, but he did keep troops at Central High for the remainder of the 1957–1958 academic year. It was into this raucous milieu that one former Lincoln Institute basketball player would soon be dropped.

12

"A World Uncertain"

The Negroes are of value economically to the South but at present the white citizens councils can only see what seems to them a danger. It will take time and a little calm for them to realize that the danger lies as much in losing this population as in retaining it and accepting the fact that integration is as inevitable as freedom.

—Eleanor Roosevelt

Heading into the 1957–1958 season, Walter Gilliard knew that his team's talent level was not yet where he wanted it to be. But his football background convinced him that the best cure for a lack of talent was superior conditioning and toughness. To transform his players into that Spartan model, he established a program consisting of heavy running combined with individual drills to improve certain physical skills. Before practice, the whole team was required to run the mile from the gymnasium down to the Blue Gate at US 60 and back. After practice, they had to repeat the two-mile round-trip.

Gilliard chided six-foot-four Ben Spalding about his lack of jumping ability. To improve that perceived fault, Gilliard sent Big Ben into practice every day wearing heavy rubber galoshes over his basketball shoes. On those rare occasions when Spalding was allowed to take off the galoshes, he felt like he was jumping through the roof. Six-foot-two Daniel Thomas was another target for extra drills. He had to wear the galoshes not only in practice but also on the team's run down to the Blue Gate and back. Then Gilliard prescribed even more running, having Thomas sprint up and down the stairs in the gymnasium.

Gilliard required his guards to wear cotton gloves during practice to make their ball handling and passing more efficient. All the starting players had to wear two-pound ankle weights during practice to improve their speed and jumping ability, which would help them execute his full-court defensive press.

On the eve of the season, Gilliard's starting five would come from a rotation that included seniors Ralph Willingham, Melvin Wilson of Louisville, and Jesse Thomas of Lawrenceburg; juniors Henry McAtee and Harry Walker of Hickman in western Kentucky; and sophomores Ben Spalding, Jewell Logan, and John Watkins. The Tigers might not win a game during the 1957–1958 season, but they would be in good shape.

Arnold Thurman's lobbying efforts came to fruition when Bagdad became the first white school in Shelby County to face Lincoln Institute during the regular season. The game was played on November 22, 1957, in Bagdad's tiny gym, which could have fit snugly into the Lincoln Institute gymnasium at Hughes Hall. One player remarked that the Bagdad gym was so small it seemed like they bumped their heads on the ceiling every time they ran down the court. The gym was as disconcerting to the Lincoln players as the fact that they were playing before a white crowd for the first time. Whatever the reason, the white Tigers easily took the measure of the black Tigers, winning the season opener by a score of 47–40.

Not all Bagdad fans had warmed to the idea of playing a black team, and some stayed away. Taking their place were new fans who considered a game between a black team and a white team a curiosity. Though accustomed to the easy manner of their black neighbors and black farmworkers, many white fans had never seen black athletes in close-up competition. Black basketball players were a novelty to these white sports fans, many of whom had never seen a live sporting event above the high school level. Television was still new in the 1950s, and televised sports was virtually limited to Saturday afternoon baseball.

Lincoln provided something else that white audiences had never seen. "Their cheerleaders were a little different than we were used to," Thurman recalled. The Bagdad fans reveled at the acrobatics and the spirited cheers of

Lincoln's cheerleaders generated their own following with their acrobatic routines and crowd-pleasing chants. From left: Anna Hite, Mary Yocum, Frances Hill, Amelia Courtney, Joyce Shelby, and Augustine Johnson. (Courtesy of Daniel Thomas)

the Lincoln girls, who "put a little more into their cheering than what our girls did. There was more of a show in them."[1]

Scheduling the game with Lincoln made Thurman a popular source of information for his fellow coaches, most of whom had never coached against black players. He received many calls after that first game and many more after a subsequent victory at Lincoln. The first question was usually: "How did you get along at Lincoln?" Thurman recalled: "The first year my telephone rang off the hook with questions from other coaches. They knew that sooner or later they would have to play Lincoln or other black schools. They'd heard stories about teams getting into fights at Lincoln, and some of that was true, but what they did not know was that the fights were never with white teams. The only trouble Lincoln had was with other black teams. There was a long-standing rivalry among the black schools, but the white coaches knew nothing about it because they had never been around it."

Thurman had some more advice for the coaches who called: they needed to be aware of their own players' attitudes toward race. "I should have been smart enough to pick up on it," Thurman said, "but I had a big, raw-boned kid who evidently didn't like blacks, and he didn't like playing against them. I didn't know that at the time. I didn't see anything on the court where he'd mouth off or throw an elbow. If it happened, I would have taken care of it real quick."

The first indication of trouble came when Thurman's old coach, Clarence Wyatt, invited him and his team to Berea for a scrimmage. After the first half the teams took a break, and Thurman went to the first-aid room to tape the ankles of one of his players. There, he encountered a black Berea player who projected an attitude of suspicion and hostility. "That kid turned me off real quick," Thurman recalled. "I hadn't done anything to him, but I realized something had gone on during the first half that I didn't know about. There was something that caused this kid to have a problem with us, and later I found out what it was."

Thurman learned the source of the problem from one of his players. "Yeah, I'm going to make sure I'm with Howard if anything happens," the player told the coach. Thurman asked him what he was talking about, and the boy responded: "Howard is a big old strong boy." Thurman fished some more, and the player finally admitted: "Howard doesn't like blacks." Thurman did not address the player directly, preferring to talk to the entire team "so we would not have those problems again."

In addition to losing their first match with a white team, the Lincoln Tigers could not post a win against their traditional rivals. Typical were humiliations such as an 80–39 loss to Dunbar on January 22, a 103–61 capitulation to Douglass on February 11, and a 74–41 pasting by Paris Western on February 15.[2] Accordingly, after bypassing the state tournament in its first year of KHSAA membership, Lincoln's performance in the 1957–1958 tournament was predictable. The Tigers fell to neighbor Simpsonville by a score of 66–59 in their first game as a member of the Thirtieth District.

But other African American teams playing in their first KHSAA tournament gave basketball fans around the commonwealth a glimpse of what had been missing from the all-white tournament. In 1958 thirty-eight African American schools participated in twenty-nine of the sixty-four district tournaments.[3] That initial group immediately proved it belonged at the dance, compiling a cumulative 34–30 record in district play and a 16–5 record in regional play.

Six former KHSAL members won district tournaments: Bowling Green High Street won the Seventeenth District title, Lebanon Rosenwald won the

Frankfort High School was integrated by the 1959–1960 season, which allowed African Americans and whites to play together. Here, George Calhoun (54) tries to block a shot by Lexington Lafayette's Jeff Mullins, while teammates Jim Brown (12) and Louis Tandy (44) look on. (Courtesy of *Lexington Herald-Leader,* University of Kentucky Special Collections)

Twenty-First District crown, Covington Grant repeated in the Thirty-Fourth District, Paris Western won the Fortieth District title, Lexington Dunbar took the Forty-Third District, and Harlan Rosenwald won the Fifty-Second District championship. More significantly, three of these district winners won their regional tournaments and became the first all-black teams to participate in the KHSAA "Sweet Sixteen." Bowling Green High Street was champion of the Fifth Region, Covington Grant won the Ninth Region, and Lexington Dunbar won the Eleventh Region.

In the 1958 state tournament played at the University of Kentucky's Memorial Coliseum in Lexington, Dunbar and High Street further distinguished themselves with opening-round victories. Dunbar defeated Meade Memorial 82–60, while High Street defeated Shelbyville 85–73. Covington Grant was ambushed 87–49 by integrated Hazard High School and its all-state center Don Smith.

In the quarterfinals, Dunbar lost a 44–25 slow-down game to eventual champion Louisville St. Xavier, and High Street narrowly lost a 67–65 thriller to Clark County. Hazard's Don Smith, Louis Stout of Cynthiana, and Julius Berry of Dunbar became the first African American players selected to the KHSAA all-tournament team.

For Lincoln Institute, however, the 1957–1958 season turned out to be even worse than Gilliard had feared. The Tigers won only four games and lost twenty-one—the worst season in school history. On the plus side, junior guard Henry McAtee had been a pest on defense, while sophomores Ben Spalding and Jewell Logan had gained considerable playing time. Other young guns such as John Watkins and Danny Thomas had benefited from a season's worth of experience on the junior varsity team.

"Wait 'til next year" was a phrase popularized by the long-suffering fans of baseball's Brooklyn Dodgers, but it was a battle cry that gave the Lincoln Institute Tigers hope for the future.

Shelby County's *Shelby News* and *Shelby Sentinel* began to report the scores of Lincoln Institute's games during the 1957–1958 season. Critics could argue that the newspapers had not changed their policy; they were begrudgingly reporting Lincoln's basketball results as part and parcel of their coverage of the local white teams. Because the white teams were now playing black schools, the latter benefited from the collateral coverage.

Doubtless, African Americans were avid readers of these local newspapers, if for no other reason than to identify the latest bargains at Steiden's Grocery or Bill's Food Market (pork brains, 23 cents a pound; ground beef, 29 cents a pound; fresh country large eggs, 39 cents a dozen). On rare occasions, events of dubious interest to black readers would appear, such as a notice in the June 10, 1955, edition of the *Sentinel* that announced: "The Colored Playground is to open this week. . . . A baseball field is being cleared at the site of the old city dump and a backstop has been erected." Typical of community journalism, neither local newspaper was bolder than its times. When front-page attention was paid to blacks, it was more likely in headlines such as these: "Negro Flees County Jail; Partner Held," or "Negro Killed, Another Injured in Brawl on Bradshaw Street."4

Lincoln Institute did not receive much recognition from its hometown newspapers. Dr. Young, himself a biblical scholar, might have referred to scripture in describing his institution's relative anonymity in Shelby County. As Jesus told his disciples in Mark 6:4: "A prophet is not without honor except in his hometown and among his own relatives and in his own household."

The disappointing 1957–1958 basketball season paled in comparison to national events that would affect Lincoln Institute students, whether they realized it at the time or not. Graduates do not recall Dr. Young spending much time talking about the national desegregation movement or the often violent resistance occurring in many southern states. Young wanted his students to take the long view beyond the Blue Gate, to find their place in a world that they would help mold and secure.

In his graduation address to the senior class of 1958, Dr. Young drew on world events and biblical references to frame a direction for his students. Time-honored institutions and pillars of the black community such as Lincoln Institute would not be necessary in a color-blind society, but, he suggested, integration had a price:

> You face a world uncertain as to its destiny, its beliefs, its goals, its concepts of democracy, its constitution and its "Bill of Rights." In fact, we are facing a new world order. The walls of Jericho are falling down, bringing with them the fate of America and the world. Never before in our history has there been so great a demand for men and women of great vision, great courage, great ideas and great faith. We must think big as well as act big. Many of our cherished dreams must go overboard to save the "Ship of State."
>
> [The Soviet satellite] *Sputnik,* with a dead dog, is only a symbol of what may some day come to pass if we allow our thoughts and acts to degenerate to the point where evil men take over government. The only

way out is absolute unselfishness, absolute purity, absolute honesty and absolute love. The choice you make may help to decide the fate of the world.

Lincoln Institute has pointed the way. It is up to you to walk therein. "I am the way, the truth and the light." This is the great challenge. In your hands, along with millions of other youth of America and the world, has been placed the tremendous responsibility of remaking the new world order. A world in which every man shall be accepted for what he really is deep within and must carry his own burden without the handicap of race, color, or creed. You will not succeed by looking down, or out. The star of hope is Up![5]

John "Slam Bam" Cunningham enlisted in the air force in January 1956 and was trained as a military policeman. On July 19 his ship docked at Yokohama, Japan. Cunningham liked the Japanese people, who did not take the measure of a man by the color of his skin. Life was good for an MP, who enjoyed a certain amount of authority on the base, but Cunningham was still a basketball player. He played in a military league, where his shooting ability and athleticism drew the attention of his superiors. The young man from Lawrenceburg, Kentucky, was assigned to the Fifth Air Force touring all-star team and saw the world from behind a basketball, traveling through Asia and the Middle East.

In the summer of 1958 Cunningham was reassigned. He had been ordered to the Little Rock Air Force Base, seventeen miles northeast of the Arkansas capital. This drew the attention of some Japanese workers at the base. "Johnny-san," they said in alarm, "you go Faubus-land?" He was amazed that the Japanese were aware of the racial problems in the United States, particularly in Arkansas. They were quick to warn him of Governor Faubus, cautioning, "He no like black GI."

Black servicemen in Little Rock learned early on where not to go and what not to do. The center of black social and economic life was Ninth Street, where African Americans owned barbershops, grocery stores, and the popular Flamingo Club. A few blocks away was the only hotel in town that permitted African American guests. The Hotel Charmaine, located at the corner

John Cunningham leaps above a taller opponent to grab a rebound during an air force all-star game in Japan. Cunningham also traveled to Korea and the Middle East with the air force all-stars. (Courtesy of John N. Cunningham)

John Cunningham was a member of a military police unit in Japan and when he returned Stateside to Little Rock, Arkansas. (Courtesy of John N. Cunningham)

of Fourteenth and Izard, was host to many African American celebrities who came to town, including Fats Domino, Joe Louis, Jackie Robinson, Willie Mays, and Sam Cooke.

Cunningham recalled that Little Rock had only two black police officers in the entire department, each working a twelve-hour shift. One of their tasks was to make sure the black servicemen who were unfamiliar with local customs and proclivities did not venture too far off Ninth Street, lest they get into trouble. The white police enforced the rules, and they too were occasionally spotted on Ninth Street, presumably during the course of official business.

Soon after his arrival, Cunningham's sergeant sent him to downtown Little Rock to pick up some special uniforms for his MP unit, nicknamed the "Hard Chargers." They were responsible for base security, and their uniforms were designed for easy recognition. Cunningham was not excited about the assignment, but he followed orders and took a military vehicle to the store. When he arrived, a man behind the counter looked up from his paper and gruffly shouted a challenge: "What do you want here, boy?" Cunningham told him his sergeant had sent him to pick up some uniforms. Recognizing a paying customer, the storekeeper no longer saw black but green, the color of money, and eased up.

"That was a strange damned place, I'll tell you," Cunningham said. "Where I grew up, I had to sit in certain seats in the movies, and I couldn't go to the white schools, but I never experienced any *real racial* stuff until I got to Little Rock! Those white people were strange down there."[6]

13

An Accepted Way of Life

When Oscar Robertson emerged from the locker room for warm-ups, the packed arena at North Texas greeted him with boos and racial epithets. The taunts grew so bad that Robertson stood at the center of the court, alone, hands on his hips, with the people of Denton spewing rage all around him. For two hours, fans behind the Cincinnati bench screamed at Robertson, introducing him to insults that he'd never heard before. Unable to pay attention in the huddle, Robertson scored twelve points, much lower than his thirty-six point average, but Cincinnati emerged victorious by a score of 70–53.

—Brad Folsom

As practice began for the 1958–1959 season, Walter Gilliard looked back only once. The previous year, his team had lost nearly every game, and his leading scorer, Ralph Willingham, had graduated. The kings of black high school basketball in Kentucky only three years earlier, the Lincoln Institute Tigers had fallen well behind longtime rivals Bowling Green High Street, Covington Grant, and Lexington Dunbar. All three had made it to the 1958 state tournament and were favored to win their regions again in 1959. Would Lincoln be able to rise to such heights before its doors closed forever? Gilliard could not dwell on past rivalries or bragging rights. He had to worry about the present and his new rivals: Simpsonville, Shelbyville, Bagdad, and Waddy.

He was expecting improvement from his team in the new season, but just how much depended on the unpredictability of youth. Lincoln's senior spark plug Henry McAtee was back, but the Tigers' success hinged on how much last year's sophomores had matured under fire. Ben Spalding had been a starter all season, and Jewell Logan had seen considerable playing time off the bench. Danny Thomas and John Watkins should be ready to contribute, and sophomore Billy Collins, up from the junior varsity team, had a combative attitude that could be useful.

But Gilliard saw something special in two new players who were also on the football team. Clyde Mosby of Maud, Kentucky, five miles south of Bloomfield, was a quarterback with a lively arm and good speed. On the basketball court, the five-foot-ten Mosby was a good ball handler who could back up McAtee. John Kavanaugh Cunningham was a dark-complexioned freshman from Lawrenceburg whom the players called "Black John" to eliminate any confusion with the legendary (and lighter-skinned) John Norman "Slam Bam" Cunningham, known as "White John." Gilliard loved Black John's toughness, and even though he might not be looking for a fight, he welcomed one when it came his way.

Gilliard's affection for the burly Cunningham might have started one day after football practice when Gilliard, a former quarterback himself, was teasing his players that they could not catch him and tackle him in the open field. The players were not wearing any pads, but that did not stop Cunningham and several other players from accepting the coach's challenge. When one of them finally grabbed Gilliard, it was Black John who piled on with all the finesse of a Friday night wrestler. Gilliard was laughing through the pain, but it was a moment that generated respect on both sides.[1]

John K. Cunningham grew up in Bucktown off Main Street, a black settlement of eight to ten families in a section of Lawrenceburg called the White Way today. Cunningham's father departed when John and his two sisters were young, leaving his mother to try to make ends meet. They lived in a small house with no electricity or running water, and trips to the outdoor privy were especially long and difficult in the winter. Every visit reduced the size of the Sears Roebuck catalog, which the family employed because they could not afford toilet paper.

Cunningham played sports as a boy, but his secret pleasure was visiting a neighbor who had the first television in Bucktown—a small, round black-and-white set. The neighborhood boys would stop by after school to watch *T-Bar-V Ranch,* a children's program on WHAS-TV in Louisville that fea-

The 1959 Lincoln football team included a number of basketball players: Ben Spalding (81), front row; Clyde Mosby, second row, fourth from left; James Crayton, second row, far right; John K. Cunningham, third row, third from left; Tyrone Handley, third row, third from right; and Billy Collins, top row, far right. Coach Joseph McPherson is seated in the third row, far right. (Courtesy of Daniel Thomas)

tured two cowboy characters, Randy Atcher and "Cactus" Tom Brooks (the brother of comedian Foster Brooks).

Growing up, Cunningham experienced the usual snubs endured by African Americans, but one left him especially angry: the books he received at the Lawrenceburg Colored School always had other children's names in them. This told him that black kids did not deserve new books, only the secondhand books used and abused by several classes of white children before them.

But Cunningham found equality on the ball fields around Lawrenceburg. White kids and black kids played together during the summer, and there was never any trouble. They were just kids playing ball and having a good time. Cunningham was a natural athlete who loved baseball, but he was not allowed to play in the white Little League. Some community leaders sponsored a Negro Little League for a couple of years, and when Cunningham turned fifteen he played first base on a men's team.

Cunningham stood six feet tall in the eighth grade and began to gravitate toward basketball. He had big hands and could do tricks with the ball, and he was athletic enough to dunk the ball on the playground rims. The white boys were duly impressed and called him "Goose Tatum," after the Harlem Globetrotters star. When the white boys went to Anderson High, they tried to recruit Cunningham, even imploring the Bearcats' coach, James D. Boyd, to sign him up for the team. But Anderson High had not yet integrated, and Cunningham's options were limited: Simmons High in Versailles or Lincoln Institute. Kids on the Versailles end of town went to Simmons, but on Cunningham's side of town, they went to Lincoln, and so did he. The county paid his tuition, and he worked in the tobacco patches during the summer to pay for his school clothes. Cunningham was the first in his family to go to high school. His mother had not finished grade school, and both his sisters quit school to find jobs. A high school education meant something to a boy growing up in hard times, and John Cunningham wanted something better out of life.

Gilliard welcomed two more new players to the varsity team in 1958: brothers from Indianapolis. Mystery surrounded their arrival, and neither James Crayton, a sophomore, nor William, a freshman, were forthcoming about their past. Out-of-state students normally came to Lincoln for one of two reasons: Lincoln Institute's positive reputation, or a troubled past. Of the latter, some had got into trouble with the law, while others had been expelled from their previous schools. These students were being sent away to what authorities and parents referred to as "reform school." White youths who got into trouble were given the option of jail or the army. Black youths could go to jail or Lincoln Institute.

Time has erased the reasons why the Crayton brothers ended up at Lincoln, but one thing remains clear: James was a decent basketball player, but William was a prodigy. The Crayton brothers were obviously well schooled in the game, having previously attended Crispus Attucks High School, a product of Indianapolis's segregated history.

James Crayton was fourteen years old and William was twelve in March 1955 when the Crispus Attucks basketball team won the Indiana state championship and became the first all-black school in the nation to win a state title. Their star was a spindly, six-foot-five sixteen-year-old who could do things with a basketball that Merlin could only do with a wand. His name was Oscar Robertson, and Crispus Attucks propelled his legendary career as three-time NCAA player of the year, Olympic gold medalist, member of an NBA championship team, and inductee into the Naismith Memorial Basketball Hall of Fame in 1980.

Robertson's early years at Crispus Attucks and the environment he grew up in are instructive in understanding the Crayton brothers. A 2009 article by Wayne Drehs that appeared on the ESPN.com website illustrates the striking similarities between Robertson's background and what we know about the Craytons:

They remember being told they could sit here but not there. They remember learning there were theaters for whites and theaters for blacks. And they remember thinking this was normal; it was an accepted way of life. Back then, Indianapolis was a ferociously segregated city, traced back to the days of D. C. Stephenson, the Ku Klux Klan grand dragon who lived in the city in the early 1920s. It was Stephenson and several Klan-supporting politicians who proposed a segregated high school for black students.

Crispus Attucks High, named after the runaway slave who was believed to be the first American killed by British soldiers in the Boston Massacre, opened in 1927. But because the school had no white students, the Indiana High School Athletic Association ruled that Attucks was not a public school, which barred Attucks from membership. Not until 1933 were member schools even allowed to play against Attucks and not until 1942 was Attucks granted membership and welcomed into the state basketball tournament.

Attucks' home gym was too small to host games, so the Tigers always played on the road. And because many of the all-white Indianapolis schools refused to play Attucks, many of those games were played in small towns outside the city. There, the Tigers were the high school version of the Harlem Globetrotters, an entertaining curiosity that filled gyms and amazed fans but who struggled to find a place they were welcome to eat after the game.

In addition to playing basketball, the Crayton brothers were members of a group called the Eckstein Norton Singers, named after the men's dormitory. From left: Jesse Harris, Fletcher Lott, William Crayton, James Crayton, and Allie Laurie. Joe Sowell backed them up on the guitar. (Courtesy of Daniel Thomas)

"It was a very prejudiced town and a very prejudiced time," said Betty Crowe, an Attucks graduate and the widow of coach Ray Crowe. "You couldn't eat in certain restaurants; you couldn't sit in certain movies. But you learned to overcome it. You learned not to use that as an excuse. You knew you just had to do better."

Many of Attucks' students, including Robertson, lived in Lockefield Gardens, a government-subsidized housing complex a couple of blocks from the school. Others weren't as lucky and lived in homes without electricity or running water. The school was the beacon of hope.[2]

Lincoln Institute would become that beacon of hope for the Crayton brothers.

"Smooth" was the word used by several former teammates who were asked to describe Bill Crayton's game. The slender six-foot-three forward could shoot from anywhere on the court, but he favored dribbling to the corner, where he would then turn and jump high, his hands guiding the ball above his head. When the ball left the tips of his fingers, it arced high like a rainbow before dropping through the nets.

Bob McDowell, who played for Simpsonville High School, recalled trying to guard Crayton. "He would dribble into the corner, and I would follow him," McDowell said. "I would be in textbook defensive position, crouched low with my eyes on his chest. But when he went up for a shot I was staring straight at his kneecaps."[3]

Gilliard's plan to restore the Tigers to their KHSAL prominence stalled for much of the season as they struggled to a 6–9 record just a few weeks before the tournament. But a 57–46 upset of Bagdad, one of the district favorites, gave Lincoln new hope. The *Shelby News* suggested as much when it reported that the Tigers had "the rather dubious distinction of being favorites to win the 30th District basketball crown."[4]

Indeed, when the Thirtieth District tournament tipped off at the Shelbyville High School gym, the only African American school in the district made an early statement, defeating Waddy 55–43 in the lower-bracket opener. According to the *Shelby News,* Lincoln's "jumping Tigers used speed, stamina and some phenomenal long shots to defeat Waddy. . . . Lincoln's pressing, rattling defense caused [Waddy] to miss many scoring opportunities and to lose the ball on several occasions on wild passes."[5]

Lincoln opened the semifinal match slowly, falling behind Taylorsville 14–6 in the first quarter before rallying to take a 31–23 halftime lead. The Bears would not fold and staged their own comeback, cutting the Lincoln margin to 1 point entering the fourth quarter. But McAtee led a full-court press that confounded their opponent, and Lincoln raced to a 67–52 victory. The diminutive senior led a balanced Lincoln attack with 16 points, while Bill Crayton scored 13 and Ben Spalding contributed 12.

In the district final, Lincoln faced the Simpsonville Bobcats, who had defeated Shelbyville 60–53 in the upper-bracket semifinal. The Simpsonville gym was located just a mile and a half from Lincoln's Blue Gate, but the two teams had never played each other until that year. The Bobcats were not as tall as the Tigers but featured outstanding guards, including Charles "Whitey" Simpson, whose 24 points had sunk Shelbyville.

Lincoln reversed its previous tournament starts, going out to a 10–5 lead by the end of the first quarter as McAtee frustrated Simpson on defense.

The Tigers maintained that small cushion throughout the game, relying on a full-court press that limited Simpson and forward Jimmy Gibbs to 4 field goals each. Meanwhile, Bill Crayton slithered open for 7 successful jump shots, mostly from the corner. Spalding and Simpsonville's tallest player, six-foot-three Jimmy Fister, battled for position underneath and traded fouls throughout the game. Both eventually fouled out in the fourth quarter, but so did Simpson, who was held to 13 points. Both teams hit 16 field goals, but Lincoln hit 21 free throws to Simpsonville's 14 for the winning 53–46 margin. Crayton's 16 points tied Fister's for game honors, while Watkins hit 7 free throws and finished with 15 points.

The new district champions were exultant, and Lincoln students and supporters treated the victory like they had won the state championship. African American fans danced and chanted in the stands; they rushed onto the floor to congratulate their team. They had been denied this opportunity for a lifetime, and now, in only their second year of mandated acceptance, the Lincoln Tigers were district champions. The victory also made them the champions of Shelby County, whose citizens had not wanted them at first but had come to respect and appreciate the "colored" school in their midst.

In winning the Thirtieth District tournament, the Lincoln Institute Tigers, composed solely of young African Americans, had defeated three teams whose players had never gone to school with black children.

Hopes were high as Lincoln traveled the following week to its first Eighth Region tournament at Oldham County High School in Buckner. Runner-up Simpsonville also advanced to the eight-team regional, and fans of both teams were rewarded for their support. The Bobcats upset Mount Washington 51–50 on Bob Walters's fifteen-foot jump shot with three seconds to go, but the Tigers did them one better, opening the tournament by knocking off top-rated Grant County, 55–53.

Simpsonville's opening victory inspired the Bobcats to play their best defensive game of the season in the semifinals against the talented Gallatin County Wildcats. Center Jimmy Fister controlled the boards against the Wildcats' star, six-foot-three Joe Lowe, and the score was tied at 34 at halftime. But too many missed foul shots down the stretch doomed the Bobcats to a 1-point loss, 61–60. Lincoln had little trouble in its semifinal game, defeating Henry Central, 69–58, behind Bill Crayton's 18 points.

The regional final between Lincoln Institute and Gallatin County had all the elements of a classic Hollywood tale. The noble black underdog—the only African American team in the Eighth Region—was playing a white team from a county known for race riots after the Civil War, when lawless Ku Klux Klan bands had terrorized the Bluegrass State and forced hundreds of blacks to flee across the Ohio River.[6] In reality, though, both teams had good arguments to claim the underdog role. Gallatin had overcome its own troubles. The county seat of Warsaw, located on the Ohio River forty miles southwest of Cincinnati, had thrived during the riverboat era, but as commercial river traffic declined after 1900, the county's population fell by 20 percent.[7] Basketball was now the biggest thing in town and the key to the community's psychological resurgence.

That year, Gallatin County had opened a new building to replace the old Warsaw High School, and the team was coached by a fiery young promoter in Charles "Jock" Sutherland. The thirty-one-year-old Sutherland was in the early years of building his own legend, which had been boosted when an article in the popular *Reader's Digest* magazine dubbed him "The Quickest Thinking Coach in America." During one game that season, Sutherland had disputed an official's call so vehemently that the referee threatened to assess a technical foul for every step Sutherland took back to the bench. Sutherland looked over at his players and motioned for two of his stronger boys to come out on the court, pick him up, and return him to the bench so he would not have to take a step.[8]

Sutherland did not win games on theatrics alone. The Wildcats had forged a 25–5 record behind a fast-breaking attack led by sharpshooting forward Lowe. But when the Gallatin players learned who they were playing for the Eighth Region title, they were concerned. "In the part of the state I was in, I had never thought about it," Sutherland said years later. "My players came to me and asked what it would be like to compete against black players. Heck, I didn't know, but I couldn't tell them that. So I just told them

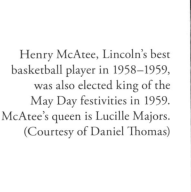

Henry McAtee, Lincoln's best basketball player in 1958–1959, was also elected king of the May Day festivities in 1959. McAtee's queen is Lucille Majors. (Courtesy of Daniel Thomas)

that they've got to run, jump, shoot and score the same as we do. At first my players were a little intimidated, but after five minutes, we just started playing basketball."[9]

Lincoln took a quick 6–4 lead and held on to a 16–15 first-quarter margin, but the Tigers inexplicably went cold in the second period, and Spalding and McAtee picked up quick fouls. Gallatin converted 8 of 10 foul shots to take a 32–29 lead, while the Wildcats' defense concentrated on stopping Bill Crayton. Johnny Watkins kept it close with some long-range goals, but Lowe countered every Tiger basket with one or two of his own. Gallatin opened a 47–39 lead by the third quarter and coasted to a 67–59 victory behind Lowe's 23 points. Watkins led Lincoln with 18 points, but Crayton was held to only 9.

The Wildcats were going to state, and the Tigers were going home.

In 1959 Hickman Riverview of the First District in the First Region became the thirty-ninth former KHSAL member to participate in a KHSAA district tournament. Five African American schools won district tournaments that year: Bowling Green High Street in the Seventeenth District, Bardstown Training in the Twenty-Fourth, Louisville Central in the Twenty-Fifth, Lincoln Institute in the Thirtieth, and Lexington Dunbar in the Forty-Third. High Street, Covington Grant, and Dunbar won their regional tournaments for the second year in a row and earned the right to play in the "Sweet Sixteen," while Lincoln and Central lost their title games. Overall, the black schools' 32–34 district record and 14–4 regional record testified to the fact that they more than belonged. This was affirmed in the state tournament, which again was played at the University of Kentucky's Memorial Coliseum in Lexington. High Street lost its opening game to Monticello by a score of 78–67, but Grant made it to the second round by defeating Pikeville 72–67. Grant narrowly lost in the quarterfinals, nipped by Olive Hill, 85–84.

Lexington Dunbar made a strong push for the championship. After easily defeating Sacramento, 82–46, and Monticello, 63–51, the Bearcats lost a 52–50 heartbreaker to Louisville Manual in the semifinals. Dunbar proceeded to annihilate Olive Hill 88–45 in the consolation game before North Marshall edged Manual 64–63 for the title. For the second year in a row, Julius Berry of Dunbar was selected to the all-tournament team, where he was joined by Tom Thacker of Grant. But other black players were making contributions to their teams, including those at integrated Maysville High School, Monticello, and Louisville Manual.

After the 1958–1959 school year, the number of former KHSAL members still operating dropped by one when Bardstown Training School closed and its students were integrated into Bardstown High School. The Bears went out in a blaze of glory, winning the Twenty-Fourth District title by defeating Springfield, Bardstown St. Joseph's, and Bardstown High before losing to Elizabethtown High, 68–63, in their Sixth Region opener.

That left thirty-eight former KHSAL members that were still operating while their local school boards deliberated their fate.

14
___

A "Progressive and Enlightened" State

A Montgomery, Ala., Negro leader predicted Wednesday that massive resistance and legal barriers to integration would break down within fifteen years, but that complete integration would take a long time. "I would say," Dr. Martin Luther King told a press conference, "that massive resistance to integration will be broken down in five to fifteen years, that legal barriers will be broken in urban areas in ten to fifteen years, and that by the turn of the century, America will have moved a long way toward integration."
—Associated Press, September 24, 1959

Kentucky was still working toward "gradual integration" on the eve of the 1959–1960 school year, which meant that Lincoln Institute was in no immediate danger of closing. The longer local school boards took to come up with plans for integration, the longer Lincoln remained the only option for African American students whose local districts could not accommodate them.

Kentucky's path to full integration was riddled with potholes. Nine Negro students were enrolled in the all-white Owen County High School, but the elementary schools remained segregated until US District Court judge H. Church Ford ordered their complete integration by September 1, 1959. When one school official complained that integration would cause overcrowding that might be rejected by the Kentucky Board of Health, Ford responded: "It's the law that controls, not the regulation of governmental agencies."[1]

In Christian County, a committee that had been formed in 1956 finally presented an integration plan that was immediately approved by the Christian County school board. It called for the integration of first graders, followed by the gradual integration of other grades at a rate to be determined annually by board officials. Approximately 177 African American students attended Hopkinsville Attucks, the county's only black high school.[2]

In the only district where violence had marred earlier attempts at integration, the Sturgis schools enrolled 44 black students and 837 whites without incident. The black students had been attending Morganfield Dunbar, fifteen miles away.[3]

The state's progress toward integration was apparently acceptable to Governor Chandler, who proclaimed that "an exemplary performance in facing the challenge of racial integration in public schools" had earned Kentucky "a reputation as one of the most progressive and enlightened states in the South." He made this statement in a special edition of *In Kentucky* magazine, a promotional vehicle distributed to news media, chambers of commerce, libraries, and businesses.[4]

The 1959–1960 school year opened peacefully in Shelby County, and that autumn, residents were occupied by the details of their everyday lives. The good news was that tobacco prices were flirting with an all-time high of 70 cents per hundredweight, and the Shelbyville tobacco market, one of the biggest in the state, was recording its highest sales volume in several years. On the downside, dairy farmers were concerned that scours, or bovine diarrhea, was afflicting their calf population. An estimated 22 percent of calves were dying before they reached two years old, representing a large loss in herd replacement and income from the sale of calves.[5]

The basketball team at Lincoln Institute had nothing to do with cash crops or livestock production, but coach Walter Gilliard was looking at the upcoming season with the sharpened eye of a commodities analyst. He was hoping the futures market for his basketball team would be more promising than its past performance indicated. Gilliard had assembled a team that showed signs it was a stock worth holding, but he wasn't yet convinced.

Four starters returned from the 1959 regional runner-up team, but the single loss was huge. Guard Henry McAtee had scored more than 400 points the previous year, and his absence would be felt. Gilliard hoped that Jewell

Logan, Tyrone Handley, or James Crayton could fill the void, but he would not know for certain until the games began. "I'm sorry I can make no predictions as to whether this team will jell, as we lost our key man, Henry McAtee," Gilliard told the *Shelby News*. "I expect all district teams to be tough, and you know Shelbyville has been picked as preseason favorites."[6]

After practice opened in October, Gilliard saw some things he liked, but he saw other things that caused him concern. Both his guards, Clyde Mosby and Johnny Watkins, could hit from outside, but Watkins was a casual defender at best. Bill Crayton was terrific when things were going well, but he was subject to mood swings and tantrums that reduced his effectiveness and reliability. The coach saw no one who could match McAtee's court savvy and scoring. Ben Spalding was a natural leader, but Gilliard was not satisfied with his rebounding efforts, so he created a drill to improve that skill. Gilliard would climb a ladder, place a dime on the rim, and then require his inside players—Spalding, Crayton, Thomas, and Billy Collins—to repeatedly jump up and pluck the dime off the iron.

Gilliard wanted an early indication of how his team would fare, so before the season started, he contacted coach Edward Adams at Louisville Central and suggested that the Tigers come to town for a scrimmage. Adams, in his second full year of coaching after replacing the legendary Bill Kean, agreed. Adams was not afraid of divulging the Yellowjackets' tendencies to the Tigers because the traditional KHSAL rivals had not played each other in any sport since 1955, when a massive fight broke out after a Lincoln-Central football game. Lincoln had defeated Central for the KHSAL football title in the autumn of 1954 and then beat Central for the basketball title five months later. Central was intent on getting even, and when its football team prevailed over Lincoln in a 34–6 runaway on October 22, 1955, they rubbed the visitors' noses in it. Tensions exploded on both sides, and a near riot ensued between fans and students. The two principals, Atwood S. Wilson of Central and Whitney Young of Lincoln, decided to suspend future competition in all sports.[7]

But memories can keep a rivalry alive as much as the games themselves. When the Lincoln bus arrived at Central High School, it was met by a crowd of former Yellowjackets who had played when the rivalry burned white-hot, and they were still itching for a slice of Tiger meat. Lincoln took the floor amid catcalls and threats from the old players. "You better not shoot that ball, boy," one of them shouted to a Lincoln player, patting his jacket as if he were carrying a weapon. "Hey, country," another shouted, "where'd you get them shoes?"

But once the ball went up, it became apparent that the insults had no effect on the Lincoln team. Even Central's best players, such as Vic Bender and Bobby Stewart, were having a hard time defending Gilliard's fast-breaking offense and cracking the Tigers' pressing defense. Mosby hustled the ball down the floor, looking for Bill Crayton or Jewell Logan for open shots. Crayton stroked smooth jumpers from all angles, while Logan found seams in the Central defense that led to easy baskets. If nothing opened up for Crayton or Logan, Mosby tossed it back out to Watkins, who was not shy about detonating a long bomb. Spalding stood like Gibraltar under the basket, ready to snag and put back the rare miss.

The crowd grew as word of the scrimmage spread, and several current Central students drifted in to watch. One in particular drew Gilliard's attention even while he was busy coaching. He had seen the tall, angular young man on a local television program called *Tomorrow's Champions*. Clad in a jacket from one of his numerous Golden Gloves championships, Cassius Clay, a Central High School senior, was a month from his eighteenth birthday and less than a year from winning a gold medal at the 1960 Olympic games in Rome.

When the scrimmage was over, Adams was ready to declare a draw, but the Lincoln players would have none of it. They knew they had outperformed the team that would attain the state's number-one ranking during the season. Even better, they had reestablished bragging rights in the close-knit African American community.

"Central was legendary in Kentucky high school basketball," Spalding recalled, "and when we stepped onto the court they looked at us like we were a bunch of country boys, just got off the hay wagon. But we stayed with them, and that helped us mentally the rest of the season. We knew if we could play with Central, we were as good as anybody."[8]

Lincoln Institute opened the season on December 5, winning by 30 points over Pleasureville High School. A few days later, Lincoln took the measure of Arnold Thurman's Bagdad Tigers, 75–66. By then, Thurman and Gilliard had forged a close relationship that was warm yet businesslike. Gilliard was straightforward and earnest—no bluff or bluster—in their dealings, and he learned to take Thurman's easy ribbing. After the game, Thurman good-naturedly admitted that his own team could not guard the high-jumping Lincoln players, who appeared to shoot *down* at the basket. "These boys can rest their elbows on the basket rim," said Thurman. Gilliard returned the banter, advising Thurman that he could expect nothing else if he relied on slow white boys. The Bagdad coach enjoyed the repartee with Gilliard, whom he called "a prince of a guy."

The Bagdad game led the local newspapers to declare that Lincoln Institute "appears to be the team to stop in the 8th Region." Sports editor Jimmy Cooke of the *Shelby News* said the Tigers' strategy "differs from the usual style of ball in this area. They use an overbearing press all over the floor, and put their two tallest men under the basket." Their pressing defense forced Bagdad to shoot from a distance, which produced missed shots that Spalding or Crayton cleared with ease. The report also noted another aspect of the Lincoln team that would be a concern later in the season: "Crayton, a sophomore, is one of the Tiger giants who is very promising. He has temper problems, but if he learns to control it, says Coach Thurman, 'He will be great.'"[9]

Bill Crayton was an enigma to his coach and his teammates. He had a beautiful voice, sang in the school choir, and was lead singer for an impromptu quartet that presented accomplished renditions of songs by the Drifters, the Isley Brothers, and the Coasters. And his skill on the basketball court was unquestioned. "He had the sweetest jump shot I ever saw," said a former teammate. "It was a high arc, and he could jump." But when Crayton lost his temper, he was a different person. And unfortunately, it occurred often during games. Sometimes when Gilliard was giving instructions to the team, Crayton would disagree and yell at the coach. Or he would throw a tantrum on the floor and start jumping up and down for no apparent reason. "He had a temper, which hurt us at times," a former teammate recalled. "You never would know what upset him, but when he had a fit he just stopped playing. When he didn't get mad, he was tough."

In a later day, a team doctor might prescribe medication to moderate a player's behavior or alter his moods, but in 1960 the only prescription was a cautionary label that read "hothead." It was bold and visible, and it made Crayton an easy target for the taunts of opposing players and fans. Crayton did not confide in many people, but Albert Minnis Jr., older son of the engineering teacher and an assistant to Dr. Young in 1960, was like a big brother to the Crayton boys. "I think Bill came from a bad family situation," Minnis recalled. "He would never talk about it, but something happened at Crispus Attucks for somebody to make the decision for him and his brother James to attend Lincoln. I visited him one time in Indianapolis, and we had to meet someplace because he wouldn't take me to his home. He was a troubled boy, and he just didn't want anybody to get too close."[10]

Lincoln had played in small gyms against other black schools, but even Gilliard was shocked at the size of some of the white schools' facilities. At Bagdad, the gym floor ended three feet from a brick wall that was covered by a cloth pad, but it provided little protection when a fast-breaking offense stormed toward the goal. The short end zones came in handy in one game, however, when an opposing player muttered racial slurs as backup Billy Collins dribbled down the floor. "He made the mistake of getting between me and the wall," Collins recalled years later. "I looked like I was taking him to the basket, but I was taking him right into the wall. He shut up after that."[11]

More often, the Lincoln players felt handicapped in smaller venues, as illustrated by a game in early December. Campbellsburg High School in Henry County played in a gym so small that its fans affectionately called it the "cracker box." In addition, the two white officials who refereed the game gave new meaning to the term "home-court advantage." According to Daniel Thomas, the officials called fouls for guarding too close. "We never touched the man, but they called the foul," Thomas said. "After that, they called so many fouls, we were afraid to get close enough to guard them." Lincoln lost to the Blue Wolves 64–63, but Gilliard did not complain. He merely commented afterward: "Just one of our cold nights."[12]

Lincoln faced a similar situation in the next game at Grant County. The Braves' impressive height gave the visitors pause during pregame warmups, but once the game started, it was not the tallness of the opposing team that had the Tigers worried. The officials at Campbellsburg may have called the game too close, but the white officiating crew at Grant County made no attempt to hide which team they favored, calling foul after foul against the Tigers. "A strange part of the contest," reported the *Shelby News*, "was that of the 30 points scored by Grant in the second half, 20 of these came on free throws." Lincoln held on to win 72–70 behind Bill Crayton's 25 points, while guards Mosby and Watkins scored 17 each. Again, Gilliard was diplomatic: "The Tigers played a good game, but I wouldn't want to make any other comments."[13]

"Get used to it," Gilliard told his players in the locker room. They had to expect catcalls from the fans, comments from their opponents, and unfair officiating. The 1959–1960 season was the first time Lincoln would play more than half its games against white or integrated schools, and the KHSAA had not yet certified black officials for such games. Unless they were playing some of their old KHSAL rivals, Lincoln could expect white officials for every game.

Fortunately, the Tigers' performance through the holidays suggested that it would take more than questionable officiating to stop them. Things were going so well, in fact, that Gilliard believed he might finally have a team that mimicked the style of his coaching hero, John McLendon of Tennessee State.

"Lincoln Institute's tall and talented Tigers have just about nailed down the favorite role in the 30th District basketball ratings," declared the *Shelby News* after Lincoln swept three games in the Eminence Holiday Invitational.[14] They survived a 71–68 scare against Waddy on New Year's Eve, handily avenged their only loss against Campbellsburg in the semifinal game on New Year's Day, and then beat previously undefeated Carrollton 73–62 on January 2 for the tournament title. Mosby and Watkins scored 18 points apiece as the Tigers dominated the Panthers, but it was a game the Carrollton players and fans would not soon forget.

15
———

Homeless Tigers

About 75 Negro college students entered their third day of efforts to be served at a midtown lunch counter. Waitresses at F. W. Woolworth Co. ignored the group, many of whom remained in the store perusing school books as they sat along the counter. A North Carolina A&T student said they plan to "visit one store at a time. If we can get one store to start serving then the others may give some service."

—*Greensboro Record,* February 3, 1960

Monday night was movie night at Lincoln Institute. The boarding students gathered in Hughes Hall, which served as both the gymnasium and the auditorium, for a night of entertainment away from their books. Bernard Minnis, a senior whose father was head of the engineering department, ran the projector. After the movie ended one night in January 1960, Bernard shut down the projector, secured the tape, and walked the half mile to his family's home adjacent to the grounds.

At about 3:00 a.m., night watchman Tom Martin noticed a suspicious glow coming from Hughes Hall. It was on fire! Lee Brown, an industrial arts instructor who lived in a small apartment on the top floor, was awakened by smoke and escaped injury. Martin alerted the campus's volunteer firefighters and the Simpsonville volunteer fire department. The Simpsonville department called the Shelbyville department, eight miles away, but in an unfortunate coincidence, those firefighters were busy battling another fire within the city limits that gutted the Scofield Pharmacy and damaged adjoining buildings.

The Simpsonville volunteers arrived within minutes, but the blaze was already raging out of control. The Shelbyville fire engines eventually arrived, but the couplings on the campus hydrants did not match their hoses, and none of their trucks could hook up. Many of the 250 boarding students, which included most of the basketball players, were out in the frigid cold, trying to save some of the sports equipment in the gymnasium. Gilliard and his wife Eleanor arrived from their home in Louisville and did what they could, but it was too late. Eleanor stood shocked and in tears as she watched the blaze destroy an important part of the school. Hughes Hall burned out of control for nearly four hours and was still smoldering at noon the following day.[1]

Named for the benefactor who had helped Lincoln stave off financial ruin in the 1930s, Robert Henry Hughes Hall was the most used building on campus. In addition to the combination gymnasium and 700-seat auditorium, the concrete-block structure housed the physical education, home economics, and music departments; the cafeteria; the kitchen; and three classrooms. In the space of a few hours, it was all gone. The cause of the fire was never determined, although Dr. Young suspected it was electrical in origin and not intentionally set. He estimated the damage at $400,000, half of which was covered by insurance.

Young insisted on resuming operations immediately while implementing recovery plans. He ordered classes back into session the next day, with an implicit appeal for patience and resilience on the part of faculty, staff, and students during this major disruption. He called in the Red Cross, which set up an emergency dining facility, and the state adjutant general supplied the school with a National Guard field kitchen that would assure hot meals for students and faculty. Governor Bert Combs dispatched state engineers and Department of Education officers to Lincoln to identify the school's immediate needs and determine how to speed the recovery. More than $1,000 in donations and other offers of help came in from both black and white neighbors, as well as from Lincoln alumni.

Dr. Young painted a grim picture in a report titled "Disaster. Fire! Fire! Fire!" that he included in his annual report to the trustees:

> At present, we are using the basement of the Boys Dormitory, which is not satisfactory. The dining room is being used as a church, activity room, class room and for social functions. Less than one-half of our students

Hughes Hall was a combination gymnasium, cafeteria, and Home Economics Department before it was destroyed by fire in January 1960. (Courtesy of Daniel Thomas)

can be housed in the room at one time. This means that we do not have an assembly room where all the students and faculty can meet. We are using an engineering room for Home Economics, the library for classes, and the Girls Student Playroom for Music Classes. The overall picture is not very bright or conducive to the building of a sound education program. Something must be done to relieve this situation immediately.[2]

On the day after the fire, Gilliard assembled his team and thanked them for saving their uniforms, pads, and balls from the gymnasium. He then informed them that he had made arrangements with the Shelby County school board to practice at the Simpsonville High School gym. One player asked the coach if a bus would be taking the players to the Simpsonville school, two and a half miles away, or if the coaches would be transporting them in their cars, as they did on road trips. Neither, said Gilliard: beginning that day, the team's conditioning program had been extended to include a run to the practice site and a run back to Lincoln when they were finished. "The coaches didn't want the program to skip a beat," one player recalled. "The basketball team was the catalyst for the whole campus; everything revolved around it. The basketball program could not shut down because of a fire."[3]

On the first day of practice at Simpsonville, the players ran down the hill in front of Berea Hall, across the railroad tracks, and up to the Blue Gate at US 60, which was one mile from campus. They turned right and ran east down US 60, crossing over the Louisville & Nashville Railroad overpass before reaching the school in the middle of town.

The unlikely troupe provided a target for some knucklehead motorists who delighted in shouting racial slurs or throwing beer cans out the window at them. The catcalls were fewer on rainy days, when the players ran wearing rubber snap-up overshoes and ponchos. Waiting for them, rain or shine, was Simpsonville's black custodian, Whitson Magruder, who let them into the gym every afternoon and locked the door behind them when they left.

"That run felt real lonesome at first," Daniel Thomas recalled. "But we started pulling together."[4] Jogging to practice every day in less than ideal conditions became a gauntlet for the Lincoln players. Mutual misery in pursuit of a worthy goal inspired camaraderie and fostered a military-like brotherhood common to boot camp or troops in combat. They suffered together, endured it together, and began to believe that they were part of something very special.

Gilliard was working the phone feverishly, trying to switch home games to the opponents' venues or to secure either the Waddy or Shelbyville gym for home games. Four days after the fire, Lincoln played at Shelbyville, where the crowd was equally divided between Red Devils fans and Tigers fans, but Lincoln embarrassed the preseason district favorite by a score of 81–62.

Shelbyville was technically a road game, but it was only a twenty-minute drive from Lincoln Ridge, and the players returned to their dormitory afterward. Their next game would be a true road test when they traveled eighty-five miles east to Paris, Kentucky, to face an old KHSAL rival, the Paris Western Tigers. The Paris fans were never hospitable to visitors, particularly those from Lincoln Institute. Earlier that year, after Lincoln's football team had won a close game, some aggressive Paris fans had chased the Lincoln players as they ran to board their bus. An unknown assailant threw a brick through an open window of the bus and hit Alfonso Wallace of Manchester, Kentucky, knocking him out cold. Wallace recovered, but relations between the two schools remained strained.

The basketball team traveled to Paris in two cars, one driven by Gilliard and the other by assistant coach McPherson. When they arrived, they were greeted with the usual taunts from the Paris fans, which continued throughout the tight game. Fortunately, Bill Crayton's jump shot was on target most of the night, and Lincoln received some unexpected help from Jewell Logan, whose game had been adversely affected by the sudden death of his fifty-two-year-old mother, who had suffered a stroke just before the season began. Crayton's 20 points and Logan's 19 led Lincoln to a narrow 79–78 victory, after which the players rushed to their cars and sped back home.

Logan's sudden emergence was welcomed, but its source might have been some unsanctioned practice in which the six-foot-two senior was engaged. Logan would sneak off campus some nights and play basketball with a semiprofessional team that charged admission to its games and split the take among its players. Practice against the older players had helped Logan's game, plus he was making a few dollars. It all sounded very innocent, until a coach from Paris recognized the high school player at one of the games; he approached Logan afterward and suggested that unless he stopped playing with the semipro team, the coach would report him. A word to the wise was sufficient, and from then on, Logan limited his basketball playing to the Lincoln Tigers.

Logan's improved play came at a good time. Gilliard had hoped someone would step up and fill the void left by the graduation of Henry McAtee, but during the first half of the season, nobody had jumped out of the pack. Not even Logan had scored in double figures in any of the first dozen games or so, but the Paris game was a turning point.

Lincoln returned to Shelbyville for the County High School Band Tournament the following Friday and Saturday nights, with proceeds going to support the bands at each of the county schools. Logan tuned up his shooting accordingly. In the opener against Bagdad, the Lawrenceburg native scored a game-high 27 points as Gilliard's black Tigers defeated Thurman's white Tigers. The following night, Logan's 15 points contributed to a balanced attack in a 70–61 victory over stubborn Simpsonville. Mosby's 17 points led Lincoln, and Crayton and Watkins also scored 15 points apiece. Logan and rebounding star Spalding headed the all-tournament team.

But the most memorable outcome of that tournament may have been a contribution from sports editor Jimmy Cooke of the *Shelby News*. Cooke was tall and thin (perhaps a former athlete himself), with close-cropped dark hair and glasses that slid down his nose as he took notes. In his white, short-sleeve shirt and thin, dark tie, he was the epitome of the local journalist. But that night, in his report of the games, he came up with a label that would follow Lincoln Institute for the rest of the season. Cooke's lead read: "Lincoln Institute's *homeless Tigers* won the Shelby County Band Tournament last weekend at Shelbyville."[5]

The team was literally homeless, in the sense that the Tigers had no place of their own to practice or to host games. But the fact that they had to play every game in unfamiliar venues, in another team's home gym, before unfriendly and often boisterous fans had a similar effect as the five-mile round-trip runs to and from practice. It was an old-fashioned gut check, a toughening process for these teenaged players.

"Everywhere we would play, there was negative energy," Spalding recalled. "Every place we played, we just felt this negative aura about us. Everybody wanted us to lose, but thank God for the people of Simpsonville and Shelbyville, because half of the black community would follow us and come to our games. That kind of positive energy helped us perform and created a positive energy within us as teammates. We supported each other. We didn't have any stars. Every one of us had a chance to perform and score."[6]

The Lincoln cheerleaders also did their part to support their team. A couple of the players dated cheerleaders, who gave special consideration to their boyfriends during games. For example, when Logan went to the foul line, his girlfriend, Augustine Johnson, would stand and lead the crowd in support, but always with a codicil: "Logan, Logan, he's our man. If he can't do it, Spalding can."

The homeless Tigers took to the road the first week of February when they headed west to play Owensboro Western and Henderson Douglass. Ten players made the trip—five each in cars driven by Gilliard and McPherson—but accommodations were rarely predetermined. Most hotels did not welcome black patrons, and some restaurants still served whites only.

The persistence of segregation in rural Kentucky is reflected in a story from historian Bill Ellis, a graduate of Shelbyville High School and Georgetown College who arrived at Harrodsburg High School in 1962 as a twenty-two-year-old history teacher and head football coach. The Harrodsburg school system had peacefully integrated a few years earlier, and the first football team he coached was about one-quarter African American. "Reality struck me early in the year," Ellis wrote, "when, returning from a scrimmage in Irvine, we stopped in Richmond for a meal on the way back to Harrodsburg. A prominent locally owned restaurant refused to admit us because we had black players. I was informed that the white players could come inside but the black players would have to eat on the bus. When I told the players what had been said, they shouted to go on to another place. We found refuge at a Jerry's Restaurant that welcomed us."[7]

Gilliard was aware of such limitations when his team traveled, and he kept his players away from confrontations. Families of the home team's players and fans volunteered to host the visiting players and coaches. This normally resulted in an enjoyable trip away from school for a few days, with basketball being the most important consideration.

During the drive back on Sunday after victories in Owensboro and Henderson, the conversation turned to Lincoln's old nemesis, Louisville Central. That very weekend, the Yellowjackets had won the prestigious Louisville Invitational Tournament, defeating Lexington Dunbar and Louisville Flaget in the process. Central would be ranked number one in that week's Litkenhous rankings carried by the *Courier-Journal*. The players talked about it, and the superstitious coaches ignored it, but all were hoping for another meeting with Central. Whether listening to the radio, looking out the window, or feigning sleep, every player knew that the last time Lincoln and Central had played for a championship, in the 1955 KHSAL finals, the Tigers had prevailed. If the two teams met again, it would not be in a scrimmage that did not count. It would be in Freedom Hall at the Sweet Sixteen. And every player wanted that meeting to be in the championship game.

Despite their celebrity status on campus, the Lincoln basketball players spent most of the week as typical high school students in an atypical atmosphere.

Dormitory life, campus activities, class work, and the rare moments of free time were wrapped around practices and games, all of which was influenced by Gilliard's discipline. Classroom attendance was mandatory for players, and missing class meant missing a game. As much as Gilliard preferred tough and courageous players, he did not countenance academic cowards.

Like most students, the basketball players rose as early as 5:00 a.m. to ensure there was enough hot water for their showers, particularly in the winter months. Late risers could experience a chilling start to the day before commencing their assigned chores. The players' regular assignment was to clean the gym, but after the fire, they were reassigned to whatever minor repairs or cleanup was required around campus. Then they returned to the men's dormitory and straightened up their rooms before dressing for breakfast. The dress code was not haphazard. Women were required to wear skirts and stockings with seams, although a few enterprising young women painted "seams" down the backs of their bare legs with eyebrow pencils until they were caught. The male students were required to wear khaki or corduroy slacks with collared shirts. Among juniors and seniors, dressing for class became a competition to crown the sharpest dresser. After a hot breakfast, students convened in home room, where they listened to the announcements of the day and recited the Pledge of Allegiance before heading to class.

Class was transformative for all Lincoln students, but especially for freshmen. For many of them, it was the first time they had been assigned new textbooks, and it was certainly the first time they had been addressed in the adult manner as "Mr. Jones" or "Miss Smith." In addition to academic lessons, most teachers were liberal with life lessons that stuck with their students. Jewell Logan recalled a lesson from biology teacher Joseph A. Carroll, which he added to his pregame preparation. "Be resilient, but don't be satisfied with the norm," Carroll told his students. "No matter whether you think you can or you can't, you are probably right!"

After lunch and afternoon classes, the ballplayers went to practice. Most of the day students went home unless they were involved with social clubs or intramural sports, which were available for both boys and girls. The boys might participate in intramural basketball or volleyball; the girls could also play volleyball or join the camera club, the modeling club, or similar activities. Music was another popular pastime, and several singing groups complemented the official Lincoln choir.

After dinner, other activities were available, such as watching television in the recreation room. Monday movie night was moved to the basement of the boys' dormitory after the fire. Some students attempted to circumvent Dr. Young's restrictions on romantic flirtations. Both boys and girls tried to sneak into the others' dormitory, although such escapades were discouraged and subject to punishment.

Students returned to their dormitories at 8:00 p.m. for a one-hour study period, supervised by monitors on each floor. At 9:00 p.m. Sears Silvertone transistor radios crackled on as the students tried to catch some late music. A favorite local station was WAKY-AM in Louisville; it launched its top-forty format in 1958 by playing "One-Eyed, One-Horned, Flying Purple People-Eater" nonstop for twenty-four hours. After dark, when more distant radio signals strengthened, the most popular station at Lincoln Ridge and for black listeners in much of the country was clear-channel WLAC-AM in Nashville. Billing itself as "the nighttime station for half the nation," WLAC's signal reached most of the eastern and midwestern United States. African American listeners were the target audience of the gravelly, drawling patter of the disc jockeys on programs such as "Randy's Record Shop," which featured popular black artists. Unbeknownst to most listeners, the station's disc jockeys were all middle-aged Caucasians, not the African Americans their voices suggested.[8]

At 10:00 p.m. both lights and radios were turned off, but the night was just beginning for some daring students. The older ones knew where to find the fun, and the younger ones soon learned that a willing bootlegger in Shelbyville was just a short drive away. The more adventurous embarked for nightclubs in Shelbyville, Louisville, or even the Club Cherry in Bardstown, where Ike and Tina Turner and Chuck Berry performed on a regular basis.

If students felt the need to repent such misdeeds, their best opportunity was at Wednesday vespers, when Dr. Young offered a prayer and addressed any issues the students needed to know about. Everyone knew that if Dr. Young wore his black suit to vespers, a serious message or admonishment would be forthcoming. Former students recalled that these messages seldom had to do with current events making headlines outside the Blue Gate. "Even though there was no conscious effort to shut us in, we were not aware of the things going on outside," said Gary Brown, a junior varsity basketball player during the 1959–1960 school year. "During the sit-ins and riots, you didn't hear about all that until you went home. Dr. Young didn't make a big issue about educating us about something that most of us didn't really care much about at the time."[9]

"I could read the newspaper in the library, but there was no mention of current events in class," said Victor Brown from Lawrenceburg. "They didn't talk race when I was there. We were from a segregated society, but they taught us the positive things. How to dress, how to conduct ourselves and how to become responsible men and women. They didn't bring the rest of the world into our campus. They just tried to prepare us to integrate ourselves into society. When integration came, we succeeded because of the preparation we got. We were isolated, but when the door was opened, we stepped through it."[10]

Lincoln Institute picked up more victories in the first two weeks of February, including a tight 87–85 win against Bagdad, thanks to Logan's 28 points. He did not outscore Bagdad star Johnny Wright, however, who was sterling with 34 points. Bagdad's performance prompted Bob Fay, managing editor of the *Shelby News,* to predict that the white Tigers, now 0–3 against the black Tigers, would eventually prevail in the upcoming Thirtieth District tournament: "Bagdad will defeat Lincoln Institute in the final next Saturday night," Fay wrote. "Bagdad's big trouble all season has been their inability to get started early enough, but after three losses to Lincoln they know by now how to play Lincoln and how to beat them. They came close in their last two meetings and will be ready for bear this time."[11]

Sports editor Cooke fell in line with his boss, writing: "So far this season, Lincoln Institute has had smooth sailing. They have seldom been pushed to win and may have a good chance to represent the region in the state tournament. But basketballs take some mighty peculiar bounces and because they are the [defending district] champions, every team in the tournament here would deem it a pleasure to knock the Lincoln Tigers off their throne."[12]

Indeed, the attitude at Lincoln Ridge was more cautious than confident. The enigmatic Bill Crayton was going through another funk and had rarely hit double figures in his last eight games. Ben Spalding, the six-foot-four center, had been sidelined for several games with a severe case of bronchitis. Fortunately, Gilliard was getting good play from his bench. Six-foot-two Daniel Thomas was filling in admirably under the boards for Spalding, and Gilliard loved Billy Collins's declaration that "there are no cheap layups when you play Lincoln Institute." A self-proclaimed "frustrator" with a thirty-six-inch sleeve length, Collins might grab an opponent's jersey, throw a well-placed elbow, or slap a face with one hand while reaching for the ball with the other.

Gilliard also liked "Black John" Cunningham's enthusiasm, although it often resulted in fights and other outbursts off the court. When a prankster hid the trunk that held Cunningham's clothes, the perceived offender was reproached with vulgar epithets that reached the tender ears of Mr. Carroll, the biology teacher. Cunningham was sent to the furnace room, where he shoveled coal until the lesson of patience and tolerance had sunk in.

The Tigers continued to stack up victories against their Shelby County opponents as the season wound down. Logan had secured the role of the team's most consistent scorer, achieving a personal high of 29 points in a 111–77 rout of Shelbyville. The guards were also playing well; Watkins hit a season-high 30 points, and Mosby added 20 to Cunningham's 15, in a 95–69 rout of Waddy on February 23.

But the Tigers' weaknesses were magnified on their last road trip of the season. They traveled to Campbellsville, where Gilliard had moved a regularly scheduled home game against former KHSAL member Durham High. Unlike Lincoln, which was remote from the population centers of Shelby and Jefferson Counties, Durham was at the center of the African American community in Campbellsville. On Saturdays the black community gathered at Durham High in a kind of farmers' market, where they could enjoy the company of relatives, friends, and visitors.[13]

Campbellsville's black community was also passionate about basketball. John Whiting was in his first year as head coach, having replaced Rodney K. Ivery, who had headed the Durham program for twenty years. But in

1960 Whiting had inherited what might have been Durham's best team, perhaps even good enough to challenge Larue County for Sixth Region supremacy. The Hornets' leader and best player was six-foot-three senior guard J. W. Allen, who would be named honorable mention all-state that year, but a great deal of attention was being directed toward a sixteen-year-old, six-foot-three freshman named Clem Haskins.

Haskins's story was familiar. He was born in Campbellsville, the fifth of eleven children of Charles Columbus and Lucy Edna Haskins, who were sharecroppers. The family lived in a three-bedroom house on a farm three miles outside of town; there was no television, telephone, or indoor plumbing. Haskins began working on the family farm when he was six years old, milking cows and chopping out and stripping tobacco.[14]

Because he was needed on the farm, Haskins did not attend school until he was eight years old. Like many black youths in rural Kentucky, he grew up oblivious to segregation. Then, one day, he and his younger brother Paul and two white friends, brothers David and Buck Roberts, went to the Alhambra Theater in Campbellsville to see the movie *Old Yeller*. David, who was four years older than Clem, paid for all of them, since the others had no money, and the boys went into the theater and took their seats. The movie was about to begin when the usher came up and shined a flashlight on them. He tapped the older white boy on the shoulder and told him his friends would have to sit in the balcony. Clem didn't know why, but he and Paul went upstairs and sat down. David and Buck didn't like their friends being treated in such a fashion, so they went up to the balcony and sat down with Clem and Paul. A few minutes later, the usher appeared in the balcony with his flashlight and told the white boys they couldn't sit there and would have to go downstairs. It was the first time Paul and Clem had been to the movies, and they were less worried about where they had to sit than what was happening on the screen. The boys were so excited about seeing their first movie that they didn't realize they had just been introduced to racial prejudice.

Haskins attended Campbellsville's one-room school for black children until fourth grade, when he enrolled at Durham. His attendance was irregular, and he was out of school more than in it during September, October, and November, when he was needed to cut and strip tobacco. After a teacher at the school spoke to his father, Clem's workload was cut, and he was allowed to attend school more regularly, which allowed him to play on the basketball team. Clem's father wasn't thrilled with the idea, but it was okay with him as long as it didn't interfere with his son's chores or school work.

The rest of Haskins's story is well known in basketball circles. He would go on to become the first African American to attend Taylor County High School in 1961, before becoming an all-America player at Western Kentucky University; this was followed by a long career as an NBA player and college coach. When asked about it years later, Haskins did not recall the Lincoln game, and other than Durham's rather easy 86–71 victory, not much is known about it. The game was not reported by Campbellsville's *News Journal,* probably because Friday night games were old news by the time the weekly newspaper came out the following Thursday.

Billy Collins recalled the home-team officials calling an unusual number of fouls on the visitors, and judging by the coverage of other Durham games, it is plausible that the Hornets' collapsing zone defense shut down Crayton's usual corner shooting. Indelibly etched into Jewell Logan's brain was what assistant coach Joseph McPherson told the players on the drive back to Lincoln Ridge: "We are not unbeatable."

16

Out of the Ruins

Thirty-seven Negroes and Whites, representing members of the Lexington branch of CORE, staged a sit-in demonstration at a rear lunch counter of the H. L. Green Co. store. Five police cruisers were dispatched, but no incidents occurred, and the group dispersed after three hours. The manager said the store maintains two lunch counters, an integrated snack bar at the front of the store and a segregated lunch counter in the rear, where the sit-in was held.
—*Louisville Defender,* March 3, 1960

The loss to Campbellsville Durham was only Lincoln's second of the season, but it came at an inopportune time, barely one week before district tournament play. Bill Crayton was erratic, Ben Spalding was still weakened by bronchitis, and the reserves were playing as well as they could. It is unknown whether the basketball team was the subject of Dr. Young's religious fervor and prayer, but Walter and Eleanor Gilliard attended every service, and the coach could be forgiven if he said a few prayers for his team.

By the time the Thirtieth District tournament opened on March 1, Gilliard's prayers were beginning to be answered, whether literally or figuratively. Crayton and Spalding shared the role of a latter-day Lazarus, whose rise from the dead is described in chapter 11 of the book of John. Crayton's temper tantrums had disappeared, and at practice he laughed and joked with his teammates and the coaches. He appeared to be ready for the tournament. Spalding was gaining strength and was finally recovered from the bronchial infection that had slowed him down for the past month. With Lincoln's inside presence intact, Logan's shooting eye seemed to get sharper with every practice, while Mosby and Watkins continued to display their season-long consistency at both ends of the floor.

All this was bad news for Lincoln's foes when the district tournament tipped off at the Shelbyville gym. First up were the hapless Waddy Warriors, whose 3-point loss to Lincoln on New Year's Eve was a distant memory. Since then, Lincoln had widened its victory margins over the Warriors to 15 and 26 points in two subsequent games, and with Spalding fit and Crayton apparently content, the Tigers dispatched Waddy with ease, 79–41. Spalding dominated the boards and scored 20 points, while Crayton added 19. As sportswriter Jimmy Cooke described the game: "The fast-breaking, jumping jack, hell-for-leather Tigers got their fast break into high gear and were never threatened."[1]

The next opponent was Taylorsville, which had the second-best record in the district at 17–8. It was Taylorsville's only meeting with Lincoln that season, and the Bears played like they had never before seen such a machine. Crayton was magnificent in an 86–56 walkover, sinking shots from all angles for 28 points. Logan was almost as proficient, hitting from the outside and driving the lane for 24. Spalding owned the paint and added 14 points.

In the opposite bracket, Shelbyville overcame a huge deficit and upended the Shelby *News's* sentimental favorite, Bagdad, 49–37. Trailing 31–20 midway through the third quarter, Red Devils coach Evan Settle ordered a full-court press that the Tigers could not handle. Shelbyville outscored Bagdad 29–6 over the last twelve minutes, as fourteen fouls were called on Bagdad versus zero for the home team. The Bagdad fans were incensed at the officiating, and their anger only grew when Settle ordered a police officer to remove the Bagdad cheerleaders from a spot on the floor in front of the Bagdad section, where they had been allowed to stand at previous games.[2]

Since both the winner and the runner-up would move on to the Eighth Region tournament, nobody had to tell either Shelbyville or Lincoln that the Thirtieth District championship game on March 5 did not matter. It was less than two weeks after Lincoln's 111–77 pounding of the Red Devils, and Coach Settle was still angry. He had heard stories about the Crayton brothers' mysterious arrival at Lincoln, and whether the rumors were fact or fiction, Settle wanted nothing more than to uncover some violation that would render the Craytons ineligible for the tournament. The Shelbyville coach decided to contact the KHSAA and request an investigation.

On March 2, the day before the semifinal game between Lincoln and

Taylorsville, KHSAA commissioner Ted Sanford received a handwritten note on Shelbyville High School letterhead that raised his eyebrows. The Red Devils' basketball coach informed Sanford: "I would appreciate it if you would make an inquiry at Lincoln Institute relative to the ages of the Crayton brothers. I have heard rumors that one of them has been in the Army."[3]

Sanford's response did not come before the Red Devils played the Lincoln Tigers, and Settle had his team ready for them. Employing the same pressing defense that had stymied Bagdad, the Red Devils forced Lincoln into early turnovers and poor early shooting. Brothers Ronnie and Jimmy Yount controlled the boards, and Shelbyville held a 50–41 lead late in the third period. Gilliard turned the tables on the Devils and ordered his team to start pressing, which converted several Shelbyville turnovers into baskets. The fourth quarter opened with the score tied at 50. Crayton, who had scored only 7 points in the first three periods, began to find the range, and Lincoln pulled ahead 60–54 with three minutes to go. But the Red Devils were not finished. Donnie Kays and Ronnie Yount led a rally, and Yount's basket tied the game at 62 with 1:32 to play. Kays fouled Spalding, who hit two free throws to give Lincoln the lead, and a Watkins steal and basket lengthened the margin to 4 points with twenty-one seconds remaining. Jimmy Yount and Crayton traded baskets as Lincoln squeezed out a 68–64 victory and its second consecutive district championship. Logan was the high scorer for the Tigers with 22 points, and Crayton added 18, 11 of them coming in the final eight minutes.[4]

Settle soon received another loss of sorts when the KHSAA commissioner responded to his inquiry the day before the regional tournament commenced at Oldham County High School in Buckner. Sanford advised the coach that he had contacted Lincoln, and the school was in possession of the Craytons' birth certificates, which placed James's birth date as May 22, 1941, and Bill's as February 17, 1943. As far as the KHSAA was concerned, the Crayton brothers were eligible for the Eighth Region tournament.[5]

Dr. Whitney M. Young Sr. had already proved his ability as a promoter. His early success with the Fair Plan had kept the Lincoln campus open, and later battles to secure state support had kept the school operating at a high level.

The Lincraft Fair was held each spring to highlight the crafts and activities of Lincoln students. (Archives and Special Collections, University of Louisville)

So it was not surprising when the Lincoln Institute president took advantage of the Tigers' basketball success to make some positive points about his institution, his community, and the future of race relations in America.

He offered the *Shelby News* a copy of a letter he had written to faculty, staff, and supporters shortly after the Hughes Hall fire, encouraging them to fight through their misfortune and work toward better days ahead. Employing the eloquence of a trained speaker and the fervor of a revival minister, Dr. Young recounted the trials of the past while painting a bright future for Lincoln Institute:

> The future belongs to those who dare, who dream, who live within the shadow of disaster. . . . For almost one-half century, 48 years to be exact, a small but dedicated band of teachers and workers have been

sowing the seeds of love, purity, unselfishness and honesty. Today, the world reaps the harvest of our sowing. Throughout the United States, in China, in India, in the West Indies, in Europe, in South American and in Africa our sons and daughters (Lincolnites) are giving their all as disciples of freedom and to spread the gospel of Christ.

Out of the ruins of the past—physically speaking—we will build new and better buildings for the children of tomorrow. Not tan, not white, not yellow, not black, but all of God's children who need and want our services. Through economy, self-restraint and self-denial, we will keep the candle of hope burning on the tower of Berea Hall, in the basement of Eckstein-Norton Hall, in the reception room of Belknap Hall, and wherever two or three of our members are gathered together.

Yes, out of the ruins of the past, our spirits have been resurrected. A God-given unity impels us on to greater goals than those we have achieved in the past. This is the time to think of each day as a miniature life. It comes to us now, it goes from us finished. There are three hundred and sixty five days in a year. The only way to have a well-finished year is to finish the tasks and duties of each day as it passes.[6]

Unlike the previous year, when Lincoln Institute had sneaked up on several of its Eighth Region opponents, the Tigers came into the 1960 tournament as clear favorites. They justified the consensus with an easy 77–53 win over Lebanon Junction in the tournament opener, but the semifinal game against Oldham County on the Colonels' home floor would not be so effortless. Coach Barney Thweatt's team had equaled Lincoln's 25–2 record with a similar style of play that included an aggressive defense and a team-oriented offense. Although this would be Oldham's first game of the season against a "colored" team, there were elements of a rivalry. Oldham County was still segregated, and among Lincoln's 422 students were 28 from that county.[7]

An overflow crowd of 3,200 arrived early and jammed the Oldham County gymnasium; more than 500 fans, many of them Lincoln supporters, were turned away by the fire marshal. The Colonels' record did not seem to faze Lincoln, which took an early 19–10 lead and stretched it to 38–24 by halftime. But with its hometown fans shouting encouragement, Oldham unleashed a furious rally and tied the game at 47 late in the third quarter. The Colonels' rugged star, six-foot-five Johnny Nix, outbattled Spalding on the boards, and Oldham opened a 6-point cushion. It appeared that Lincoln's dream season might come to a crashing halt.[8]

But the Tigers refused to quit and closed the deficit to 53–50 before running off 9 points in a row with four minutes to go. Thweatt called his last time-out, and the Colonels came roaring back to within 2 points when Spalding committed his fifth foul with 2:54 remaining. Nix tied the score at 61, and after rebounding a Lincoln miss, guard Terry Barrickman hit a driving layup to put Oldham in front 63–61. Another Tiger miss led to a basket by Nix that gave the Colonels a 4-point lead, but Logan and Watkins answered, and the score was tied again at 65 with 1:44 remaining.

The teams traded baskets until a Watkins layup gave the Tigers a 69–68 lead with fifty-three seconds remaining, but with Spalding on the bench, Nix ran free. The burly center hit a short jumper for his 28th point and a 70–69 Oldham lead with sixteen seconds remaining. The Colonels' defense was relentless, and six seconds ticked off the clock before Mosby threw cross-court to Crayton, who missed a fifteen-foot jumper. Fortunately, the ball bounced back to him, and he put it up again—and missed again. But Crayton, not to be outdone, outfought Nix for the rebound. He had one more opportunity, a "third time's the charm" bank shot that sliced through the net as the buzzer sounded.

The Tigers were joyous, jumping and dancing and hugging one another at their 71–70 victory. But some Oldham County fans, angry at the Lincoln comeback and offended by the players' exuberance, began pelting them with crumpled cups and yelling obscenities and racial slurs. Gilliard quickly hustled his players off the floor to avoid any trouble, then lectured them in the locker room for letting their big lead slip away.

The championship game was against 27–4 Carrollton, which had nipped Campbellsburg after the Blue Wolves eliminated Shelbyville in the opening game. The Panthers' players and fans were still stinging from their loss to Lincoln in the Eminence Invitational, but they could not do much about it. Lincoln started out hot, and Crayton was on fire, hitting shots from all over the floor. Lincoln took a 36–22 halftime lead and widened it to an

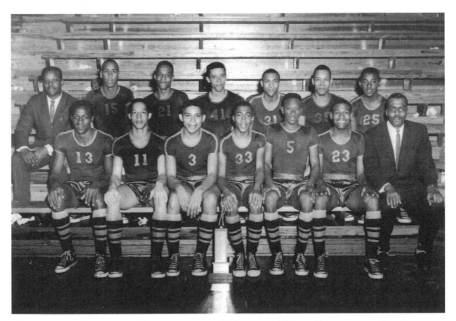

The 1960 Eighth Region champion Lincoln Institute Tigers. Bottom row, from left: Carl Williams, Tyrone Handley, Billy Collins, Howard Barlow, John Watkins, James Crayton, and coach Walter Gilliard. Top row, from left: assistant coach Joseph McPherson, Ben Spalding, William Crayton, Jewell Logan, John Parker, Clyde Mosby, and Danny Thomas. Not pictured: John K. Cunningham. (Courtesy of the Walter Gilliard family)

eventual 85–64 victory over the outmanned Panthers. Crayton finished with 26 points and had ample support as every other starter scored between 14 and 16 points.[9]

Carrollton's players and fans might have been beaten, but they were not going to take the loss gracefully. When it came time for the customary cutting down of the nets by the winning team, Lincoln's players received a shock. As they carried a ladder to one of the baskets, some Carrollton fans and players tried to grab the ladder and stop them, shouting racial slurs and threats. Fans left the stands as two sheriff's deputies on the floor watched but did nothing. Some of the white fans from Shelby County who had come to support Lincoln began to scuffle with the Carrollton supporters, who streamed onto the floor. Failing to deter Lincoln's celebration, the Carrollton players and fans went to the other basket and had their own celebration, cutting down the nets on the opposite goal.

"When we looked at the other end, their men were up there swinging knives, cutting the nets down," recalled Daniel Thomas. "I never saw the loser trying to cut the nets down before, but they didn't want us to get the nets. That's the worst incident that I remember all season. Oldham was supposed to win the Regional on their home floor, but after we beat them I guess Carrollton thought we shouldn't have beat them." Reserve Billy Collins put it another way: "Those fans didn't want a speck of darkness left on that floor!"[10]

The Kentucky High School Athletic Association investigated the incident and suspended Carrollton High School's athletic teams for thirty days of competition and placed the school on probation for one year. Commissioner Ted Sanford said the penalties resulted from "a rules violation that occurred after the Lincoln Institute–Carrollton basketball game in the finals of the 8th Region Tournament March 12."[11]

That did not matter to the new Eighth Region champions. Gilliard's team had achieved the first part of their mission: they were going to state.

17

Secret Ballot

U.S. Senator Lyndon B. Johnson is under pressures and cross-pressures of a force and savagery never to beat upon any member of the Senate in any party for any reason. The task Johnson has assigned himself is to pass a civil rights bill that will genuinely and totally guarantee the voting right of the Negroes in his native South while not destroying his own prospects as a Democratic presidential aspirant.

—William S. White

Louisville's Freedom Hall might have been the site of the two most recent NCAA men's basketball championships in 1958 and 1959, but it was not a popular venue for the Kentucky state high school championship. The last time the "Sweet Sixteen" had convened in Louisville had been in 1950, when the tournament had been played at the old armory. Then it moved to the University of Kentucky's brand new Memorial Coliseum in Lexington for the next six years. Lexington was in central Kentucky, convenient to schools in the Bluegrass region and in the eastern Kentucky mountains. But Lexington enjoyed another advantage: the aura that surrounded coach Adolph Rupp's University of Kentucky Wildcats, the reigning kings of college basketball. The opportunity to watch a game in the "house that Rupp built" was high on the wish list of Kentucky basketball fans from the Big Sandy to the Mississippi.

Louisville gained an advantage of its own when Freedom Hall opened in 1956 as part of the new Kentucky Fair and Exposition Center. Freedom Hall's unofficial seating capacity of more than 18,000 dwarfed the 11,500 of Memorial Coliseum. The additional revenue that could be derived from a bigger arena was enticing, and Louisville interests persuaded the KHSAA to bring the 1957 tournament back to Louisville. But after Lexington Lafayette defeated Eastern High School of Jefferson County in the 1957 championship game, fans expressed an overwhelming displeasure at the new venue.

As expected, attendance was up, but the expanded seating was less a blessing than a curse. Fans thought the arena was too big! Freedom Hall had been designed for the nation's premier equestrian competition, the Kentucky State Fair World Championship Horse Show, and its permanent seats were arranged around an almost 300-foot-long show ring. A high school basketball court, measuring 84 feet by 50 feet, had been plopped into the middle of the ring, leaving a wide band of concrete around it. With the exception of temporary end-zone seating for the participating schools, most of the basketball fans—accustomed to watching games in high school gyms that seated hundreds of spectators—were so far away from the court that they could see the players' numbers only with great difficulty, if at all.

"I am writing to tell you how lousy it was this year (accommodations, not the teams)," one fan wrote to KHSAA commissioner Sanford. "It was impossible to see the players and recognize them unless you had a seat right along the playing floor, as the place was so huge. I am sure all the good seats were sold to the local people. We hope you return the tournament to Lexington next year where we poor Grant Countians can enjoy the games, and return home with a penny or two in our pockets!"[1]

Another letter writer from Paintsville, who identified herself as part of a "family of high school basketball fans," deplored the traffic congestion and the public drinking of alcoholic beverages. "This is the first time we ever saw an open bottle of whiskey being passed from person to person in full view," she wrote. Even a dance for teenagers sponsored by tournament organizers received a thumbs-down from one writer, who claimed to have seen the "police break up two fights, a most uninhibited necking exhibition and some extremely vulgar dancing."[2]

Still more complaints were addressed to the Louisville Chamber of Commerce. "Getting out of the parking lot is hell," wrote one critic. "It is every man for himself, and the Devil take the hindmost. . . . Where were the ushers? When, if ever, will the Louisville Police learn that every high school kid is not a delinquent? Every kid I heard talking about the tour-

Fayette County judge Bart Peak draws for the 1960 state high school basketball tournament brackets at the KHSAA office. Observing, from left, are assistant commissioner Joe Billy Mansfield, commissioner Ted Sanford, and Ernie Coyle, *Herald-Leader* sportswriter. (Courtesy of *Lexington Herald-Leader,* University of Kentucky Special Collections)

nament was mouthing about the way Louisville Police were pushing them around."[3]

The partisan *Lexington Herald* used such criticism to editorialize that "the many problems associated with conducting a basketball tournament seem to have been multiplied in Louisville this year, and the inexperience of those conducting the affair did not make things any easier on the thousands of high school boys and girls and their parents who attended. . . . After all is said and done, we believe that many tournament visitors would welcome a return to the coliseum at the University of Kentucky."[4]

One candidate for state representative even proposed legislation as a solution to the bickering. He recommended passage of a law whereby the tournament would have to be played at the University of Kentucky every year, with no changes.

The issue of where to hold the tournament was just as contentious in the boardroom of the KHSAA. The Board of Control returned the 1958 tournament to Memorial Coliseum, where Louisville St. Xavier defeated Daviess County, 60–49, for the title. The issue of where to hold subsequent tournaments was tabled until the Board of Control's summer meeting in July 1958, when board member W. H. Crowdus proposed that the 1959 state tournament be held in Lexington and the 1960 tournament return to Louisville "if satisfactory arrangements could be made." When the board was polled, the votes were split 4–4 on a strictly geographical basis. The one member who lived in Louisville—Jack Dawson—and the three from western Kentucky—Crowdus of Franklin, Robert P. Forsythe of Greenville, and Louis Litchfield of Marion—voted aye. The four members who lived east and south of Lexington—Kenneth G. Gillaspie of Georgetown, W. B. Jones of Somerset, Cecil A. Thornton of Harlan, and board president Russell Williamson from Inez—voted nay. Crowdus then amended his motion to suspend any discussion of the 1960 tournament and to vote only on holding the 1959 event in Lexington. The amended motion carried unanimously.[5]

In an effort to avoid controversy, Sanford put the vote up to KHSAA member schools, but that resulted in a predictable split along the same regional lines. Schools in the central Bluegrass region and east favored Lexington, while the western schools generally favored Louisville.

With the location of the 1959 tournament settled, the Louisville business community focused on bringing the 1960 tournament back to Freedom Hall. A month after North Marshall's 64–63 upset of Louisville's DuPont Manual in the 1959 championship game, Clyde Reeves of the Kentucky State Fair Board led a delegation representing Louisville hotels, transit agencies, and the Chamber of Commerce in an effort to persuade the Board of Control to give Kentucky's largest city one more chance to host the commonwealth's most popular grassroots event.[6]

The eight board members grilled Reeves and other members of the delegation, who were then asked to leave the room. Board member Robert Forsythe, a Louisville advocate, moved that the 1960 tournament be held at Freedom Hall. He then recommended that the board suspend its normal voice vote and vote by secret ballot. Whether he knew that one of the pro-Lexington voters was going to switch his vote to Louisville is unknown, but a secret ballot would keep the turncoat's identity confidential and probably save him from criticism by other members and in his home district. Sure enough, when the ballots were counted, five members had voted to give Freedom Hall another chance, while three had voted to keep the tournament in Lexington. Member W. B. Jones moved that a rental fee of $9,000 be offered for the use of Freedom Hall, which Reeves accepted. The 1960 tournament was headed back to Louisville.

The Louisville group still faced criticism stemming from the 1957 tournament experience. Reeves and his committee knew they had to blunt any past objections with proper planning, new features, and an entirely different approach. To combat the higher prices that had shocked previous visitors, the Louisville Chamber of Commerce established a State Tournament Housing Bureau to make housing available for followers of the participating teams. Fans who required accommodations had the option of hotel, motel, YWCA, or private home. Housing for the teams had already been arranged. A Hospitality Committee was organized, and events and activities surrounding the four-day tournament were created. Chaired by Board of Control member Jack Dawson, the committee reported progress on such events as a teen dance at the Knights of Columbus hall and swimming privileges for guests of the tournament at the Henry Clay Hotel. The hotel had assured the committee that its swimming pool was nonsegregated. The Kentucky Movie Theater, which was segregated, had agreed to admit all tournament visitors, regardless of race.[7]

Recent events had made attention to African American attendees critical to the tournament's success. On Christmas Day 1959 the popular Brown Theater had hosted the Louisville premiere of the movie *Porgy and Bess.* Although the production featured an all-black cast and such stars as Sidney Poitier, Dorothy Dandridge, and Sammy Davis Jr., the management of the segregated theater refused to allow African American patrons inside to see it. The NAACP established a picket line to underscore the irony of excluding blacks from viewing an all-black production, and students marched outside the theater carrying placards stating, "This Theater Does Not Admit Negroes." This boycott was one of the first such protests in Louisville, and it spurred a series of new campaigns challenging segregation in public accommodations, employment, and housing citywide.[8]

On January 4 black activists gathered at city hall to ask new mayor Bruce Hoblitzell to introduce an ordinance banning discrimination in public accommodations. The mayor responded that he would not tell businesses which customers they could or could not deal with. The mayor's reticence prompted local black leaders to ask black alderman William W. Beckett to introduce an ordinance seeking to end segregation in public places. Beckett resisted, knowing that his eleven fellow aldermen, all white, would reject any such proposal. Only when black leaders threatened to boycott Beckett's funeral home did he agree to introduce the measure. On February 9 Beckett presented an ordinance making it unlawful to deny patronage to any person because of race or religion and calling for the complete desegregation of downtown restaurants, hotels, and theaters. As expected, the white aldermen opposed the measure, which failed 11–1. Beckett attempted to revive the proposal, but it was scrapped in a procedural move by the Board of Aldermen's legal committee.[9]

Ironically, the aldermen's vote came two weeks after a progress report presented at the KHSAA's winter meeting had put Board of Control members' minds at ease. "The cooperation of the Louisville group to date had been outstanding," Commissioner Sanford reported to the board. His assistant, Joe Billy Mansfield, concurred, saying that advance ticket sales were strong, "possibly better than ever before at this time."[10]

The 1960 state tournament fell just short of being a memorial tournament for the old Kentucky High School Athletic League. Hopkinsville Attucks of the Second Region joined Lincoln Institute as the only former KHSAL members to win their regional tournaments, but three other all-black schools had missed by only a hair. In the Sixth Region, Campbellsville Durham, which had handed the Lincoln Tigers their second loss, lost a heartbreaker to Larue County, 54–52, in the regional finals. Freshman star Clem Haskins scored 22 points, but the Hornets could not stop a hot second half by the Hawks. Another favorite, Covington Grant, the two-time Ninth Region champion, was upset by Newport High School, 55–46. Three other regional winners with African American starters helped make the case for integration: Maysville in the Tenth Region, Harrodsburg in the Eleventh Region, and Monticello in the Twelfth Region.

If Lincoln ever had reason to pull for its archrival Louisville Central, it was in the Seventh Region tournament, where a Central victory could have led to their long-anticipated rematch at Freedom Hall. However, the top-ranked Yellowjackets were upset by Flaget High School, 58–49, in the regional semifinals. Central had defeated the Braves three times during the season, but in the regional game the Yellowjackets could not stop hot-shooting Tom Finnegan, who scored 27 points. Yellowjackets players and fans did not take the loss well. In the closing seconds, Central's Bobby Stewart was ejected after talking back to official Red Hagan, who had called a technical foul. Another technical was called against Randolph Redwine for threatening Finnegan, and a Central fan came onto the floor and took a swing at the other official, Irwin Spencer. After the buzzer sounded, Central's Vic Bender jumped on Flaget guard Buddy Weihe and wrestled him to the floor. At that, fans of both teams rushed out of the stands to join the melee, but city and auxiliary police and officials of both schools intervened to defuse the budding riot.[11]

Heading into the victorious Flaget dressing room, separate from the fracas but loyal to their teammates, were the Braves' three African American players: starter John McGill and reserves Don Turner and James Montgomery. McGill, a five-foot-ten guard, averaged 13.2 points per game, but he was the third scoring option after the more talented Finnegan and six-foot-four Ted Deeken. The offense revolved around Finnegan, a 20-point scorer who would later play for the University of Louisville, and Deeken, who averaged 16.7 points during the season and would become a star at Kentucky. But McGill was at the center of the Braves' defense, and his quickness made him a major disruptor in first-year coach Jim Morris's pressing scheme. McGill was free to badger the dribbler into turnovers and steals that led to quick baskets on the other end. McGill's impact, however, was even more impressive considering that basketball was not even his best sport.

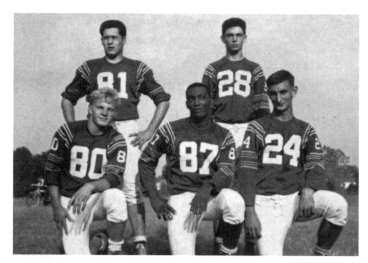

John McGill (87) was a three-sport star, including all-state wide receiver and cocaptain of the Flaget football team. (Courtesy of Flaget Museum)

John McGill's parents—John Sr. and Doris—grew up in the New Haven community near Bardstown, about forty miles south of Louisville. After they married, the McGills moved to Louisville, where John Sr. took a job at International Harvester. They moved into a house at 3705 Greenwood Street in Louisville's predominantly black West End and immediately started a family. John was born in 1942 and another son, James, was born a year later.[12]

John McGill Sr. was a devout Catholic—his sister Rebecca was a nun—and he vowed that his children would be raised Catholic. Although only 3 percent of Catholics in the United States are identified as African American, they have maintained a significant presence in Kentucky.[13] The first African American Catholics in Kentucky were slaves who arrived with settlers from Maryland in 1785. In 1869 Father John L. Spalding was appointed to organize African American Catholics in Louisville, and a year later he had raised enough money for a new church. St. Augustine became the first African American Catholic church in Louisville and one of only six in the United States. St. Augustine School opened in 1921 at Thirteenth and Broadway, along with Catholic Colored High School.[14] John McGill attended elementary school at St. Augustine, but Catholic Colored High School closed after the Louisville schools integrated. John enrolled at Flaget High School, named for Benedict Joseph Flaget, the first Catholic bishop of Kentucky.

While John grew strong and participated in sports at St. Augustine and

Flaget, his brother James lived a totally different life. He had cerebral palsy and suffered from its effects, including bone deformities, misaligned joints, and stunted speech. James was a big, strong boy who never had the opportunity to play sports, but he worshipped his older brother. Every day when John got home from school, James would greet him happily and give him a big hug. However, when sports kept John at school past his normal arrival time, the disruption in James's schedule sometimes caused bouts of nervous anxiety and episodes of vomiting. When John came home, he would cradle his brother in his arms until the attack passed.

At Flaget, John excelled in football and basketball, but he gravitated toward a sport not ordinarily associated with young African Americans in the 1950s. John fell in love with tennis, which he played on the public courts at Chickasaw Park, eleven blocks from his house. Formerly the riverfront estate of political boss John Henry Whallen, the property had been developed into a park in 1922. The City Parks Commission passed a resolution in 1924 making Chickasaw Park and a few other small parks black only, leaving the larger parks in the city for white patrons. For the black youths of the West End, the park—with basketball courts, ball fields, and the only free clay tennis courts in the city—was heaven.

Hitting the ball back and forth with friends at the park, McGill drew the attention of Arthur Lloyd Johnson Jr., the part-time tennis coach at Central High School. A native of Lawrence, Kansas, Johnson had graduated from the University of Kansas and then earned a graduate degree at Hampton Institute before moving to Louisville as first violinist with the Louisville Civic Orchestra.[15] Johnson became better known to generations of black boys and girls as the godfather of black tennis in Louisville. He taught his students at Chickasaw Park, while the white tennis players practiced at the prestigious Louisville Boat Club. In 1951 the Boat Club was the site of the Davis Cup tournament, where Dick Savitt, Herb Flam, Bill Talbert, and Tony Trabert led the US team to victory over Japan. The tournament returned to the Boat Club in 1955, when Lew Hoad and Ken Rosewall led Australia to a win over Brazil.[16]

Although African American tennis players were allowed to play in public parks other than Chickasaw, the only blacks permitted at the Boat Club were service and maintenance workers. Fortunately, Johnson's contacts in the tennis world extended far beyond his adopted city. Before the summer of 1959, Johnson contacted Dr. Robert Walter Johnson of Lynchburg, Virginia, a black physician who had founded and funded the American Tennis Association's Junior Development Program for African American youths. As part of this program, promising young players who had no public courts where they could learn to play tennis and no money for lessons could qualify for an all-expenses-paid summer tennis camp.[17]

Dr. Johnson had a proven reputation of nurturing young black tennis players. In 1946 he had discovered a young girl from South Carolina who showed some promise. Althea Gibson became the first black player to cross the color line of international tennis, and in 1956 she became the first person of color to win a Grand Slam title. Although Dr. Johnson had no Gibsons in his current group of female players, he had a sixteen-year-old boy from Richmond, Virginia, who showed just as much promise: Arthur Ashe.

When John McGill arrived in Lynchburg in June 1959, he was paired with the young Virginian and spent the summer as Arthur Ashe's doubles partner. They attended tournaments throughout the middle Atlantic states, but McGill found that playing with a prodigy had its drawbacks. In one tournament, McGill and Ashe made it to the doubles finals, but Dr. Johnson forfeited their match because he wanted Ashe to be fresh for his singles final that afternoon, which, of course, he won.

When the summer was over, McGill returned to Louisville and put away his tennis racquet until the state tennis tournament the following spring. The first sport in the fall was football, and McGill's teammates voted him co-captain along with his best friend on the basketball team, Kenneth T. "Buddy" Weihe. The Braves finished with a commendable 7–2 record, and McGill was named all-state wide receiver. Once football season was over, McGill's attention shifted to basketball.

The Braves opened the basketball season with eight wins in a row, including a 58–52 victory over eventual Tenth Region champion Maysville. But Louisville had the most competitive teams in the state, and over the next two months, Flaget faded. It lost two of three games to St. Xavier, split two games with Manual, and lost twice during the season to Central. The Cen-

Flaget started five seniors when it won the state tournament: Buddy Weihe (23), John McGill (25), Don Kalmey (32), Ted Deeken (12), and Tom Finnegan (13). (Courtesy of Flaget Museum)

tral Yellowjackets then swept the finals of the Twenty-Fifth District tournament with another easy win, 84–69.

The Braves caught fire in the regional tournament, however, defeating Manual 59–51 before pulling the upset of the year when they stung Central. The 56–52 victory over Butler in the Seventh Region final was anticlimactic, but it sent Flaget to Freedom Hall, where the Braves' task would not get any easier. Their opening game would be against Fourteenth Region champion Breathitt County, which the *Courier-Journal* sports staff had picked to win the tournament. But according to Dr. Litkenhous's ratings machine, the two teams that had the best chance to win the state tournament, based on their district and regional play, were the Flaget Braves and the Owensboro Red Devils, who opened the tournament against Eighth Region champion Lincoln Institute.

18

A Whistle from Midcourt

Gov. Bert Combs' administration suffered its first legislative setback Wednesday as the Kentucky House defeated a bill to create a human rights commission. The administration had announced its endorsement of the bill introduced by the only Negro legislator, Rep. William Childress (D-Louisville). An opponent of the bill, Rep. William Edmonds (D-Hopkinsville), argued that such a commission was not necessary and would hinder relationships now improving between the races.

—Associated Press, March 10, 1960

Nobody expected Lincoln Institute to be just minutes away from defeating one of the tournament favorites—and a wounded one at that. Another field goal by Clyde Mosby had pushed the Lincoln lead to 68–63 with 5:15 left in the game. Owensboro's big man, Jan Adelman, had fouled out with 17 points and 12 rebounds, and six-foot-one forward Richard Anderson had been disqualified on fouls in the third quarter. Lincoln could not have been in a better position, and it seemed remarkable that just a few years ago, an opportunity to play in the state tournament would have been unthinkable.

At that moment, Lincoln represented all the great black high school basketball teams that had toiled for years without recognition—until a Supreme Court decision wiped away decades of injustice and gave them the opportunity to compete with the best white teams. As historically significant as Lincoln's appearance might have been, none of the Lincoln fans in Freedom Hall that Thursday morning were thinking about civil rights or social wrongs. There was a game to be won, and their Tigers were on the cusp of victory.

Owensboro missed another shot, and Lincoln had the ball. The Tigers prepared to attack the offensive basket once again, hoping to widen their lead and assure victory. But Coach Gilliard called a time-out. He feared the offensive firepower of the Red Devils' hot-shooting star Randy Embry, and he wanted to keep the ball out of his hands. Lincoln's guards had been unable to stop Embry, and Gilliard had even substituted the "frustrator," Billy Collins, to try to stay with him. Nothing had worked.[1]

This time, Gilliard changed the team's offensive approach. Instead of continuing to run his offense against a weakened defensive team, Gilliard ordered his players to freeze the ball. Crayton threw his arms into the air in protest, and the other players were puzzled by this strategy, but the coach believed the best game plan was to deny Embry the ball and force Owensboro to foul. It was the first time during the season that Gilliard had ordered his team to hold the ball. It was not a tactic they had practiced; nor was it a strategy they had ever considered implementing. Playing "not to lose" was not playing to win for the Tigers.

Owensboro coach Bobby Watson immediately saw an opening, and he ordered his smaller Red Devils to press. Embry stole a pass and scored, and suddenly Owensboro had cut the deficit to 3 points, 72–69, with four minutes to play. Two more possessions ended in similar disasters for the Tigers, and Embry's twenty-foot jumper tied the contest at 73 with 3:01 remaining. Back on the attack, Bill Crayton buried a jump shot to put Lincoln back in the lead by 2 points, and then he rebounded an errant Owensboro shot. But the Red Devils continued to press, and David "Whip" Yewell stole the ball and drove the length of the floor for a layup, tying the game at 75 with 1:05 to go.

Nearly every fan in Freedom Hall was standing, regardless of which team they were rooting for, but none of them could have predicted the final minute of chaos. Lincoln held the ball for a good shot, but Crayton missed a fifteen-foot jumper with twenty-five seconds left. Owensboro rebounded and was headed the other way, but Watkins intercepted a pass. He flipped it to Crayton, who drove for the basket, but the Red Devils' Jerry Brooks slipped in from behind and took the ball out of Crayton's hands. Yewell reacted immediately to the steal and ran a post pattern straight down the middle of the floor. Brooks turned and unleashed a pass to the streaking Yewell, who had gotten behind the Tigers defenders. If that play had been executed in some other sport, it would have been remembered in slow motion, like Johnny Unitas to Raymond Berry, with sweat spraying off Yewell's face as he gracefully settled under Brooks's pass. The ball traveled more than seventy-five feet in the air—a perfect strike—as Yewell took two steps and laid it in the basket for a 77–75 lead.

Gilliard called a time-out with only eleven seconds showing on the clock. Lincoln had one more chance, and Gilliard called for the "figure eight," a pass-first, no-dribble offense designed to get the ball up the floor quickly. The play required two men at half-court awaiting the throw-in and two men at the foul line waiting for an opportunity. If executed properly, after three or four quick passes, one of the men on the foul line—either Crayton or Logan—would be open with a clear lane to the basket. It was high-speed, pass-only basketball at a dead run, and the Tigers' season depended on it.

The play worked to perfection. Logan caught the final pass as a sliver of daylight emerged off the right side of the key. He dribbled close to the ground to prevent a steal, drove hard to the basket, and went up as Yewell stretched in an attempt to block the shot. Yewell's right arm came across Logan's right wrist just as he flipped the ball onto the backboard. The ball banked soundly into the basket with two seconds to go as a referee's whistle trilled from midcourt. The official under the basket signaled "good," and the scoreboard flashed the 77–77 tie.

The Lincoln bench and their fans erupted at the apparent tie, and the reliable Logan headed to the line. But referee George Conley came running in from midcourt, making a sign that nobody in Freedom Hall expected. Conley did not call a foul on Yewell. Instead, he signaled that Logan had taken one too many steps on his final drive to the basket. The shot was nullified, and Owensboro won a game that suddenly fit comfortably into the lore of state tournament heart-stoppers.

Now it was the relieved Owensboro side that celebrated. The players from the bench crowded those on the floor, particularly Embry, who had scored 34 points, 10 of them in the final quarter, and grabbed 11 rebounds after the Red Devils' big men had fouled out. The other hero was Yewell, who had scored Owensboro's last two field goals on driving layups and tallied 17 points. In the Red Devils' locker room, Yewell grabbed teammate Brooks, whose steal and long pass had set up the winning basket, and gave him credit for the victory. "Here's the arm that did it," Yewell shouted as he playfully raised Brooks's right arm in a victory salute.

The mood was much different in the Lincoln locker room. Players buried their heads in towels, and some wept openly as Gilliard went around the room trying to console each one. Their grief at that moment crowded out memories of a burning gym, weeks and weeks of running five miles to and from practice, and enduring racial taunts and slurs to emerge in victorious dignity. Players understand that defeat is 50 percent of the game. Sometimes it comes when your team is beaten by superior talent, and sometimes you lose on a cold shooting night. But defeat is difficult to accept when you believe victory was taken from you. Such a defeat is doubly hard when it comes in a player's final game with his teammates. Reporters gathered around Logan to ask about the questionable call, but the senior gracefully responded: "The referee said I walked." It became the play that has lived in infamy for a generation of Lincoln graduates.

"A lot of black folks from Louisville were at the game, and they didn't like it," a Lincoln player recalled years later. "They still talk about that game and how we got a bad call at the end. We were on fire, and we changed our whole game plan." Bob McDowell, then an eighteen-year-old senior at Simpsonville High School, whose Bobcats had lost to Lincoln three times during the season, remembered, "I was at the game, and Lincoln was robbed. It was a bad call."[2]

Walter Gilliard remembered it fifty-five years later. Through the cloud of vascular dementia, which robs the brain of the chronology of events but not the events themselves, Gilliard nodded at a question posed by his daughter. "The official made a bad call," he said.

Owensboro High School won its next game in the tournament, a 48–47 overtime squeaker over Symsonia High School as Embry scored the final 5 points. But the Red Devils' hopes of a championship were thwarted in the semifinal round when integrated Monticello High School beat them 61–56.

Flaget surprised Breathitt County in the opening round, 76–59, as Tom

John McGill (25) and his Flaget teammates celebrate their state tournament championship victory over Monticello High School. (Courtesy of Flaget Museum)

John McGill drives for a layup against St. Xavier during the season. In three games against their biggest rivals, the Braves lost twice (by 2 points and 1 point) and won once (by 2 points). (Courtesy of Flaget Museum)

Finnegan scored 23 points and John McGill added 14. The Braves encountered a more serious challenge against Maysville and its African American stars Robert Alexander and Chuck Hall. With the game tied at 56, McGill hit two free throws to seal the 59–56 victory. In the semifinal round, the

Monticello's Junior Peyton (32) battles for the ball with Pikeville's Jack Jones in a January match. Monticello lost to Flaget in the state finals, which cost Peyton the chance to be the first African American player to start for a KHSAA state champion. (Courtesy of *Lexington Herald-Leader,* University of Kentucky Special Collections)

Braves had a surprisingly easy 96–72 win over Hopkinsville Attucks and its all-state guard Walter Gee, whose 31 points were doubled by the combination of Finnegan with 27, Deeken with 23, and McGill with 12.

In the championship game, the Braves prevailed over Monticello 65–56, and Finnegan, Deeken, and McGill were named to the all-tournament team. Flaget's victory gave McGill the honor of being the first African American starter on a KHSAA state champion team. But he still could not play tennis at the Louisville Boat Club.

Suggestions that the call on Logan had been racially motivated were raised mostly in casual conversation among the Lincoln Institute family. The referee who made the call, George Conley, was one of the most respected officials in the state (and the father of future Kentucky star and broadcaster Larry Conley). Any suggestions of prejudice could be countered with the final statistics, which showed that Lincoln had been assessed only nine fouls, compared with eighteen for Owensboro, which included the early losses of Adelman and Anderson. The real villain was Lincoln's poor shooting. The Tigers hit only thirteen of twenty-five free throws and 41.1 percent from the field (hitting thirty of seventy-three shots). Owensboro hit nine of fourteen free throws and 44.7 percent from the field (hitting thirty-four of seventy-six shots).

But one Lincoln fan would not accept the loss. A few days after the tournament, Hattie Bell Boyd wrote an irate letter to KHSAA commissioner Sanford, alleging a conspiracy against African American teams. Sanford sent a copy of the letter to Dr. Young on March 23, a week after the game, along with a cover letter. "Enclosed is a letter which we received recently from one of your students or patrons which speaks for itself," Sanford wrote. "Some of the implications made in the letter are too ridiculous for me to take time replying to the letter. I know that you will be embarrassed when you read the letter. Will you please return it for my files. I would also like to know just who Hattie Bell Boyd is." Sanford also attached a footnote: "Your representatives at the recent State Tournament were very fine, both faculty and players. They were indeed a credit to your institution."[3]

Young's response a few days later distanced the institution from Boyd's incendiary comments. "Miss Boyd is a patron," Young wrote apologetically, "and I regret very much that she allowed her enthusiasm to overcome her logic. This letter does not, in any way, reflect the official sentiment of Lincoln Institute. As you perhaps already know, the officials of Lincoln Institute have considered it more important to learn to play the game and to accept official rulings than to win. To me, winning is only incidental. We want our boys to play hard and to develop good character." Young claimed that Lincoln's true attitude was exemplified by Logan's postgame comment—"The referee said I walked"—at a time he could have been excused for expressing his frustration with vitriol. Young wrote to the commissioner: "I cannot help but admire this youngster for his bold statement."[4]

Dr. Young knew Hattie Bell Boyd a bit better than he suggested to Sanford. She was a Lincoln graduate and an assistant to Young's wife, Laura, in the Lincoln Ridge post office. One former staff member suggested that Boyd had written the letter in an effort to please Dr. Young, although the president reprimanded her later. Boyd was a frequent contributor to Lincoln publications and in 1962 became the postmaster of the Lincoln Ridge post office after the death of Laura Young, who had held the position since 1940.[5]

Interestingly, although the *Shelby Sentinel* carried pictures of the Tigers in action against Owensboro, the *Shelby News* ignored Lincoln Institute's defeat altogether. However, the newspapers did not ignore the bigger news in local education that week. Both carried front-page articles about the consolidation of schools in Simpsonville, Bagdad, and Waddy into the brand-new Shelby County High School, scheduled to open in September 1960 north of Shelbyville on US 60, the old Midland Trail.

The paradox of integration, as experienced by Kentucky's African American high schools in the years after *Brown,* was this: when basic human rights are denied, the process to achieve those rights sometime requires the sacrifice of other accomplishments. When African American leaders persuaded the US Supreme Court to prohibit segregation in public schools, it meant that much of what they had achieved in their separate universe would disappear.

Integrated education was long overdue and was the proper course to take, but the price was the loss of traditional institutions such as African American high school basketball. Many African Americans who endorsed integrated schools rejected the idea that their own schools, whose identity was often measured by athletic achievement and standing within the black community, would have to be sacrificed. Basketball was a small price to pay for social justice, but for those engaged in the transition, it was a bittersweet solution, an irrational dissonance created when emotion meets logic.

A related argument could be made by hundreds of young African Americans: the elimination of their schools denied them the opportunity to participate in certain activities, such as basketball. Young men who sat on the bench at Lincoln Institute or Lexington Dunbar were unlikely to make the team at all when competing in a much bigger pool at larger, integrated schools. Again, that was a small price to pay.

The US Supreme Court's 1954 ruling against segregated public schools gave African American high schools an indefinite time frame in which they could continue to operate. But they did so with a sword of Damocles hanging overhead, with no ability to control or influence its descending swipe. Until they found locks on the gym doors, the teams at those institutions continued to work, sweat, and sacrifice to achieve excellence. Therefore, for Kentucky's black high school basketball teams, the transitional period presented both an opportunity and a curse: an opportunity for players and coaches to compete at the highest levels of their sport, and the curse of an inevitable but uncertain termination.

Nonetheless, the years of transition represented the high-water mark of black high school basketball in Kentucky. The powerful teams from the old Kentucky High School Athletic League finally had an opportunity to participate against white schools and prove they belonged. A handful never won a game in a tournament during the transition, but their records are less important than their participation. They were there, providing their students with an opportunity to succeed, and sometimes that is enough. Having the chance and falling short of the goal is far better than never having the chance at all. For twenty-five years, the KHSAL schools never had the chance, and when it came, it came with strings. But at least when they got the opportunity, they made the most of it.

Champions are forged by superior performance in difficult circumstances. By that measure, the African American teams that transitioned from the only league in which they were permitted to play to the one that had rejected them for so long were champions. The extension of their grand tradition was subverted by the greater good—a necessary movement toward desegregation. In that sense, all the African American schools that survived the first wave of desegregation became "homeless tigers," existing in the uncertainty between the first draft of their obituary and their death. To paraphrase Whitney M. Young Sr., Lincoln Institute and its contemporaries were founded amid the constraints of segregation, and they were destroyed by the deliverance of integration.

Epilogue

The accomplishment of playing in a state tournament was still warm at Lincoln Institute later in the spring of 1960 when the inevitable question arose: how much longer would Lincoln function as a high school for African American students?

A month after the state tournament, Governor Bert Combs named a committee to study the question of what to do with Lincoln Institute. The committee's recommendation: transform Lincoln into a vocational high school for young people of all races from around the state. The committee, headed by Mrs. Craig Schmidt of Shelbyville, suggested specialized trades courses in addition to a regular high school curriculum.[1]

They were planning the funeral, even though the patient was still breathing. How many ticks were left on the clock before Lincoln Institute would be forced to close?

On June 1, 1960, Lincoln Institute held its forty-sixth commencement program. The graduates walked in to "War March of the Priests" by Felix Mendelssohn and listened to the commencement address by Frank L. Stanley Sr., editor and publisher of the *Louisville Defender*. Graduates who had achieved special honors were recognized, including class treasurer William Ben Spalding, who received the Dr. Maurice Rabb Best Sportsmanship Award, given to the school's outstanding senior athlete. John Wesley Watkins, who received a vocational engineering certificate, was awarded the Gold Star Citizenship Award. Jewell Francis Logan and Daniel Eugene Thomas also received vocational engineering certificates.

John McGill enrolled at Bellarmine College in the fall of 1960 to play basketball and tennis, but his grades fell and he was forced to leave school. He continued to play tennis just as Louisville's prestigious tennis community was undergoing a change of its own. In 1961 twenty-four-year-old Yale graduate Sam English agreed to accept an offer to become director of Kentucky's state tennis tournaments only if African Americans like John McGill were allowed to enter the tournaments.[2] That same year, McGill became the first African American to play in the men's state tennis championships. He reached the semifinals at Louisville's Central Park by winning a morning match, then went home and took a shower. McGill returned that afternoon for the championship match against John Evans of St. Xavier, but he was forced to default because of leg cramps.

John McGill left his mark on the Louisville tennis community, even though he never achieved his ambition "to become a tennis pro," as he stated in his Flaget High School yearbook. After McGill's brother James died in 1965 at age twenty-two, his father helped him get a job at International Harvester, where McGill worked until he retired.

After the 1960 spring semester, Walter Gilliard resigned as Lincoln Institute's athletic director and head basketball coach. The reason had less to do with Lincoln's uncertain future than with the fact that his marriage to Eleanor was on the rocks, and his decision to leave Lincoln was likely mutual.

Gilliard was replaced by Alvin Hanley, who came to Lincoln Ridge with impressive credentials. A two-time football all-American at Kentucky State College, Hanley had scored forty touchdowns at KSC and in 1951 had been the thirtieth-round draft choice of the Los Angeles Rams. After failing to make it in the NFL, Hanley became head coach at Frankfort Mayo-Underwood High School in 1953 and wasted no time building on the basketball heritage he had inherited from longtime coach James B. Brown.

When Hanley took over at Lincoln, the Tigers had been rated the 1960–1961 preseason favorite by Eighth Region coaches. They ranked Bill Crayton the number-one player and Clyde Mosby the number-three player in the region. But not everyone could adjust to Hanley's abrasive coaching style. During one game, Hanley called a time-out, and when the players approached the bench, he slapped John Cunningham hard in an effort to get his attention. "Black John" took offense and quit the team the following day.

After meeting with Dr. Young, he agreed to return for the next game, which was against the newly consolidated Shelby County High School.

The Shelby County Rockets hosted the game in their new 4,500-seat gymnasium, the largest high school gym in the state. They had the game well in hand until the school's enterprising band director began taunting the Lincoln players with repeated renditions of "Sweet Georgia Brown," the Harlem Globetrotters' signature song. The song energized the Tigers, who came back to win the game. Bill Harrell, the Shelby coach, later told the band director never to play that song again.

But the loss of graduating seniors Jewell Logan, Ben Spalding, Johnny Watkins, and Daniel Thomas was too much for the Tigers to overcome. Lincoln finished with a disappointing 13–11 record after being bounced out of the Thirtieth District tournament by Shelby County in a 77–55 rout. The Rockets would go on to win the Eighth Region title in their first year.

Hanley's aggressive style would get him into more trouble the following season. After a game with Lexington Dunbar in the new gym at Lincoln Ridge, one of the referees wrote a letter to KHSAA commissioner Ted Sanford complaining about Hanley's actions during the game. "Mr. Handley [sic] outwardly used profane words in front of his team, visiting team, my co-official, student body and [Dunbar] coach [S. T.] Roach." John W. "Scoop" Brown, whose regular job was supervisor of the Lexington parks and playgrounds, had ordered Hanley to leave the bench, but the coach had refused. Brown, a respected official who became the first African American to officiate at the state high school tournament in 1963, backed off. As he informed Sanford, he had allowed Hanley to remain in the game "due to a lack of police protection, and not knowing what the reaction of the spectators if the game was forfiet [sic] for his failure to leave the bench."[3]

Sanford sent a copy of the letter to Dr. Young, who promised to have a talk with Hanley. The coach sent a letter of apology to Sanford the following day.

All thirty-eight African American schools that finished the 1959–1960 season returned in 1960–1961, and it was a banner season for the former KHSAL members. Three won regional tournaments and spots in the Sweet

Sixteen held in Lexington. Previous Ninth Region champion Covington Grant and two-time Eleventh Region champion Lexington Dunbar returned to the tournament, where they were joined by newcomer Glasgow Bunche of the Fifth Region. Grant and Bunche lost their opening games, but Dunbar made a run for the championship behind all-state forward Austin Dumas. The Dunbar Bearcats defeated Harrison County 68–56 in the opener and then took the measure of Beaver Dam and its own all-stater, six-foot-three Butch Hill, winning by a score of 83–74 in the quarterfinal.

Dunbar and Fourteenth Region champ Breathitt County, out of the eastern Kentucky mountains, engaged in a classic semifinal match before Dumas hit one of the most memorable shots in state tournament history. With time expiring, Dumas launched a one-handed heave from midcourt that found the bottom of the basket as the clock hit zero, giving Dunbar a 55–54 victory. The Bearcats' dream to become the first African American school to win the KHSAA state tournament ended in the championship game, which they lost to Ashland High School, 69–50. The Ashland Tomcats were led by all-state first teamer Larry Conley, son of referee George Conley. The elder Conley continued to officiate college basketball into the mid-1970s, but he never again worked the Kentucky state high school tournament.[4]

Dunbar's run to the championship game was the last opportunity for a former KHSAL member to win the state tournament during desegregation's transitional years. The evolutionary effects of public school integration in Kentucky became apparent after the 1960–1961 academic year. As more public school districts made their peace with integration, African American schools with active sports programs gradually began to disappear as their students were absorbed into white schools.

After the 1960–1961 school year, four more African American schools closed. Lebanon Rosenwald, Versailles Simmons, Barbourville Rosenwald, and Ashland Booker T. Washington shut their doors forever, and their students were integrated into previously all-white schools. The snowball of integration had begun to roll and would not stop.

The year 1961 was not without its proud moments for Whitney M. Young Sr. On January 26 his son and namesake succeeded the retiring Lester Granger

Dr. Whitney Young and his wife, Laura, greet their son, Whitney M. Young Jr., and his wife, Margaret, at the fortieth anniversary celebration of Lincoln Institute in 1952. (Courtesy of Center of Excellence for the Study of Kentucky African-Americans, Kentucky State University)

as executive director of the National Urban League. Young Jr., only thirty-nine, outlined his plan during a visit to Cleveland later in the year:

> I pledge that I will give to the League not only that which I have gained by way of experience, skills and knowledge. But with equal zest all my loyalty, devotion and dedication. At stake is the future and reputation of an agency whose past contributions are reflected not in monuments of stone, but in the lives of hundreds of thousands of young people and adults who have been lifted from the throes of despair and distress to fuller, more productive lives.
>
> Ours is a crusade for justice, for decency, for morality, honesty and

frankness. It is a crusade to put into operational framework on a day to day, person to person basis the American creed and democratic promise. Ours is an obligation, most immediate to the Negro citizen or other minorities whom we serve, but in the final analysis it is a responsibility to America as it faces its greatest hour of challenge.[5]

Since 1954, Young Jr. had served as the dean of social work at Atlanta University, where he supported alumni in their boycott of the Georgia Conference of Social Welfare in response to low rates of African American employment within the organization.

Although its own future was limited, Lincoln Institute's legacy would live on through men and women like Whitney M. Young Jr.

Lincoln Institute's basketball team limped through the 1961–1962 season with an 8–13 record, although they rallied to win the Thirtieth District tournament by defeating Taylorsville and Shelbyville. They lost a 42–41 squeaker to Eminence in the Eighth Region opener. Five other black schools in the state, including 1960 state tournament semifinalist Hopkinsville Attucks, won district tournaments. However, none of the six came out of their regions to participate in the 1962 state tournament. At the end of the 1961–1962 school year, two more former KHSAL members closed: Providence Rosenwald and Owensboro Western. That left thirty-three former KHSAL members alive, and that number would drop drastically in the next two years as the national civil rights movement gathered momentum and local school boards rushed to keep pace.

Lincoln won the Thirtieth District tournament again in the 1962–1963 season, defeating Shelby County, before falling in the Eighth Region opener to Grant County. But the 1963 state tournament became the most historically significant one with regard to the impact of African American players. For the first time, blacks outnumbered whites on the all-tournament team, eight to two, and for the first time since John McGill, black players finished in the winner's circle. Louisville Seneca, led by African Americans Mike Redd and Westley Unseld, defeated Lexington Dunbar, 72–66.[6]

After the 1962–1963 school year, eleven more African American schools closed when their local districts integrated: 1963 state tournament participant Princeton Dotson, Campbellsville Durham, Harlan Rosenwald, Murray Douglass, Paris Western, Nicholasville Rosenwald, Lexington Douglass, Middlesboro Lincoln, Lynch West Main, Stanford Lincoln, and East Benham. Eight more closed after the 1963–1964 school year: Earlington Million, Todd County Training, Morganfield Dunbar, Drakesboro Community, Danville Bate, Lancaster Mason, Jenkins Dunham, and 1961 state tournament participant Glasgow Bunche.

Two other former KHSAL members closed before the new school year started, and only partly because of integration. Mount Sterling DuBois High School, which had served African American students since 1929, was destroyed by fire—a probable case of arson—on September 3, 1964. There were three fires in the Negro section of town within twenty-four hours, including one at the Negro Masonic Lodge and one at a four-room frame residence owned by an African American. As a result of the school fire, the Mount Sterling board of education announced that it would integrate all city schools when registration and classes started the following week.[7] Somerset Dunbar, which never joined the KHSAA, also closed. The avalanche of closures would continue after the 1964–1965 school year.

When John Norman "Slam Bam" Cunningham was discharged from the air force and returned home to Lawrenceburg, he had no idea what he was going to do with his life. Cunningham was unaware of the program commonly called the GI Bill, which provided governmental assistance to former military personnel pursuing an education. But Cunningham took his industrial arts education at Lincoln Institute, along with his air force training, and came up with a plan. He enrolled at the University of Kentucky and used the credits to highlight a résumé that he took to Lexington's largest employer at the time, IBM. He was hired on the spot and, as an added bonus, found out that IBM had a company basketball team.

Soon, Cunningham was immersed in the Lexington culture of "Big Blue," which combined IBM's corporate nickname with the nickname of the hometown college basketball team. Coach Adolph Rupp held the color line at the University of Kentucky because he could not take black players

John Cunningham drives for an easy layup during an armed forces tournament. After Cunningham left the service, he played on IBM's corporate team and delighted in tweaking the nose of Kentucky coach Adolph Rupp. (Courtesy of John N. Cunningham)

into the resistant stronghold of segregation in the Southeastern Conference, of which UK was a member. But Rupp hosted teams with African American players, and his freshman team, the UK Kittens, did the same.

The UK freshman schedule included games with other freshman teams from the University of Tennessee, Vanderbilt, Cincinnati, and Dayton, as well as a number of squads that were a few notches above "shirts and skins." The UK Kittens played teams from the Lexington YMCA, the UK Dental School, and Southeastern Christian College.

On January 2, 1965, IBM's corporate team went into Memorial Coliseum to play the Kittens. Rupp had recruited well that year, and his freshman lineup included six-foot-five center Thad Jaracz of Lexington Lafayette, six-foot-four Bob Tallent of Maytown High School, and six-foot-two guard Jim Lemaster from Bourbon County.

Cunningham was ten years older than the UK freshmen, but once the game began, it was evident that none of the young players could stop the IBM star. "Slam Bam" was slicing behind the UK guards on fast breaks, stealing the ball, and taking rebounds away from the taller Jaracz and six-foot-eight Cliff Berger. Tallent's hot shooting gave the Kittens an early lead and a 51–31 halftime bulge, but he was not necessarily the best player on the floor. As the *Lexington Herald*'s Bob Ryans reported, "If Tallent was hot, IBM's John Cunningham was even hotter. The 6–3 forward ripped the baskets for 17 points in the first half to keep his team within range."[8]

At one point, Rupp, who was watching the game from under a basket while his assistant, Harry Lancaster, coached the team, shouted out at his players: "Can't anybody stop that guy?"

Cunningham looked over his shoulder and shouted back at Rupp, "You can put all your kittens on me, but you can't stop me!"

The Kittens were not threatened and rolled to an easy 98–59 victory, with Rupp's prized scholarship players leading the way. Tallent scored 20 points, Lemaster 19, and Jaracz 17. Game honors, however, went to John "Slam Bam" Cunningham, who scored 24 points, grabbed 18 rebounds, and acquired a story that summarized his career.

Five months later, after the 1964–1965 school year ended, six more former KHSAL members that had participated in the KHSAA closed their doors: Paducah Lincoln, Mayfield Dunbar, Henderson Douglass, Franklin Lincoln, two-time state tournament participant Bowling Green High Street, and three-time state tournament participant Covington Grant. That left only a thin black thread still hanging.

Lincoln Institute had managed to survive as its brethren were falling, but its time was at hand. When the 1964–1965 school year opened, African American students in Shelby County were given the option to attend Shelby County High School, but only one student, a freshman from Shelbyville named Bruce Marshall, chose to do so. Marshall had an easy manner and an infectious sense of humor, and he quickly became popular among his white classmates. The following year, African American students in the county were given the same option, and they responded en masse. Enrollment at Lincoln dropped from 562 in 1964–1965 to 309 in 1965–1966.[9]

Lincoln Institute and the entire county already knew what was coming, but a legislative pronouncement dated February 16, 1966, and innocently titled "House Bill No. 89" made it official: "Be it enacted that a new section of Chapter 166 of the Kentucky Revised Statutes is created to read as follows: The state institution formerly designated as Lincoln Institute and located in Shelby County, Kentucky, shall hereafter be established, utilized and maintained as a secondary school for the education of exceptionally talented but culturally and economically deprived children of the Commonwealth of Kentucky."[10]

Lincoln's closure as a high school and its redirection had been mandated by the state, and the African American community of Shelby County and Shelbyville accepted the loss of its most treasured institution. Integration had finally come, a dozen years after the Supreme Court of the United States had declared it the law of the land.

Dr. Whitney M. Young Sr. knew that when his beloved Lincoln Institute closed, it would be time for him to say good-bye. Two months before the end of his final term, he penned the following letter to the Lincoln Institute Board of Regents:

June 8, 1966 will mark the end of 51 years of my association with Lincoln Institute as student, teacher, dean and president. The 31 years as President have been filled with rich and glorious experience. We have passed through floods, fires, financial crises and 11 years of desegregation. My wife, who passed in 1962, and

Whitney M. Young and Governor Louie B. Nunn flank President Richard Nixon at this meeting at the White House in May 1971. Nixon pledged $1 million in federal funds to help Lincoln Institute reopen as a vocational center. (Courtesy of Center of Excellence for the Study of Kentucky African-Americans, Kentucky State University)

my daughter Eleanor have played an important role in the success of the school.

We have seen the enrollment increase from 85 in 1935 to 562 in 1965. We have witnessed an increase in the appropriation from $42,000 annually in 1936 to $250,000 in 1966. We have seen three fireproof buildings replace old fire traps. We have achieved the highest rating attainable by any high school in the state. The journey has been long, hard and often trying, but always it has been gratifying. We can never repay our many co-workers, association and friends for their help and encouraging messages.

The time has come for a younger person to take over the leadership of the school. It is with deep regret that I must tender my resignation as of June 8, 1966. With deepest gratitude to Dr. Carl Hill, the Board of Regents and the Lincoln Foundation for their valuable assistance and confidence.

Very respectfully submitted,
Whitney M. Young

After the 1965–1966 school year, Lincoln Institute was joined in the ever-after by 1965 state tournament participant Madisonville Rosenwald and Hickman Riverview. Only three former KHSAL members would open in the fall of 1966, but it would be the last year for two of them: Lincoln's fellow 1960 state tournament participant Hopkinsville Attucks and Lexington Dunbar. The storied Lexington school, which had participated in six state tournaments during the transitional years of desegregation, would reopen in 1990 as integrated Paul Laurence Dunbar High School, pursuant to an agreement between the Lexington school board and the local black community.

Perhaps it was fitting that Louisville Central was the last former KHSAL member left standing. Central was the oldest African American high school in Kentucky, having opened in October 1873 at Sixth and Kentucky, and it had been the most successful KHSAL member. Although the Yellowjackets participated in only one state tournament (1965) during the transitional years, the newly integrated Central High School continued its sterling basketball tradition, winning the 1969 and 1974 state high school basketball tournaments. Central's principal during the latter season was Joseph McPherson, Walter Gilliard's assistant basketball coach. McPherson had joined the Central faculty in 1962 and was named principal in 1972; he retired from the school in 1982. Central remains open to this day.[11]

In the early years of integration, black athletes were accepted much more quickly in white schools than were black teachers or even black game officials. During a roundtable discussion in Louisville at a 1955 desegregation conference attended by 150 Kentucky educators, C. D. Redding, superintendent of the Frankfort schools, issued some prophetic remarks about the "peculiar situation in Kentucky." "Most schools are small and the teaching

Louis Stout went from Banneker High School in the KHSAL to integrated Cynthiana High School and then to Regis College, where he played for fellow Cynthiana native Joe B. Hall. Stout became the first African American commissioner of the Kentucky High School Athletic Association in 1994. (Courtesy of Kentucky High School Athletic Association)

load is small," Redding told the conference. "Negro teachers are better qualified than the white. A higher percentage of white teachers have emergency certificates than Negro teachers. In any form of desegregation, a good many school districts are going to have some surplus teachers. We have the practical problem. Which ones are you going to eliminate? Somebody, under any plan of desegregation, is going to lose a job."[12]

For several years extending beyond 1956, black game officials fought to gain a place alongside their white counterparts. Black officials were banned from working at high school games in many areas of the commonwealth, and it was not until a federal court decree in 1971 that they were actually permitted to officiate at athletic contests with the full support of the KHSAA. The Kentucky Civil Liberties Union and the Black Coaches Association filed the federal lawsuit, which drew the concurrence of judge Max Swinford. "Something is wrong when Negroes make up 50 percent of the players and only 1 percent of the officials," Swinford said in condemning the KHSAA. The court mandated that the KHSAA appoint at least one black administrator to take affirmative steps to train and employ more African American officials.[13]

To comply with the court order, the KHSAA called on Louis Stout, the former player at Cynthiana Banneker who had succeeded the legendary S. T. Roach as head coach at Lexington Dunbar. Stout joined the KHSAA in 1971, focusing on issues of diversity and inclusion. He reconstituted African American officials and gave the so-called minor sports greater importance. In 1994, in recognition of Stout's efforts and perhaps as a bit of redemption, the KHSAA, which had administered the athletics of segregated white schools for decades, named Louis Stout its first African American commissioner.

After Walter Gilliard left Lincoln Institute, he was hired as head basketball coach by Jefferson High School in Pontiac, Michigan. Gilliard remarried, and he and wife Patsye had four daughters: Michelle, Renee, Carolyn, and Beverly. Gilliard left Pontiac in 1964 to become director of physical education and athletics at Kent State University High School, a selective private school connected with Kent State University's College of Education. For the first time in his career, Gilliard found himself in the unique position of being the black coach of an all-white team, but all players respond to good coaching, and in 1965 Kent won its sectional championship. More important, Gilliard's position at the school gave him an opportunity to continue his education.[14] In 1973 he received a master's degree in counseling psychology and became the first African American in the PhD program.

Gilliard later moved his family to Western Illinois University in Macomb, where he became a full-time administrator and teacher. His only athletic duties consisted of umpiring his daughters' Little League softball games. After spending some time as dean of students at Central State University, Gilliard moved to the University of Dayton in 1980, where he was associate dean of students until he retired in 1992. After Gilliard's wife Patsye passed in 2012, he moved to Silver Spring, Maryland, to live with daughter Michelle. Shortly before his death at age ninety on March 8, 2016, Gilliard was still singing in his church choir at Scotland African Methodist Episcopal Zion Church in Potomac, Maryland.[15]

Gilliard outlived his old friend Arnold Thurman, the first white coach to schedule a game against Lincoln Institute. Thurman died on May 30,

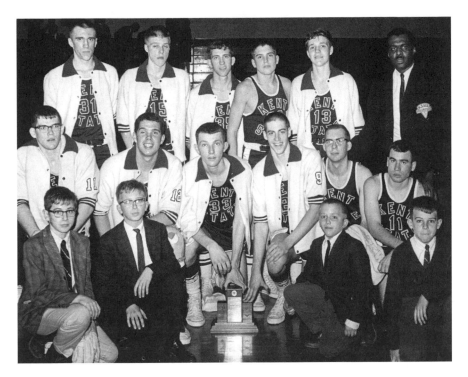

Walter Gilliard found himself in a unique position at Kent State University High School in 1965, where he was the black coach of an all-white team. (Courtesy of the Walter Gilliard family)

2015, at age eighty-two. Among the eulogists was the Reverend Norris Beckley, an African American starter when Shelby County High School won its second state championship in 1978 under athletic director Thurman. In a fitting tribute, Beckley told the assembly at Christiansburg Baptist Church: "Arnold Thurman was my friend, my mentor, and my coach."

In late May 1966 Lincoln Institute's baseball team took the field in the district tournament against Shelby County High School at the Shelbyville High School field. Al Minnis Jr., son of the engineering teacher at Lincoln, was the Tigers' baseball coach. The Shelby County Rockets were heavily favored. Four Rockets were members of the recently crowned 1966 state champion basketball team, including shortstop Mike Casey, who had been named the state's Mr. Basketball. Another starter on the basketball team was Shelby's best pitcher. Ron Ritter, a six-foot-three, 220-pound right-hander, was drawing the attention of major league scouts for his 92 mph fastball.

Surprisingly, in the top of the first inning, infielder Scott Jones keyed in on one of Ritter's breaking pitches and sent it over the fence with a man on base, giving the Tigers a quick 2–0 lead. Ritter dispensed with the cute stuff and went back to his fastball, which stymied the underdogs long enough for the Rockets to come back and take a 4–2 victory to advance in the tournament.

The last play of the game was a pop fly to right field, where a pudgy senior outfielder drifted under it, shaded his eyes from the late-day sun, and squeezed it for the final out.

The loss was Lincoln Institute's last varsity athletic event before the school closed that summer. Scott Jones would transfer to Shelby County, where he would become a reliable contributor to the baseball team and a starting guard on the basketball team.

In the spring of 1966, Shelby County's Mitchell Bailey was living a high school coach's dream. As the assistant basketball coach, he had celebrated a state title, and as the head baseball coach, he nearly took a second one, his team falling to Ashland 2–1 in the championship game. Before coming to Shelby County, Bailey had served as head basketball coach at Campbellsburg High School, which closed after the 1959–1960 school year. Until that halcyon two months in 1966, Bailey's greatest thrill as a coach had come in his final year at Campbellsburg, when, in December 1959, his Blue Wolves had handed the Lincoln Institute Tigers their first loss in what would become their greatest season.

The pudgy outfielder who caught the final fly ball in Lincoln Institute's last varsity event went on to have a long career in and around sports as a writer, National Football League executive, and college athletic director. His most cherished accomplishment, however, is writing the book you hold in your hands.

Acknowledgments

My father, Charles E. Miller, introduced me to Lincoln Institute. My brother Jerry and I rode shotgun on our father's truck that transported milk from the Lincoln dairy to the processing plants in Louisville, and Dad took us to see the Lincoln Tigers play in the 1959 and 1960 district and regional tournaments. I did not know until I started researching the subject that our family's association with the school went even further back. During my first conversation with Al "Junior" Minnis, I learned that my grandfather, Chester C. Miller, had moved the Minnis family's furniture from Louisville to Simpsonville in his produce truck after Albert Minnis Sr. became Lincoln's engineering teacher in 1939. That revelation should have come as no surprise, since the heart of this book comes from the reminiscences of many former Lincoln Institute players, coaches, and staff members who were gracious enough to let me into their homes and into their memories.

Gary Brown, a Lincoln graduate and longtime director of the Lincoln Foundation, was my first interview with a Lincolnite, and his insight and perspective were invaluable. Albert Minnis Jr. offered other thoughts from his various platforms as a Lincoln student, faculty member, and assistant to Dr. Young and as the Tigers' last baseball coach. Michelle Gilliard allowed me into her Maryland home to discuss her father's career as well as his strength in fighting a debilitating illness. Former players John N. Cunningham, Ben Spalding, Jewell Logan, Daniel Thomas, Billy Collins, the Reverend John K. Cunningham, and Dr. Bernard Minnis all offered personal insights that deepened the narrative.

Two other participants in the 1960 state tournament offered another perspective that contributed greatly to my understanding. I sat down with John McGill at his Louisville apartment to discuss basketball, and he revealed his role as Arthur Ashe's tennis partner and the discrimination he faced in his own hometown. Kentucky basketball legend Randy Embry was generous with his insight and stories about the tournament from the Owensboro perspective.

Special recognition goes to two of my old high school coaches. Dr. Bill Ellis, my head football coach at Shelby County High School, smartened up early and became a historian and college professor. His *History of Education in Kentucky* filled many holes in my research, and his guidance and comments on the manuscript were invaluable. Arnold Thurman's character and his propensity for doing the right thing are reflected in his early efforts to ease the transition of desegregation. I regret he did not live long enough to see the fruits of his insight.

Others contributed on a less personal, but no less essential, basis. The research task would have been long and arduous without the prior groundwork of two individuals. Louis Stout's book *Shadows of the Past* will forever keep the memory of the Kentucky High School Athletic League alive, and Jeff Bridgeman's *Encyclopedia of Kentucky High School Basketball* was a treasure chest of tournament games, team histories, and coaching records.

Joe Angolia of the Kentucky High School Athletic Association was always available to answer questions or to suggest another person to contact if he did not have the answer. Special thanks to the staff at the Shelby County Library in Shelbyville, Kentucky, for allowing me to monopolize the microfilm machine to read back issues of the *Shelby News* and the *Shelby Sentinel* whenever I was in town. My cousin Sharon Hackworth and her husband Neil, the former mayor of Shelbyville, offered early encouragement as well as advice and contacts in Shelbyville's African American community.

Another Shelby County native and longtime friend, Steve Doyle, took time from his job as managing editor of the *Greensboro (NC) Record* to edit the manuscript and offer valuable suggestions that tightened the narrative. My friend and former colleague David V. Hawpe, retired editorial page editor of the *Louisville Courier-Journal,* offered insight on Louisville's integration process from a high school student's perspective. Thanks also to two of my old SAE fraternity brothers at the University of Kentucky: Bill Gorman, who put me in touch with former Hazard High School star Don Smith, and

Dr. John "Sparky" McDowell, who led me to Dwayne "Nug" Faris, a former Maysville High School athlete with knowledge of Bobby "Toothpick" Jones. My appreciation also goes to Bob Ullrich of the Flaget High School Alumni Association, who put me in touch with John McGill. My friend Jim Richards, former head coach at Western Kentucky University, whose Glasgow Scotties won the 1968 state tournament, shared his recollections of the racial transition of Kentucky high school basketball in the 1950s and 1960s.

Sometimes overlooked, but invaluable to any research, are the men and women who help researchers navigate the historical collections that contain so much information to enrich the people and times depicted in their work. Irma Johnson of Kentucky State University's Center of Excellence for the Study of Kentucky African-Americans cut her own vacation short to accommodate my travel schedule and allow me to review the Whitney M. Young Sr. Collection. Jackie Couture of the Special Collections Office at Eastern Kentucky University was instrumental in my examination of the Kentucky High School Athletic Association files and Board of Control minutes. Supervisor Jennifer Patterson guided me through the Kentucky State Archives in Frankfort and helped me locate many pertinent Lincoln Institute records. Harry Rice, sound archivist of the Special Collections at Berea College's Hutchins Library, sent me a dozen CDs that contained the bulk of Professor Andrew Baskin's Lincoln Institute Oral History Project, excerpts of which were used liberally herein. Matt Harris of the Kentucky Education Collection at the University of Kentucky's Margaret I. King Library located old publications and records that pertained to Lincoln Institute and education in Shelby County. His University of Kentucky colleague Jacqueline Doucet, manager of the lending unit at the William T. Young Library, executed my interlibrary loan requests for local Kentucky newspapers. Joe Hardesty made my visits to the Louisville Free Public Library a joy not only because of his guidance but also because he repeatedly showed me how to get his cutting-edge microfilm machines to print.

My ongoing thanks to the staff at the Earl K. Long Library at the University of New Orleans, who coordinated my interlibrary loan requests for books and microfilm and allowed me unlimited access to the UNO microfilm center for viewing.

Major databases such as the Notable Kentucky African-American Database, the Kentucky Digital Library, the African-American Oral History Collection of the University of Louisville, and the Genealogy Bank provided access to a wealth of resource material and newspapers of the day.

On a more personal note, my brother Jerry is an ongoing inspiration for his love of Kentucky history and his service to the African American community through his membership on the Louisville Metro Council and in the Kentucky house of representatives. Last, but far from least, I want to thank my wife and best friend, Jean Miller, for her encouragement, for her patience during my research trips and hours of writing, and for her love for me and our children.

Appendix

Where Are They Now?

Whitney M. Young Sr. remained active after he retired from Lincoln Institute. He served on the Chief Justice's Housing Commission, the State Vocational Advisory Board, and the Black History Committee of the Kentucky Commission on Human Rights, which published the 1971 textbook *Kentucky's Black Heritage.* Dr. Young died at age seventy-seven on August 18, 1975, and is buried in Cove Haven Cemetery in Lexington.

Dr. Arnita Young Boswell taught social work for nineteen years at the University of Chicago and was active in the civil rights movement. In 1966 she led the women's division of a massive demonstration led by the Reverend Martin Luther King. She also served as director of social services at the University of Illinois at Chicago. She died in 2002 at age eighty-two.

Dr. Eleanor Young Gilliard Love left Lincoln Institute for the University of Louisville and became the first African American dean at the university. At the time of her death in 2006 at age eighty-three, she was professor emeritus at the University of Louisville and a member of the Lincoln Foundation Board of Trustees and the Kentucky State University National Alumni Association.

Whitney M. Young Jr. became director of the National Urban League and was one of the nation's foremost civil rights leaders. At age forty-nine, Young died of a heart attack on March 11, 1971, after swimming with friends in Lagos, Nigeria, where he was attending a conference sponsored by the African-American Institute. President Nixon sent a plane to Nigeria to collect Young's body and traveled to Kentucky to deliver the eulogy at his funeral.

Coach Walter Gilliard lived with his daughter, Michelle Gilliard Sheehan, in Silver Spring, Maryland, until his death on March 8, 2016, at age ninety (see the epilogue).

Assistant coach Joseph McPherson joined the Louisville Central faculty as a teacher and coach in 1962. He was named principal in 1972 and retired from the school in 1982. McPherson is deceased.

Jewell Logan, seventy-four, played basketball in the US Air Force and was named to an air force all-star team before his discharge in 1966. Logan received a degree from Central State College in 1970 and worked in sales for the AC Delco division of General Motors. After he was transferred to Seattle, he obtained a real estate broker's license in 1982 and is still active in the real estate business in Portland, Oregon.

Ben Spalding, seventy-four, became a social worker. He lives in Tucson, Arizona, where he works for Pima County Social Services.

Bill Crayton returned to his hometown of Indianapolis and served in the US Army from 1963 to 1966. Logan saw Crayton at an Air Force–Army basketball game in Washington, DC, in 1965—the last time any of his former teammates saw him. Crayton died in Indianapolis in 1993.

The whereabouts of John Watkins and Clyde Mosby are unknown, but both are believed to be deceased.

Billy Collins, seventy-three, joined the US Air Force in 1961 and retired from the military in 1984. He worked in the construction business and drove long-haul trucks until he retired for good in 2005. He lives in Oklahoma City.

Daniel Thomas, seventy-four, retired from Buffalo Trace Distillery in Frankfort, Kentucky. He serves as a doorman for the Kentucky house of representatives.

"Black John" Cunningham, seventy-four, retired from Wild Turkey Distillery in his hometown of Lawrenceburg, Kentucky. He has served as minister of the First Baptist Church of Berea since 1994.

Dr. Bernard Minnis, seventy-five, was a classroom teacher, middle school principal, and deputy associate superintendent for instruction with the Kentucky Department of Education. In 2009 Metro Louisville awarded him its Dr. Martin Luther King Jr. Freedom Award for "promoting justice, peace, freedom, nonviolence, racial equality and civic activism." Dr. Minnis is professor emeritus at Bellarmine College, where he taught instructional leadership and social justice. He lives in Louisville.

Albert Minnis Jr., eighty-three, graduated from Lincoln, served as assistant to Dr. Young, and was Lincoln's last baseball coach. He is retired and lives in the same house he and his brother grew up in, just off the Lincoln campus in Simpsonville, Kentucky.

John N. "Slam Bam" Cunningham, seventy-nine, retired from IBM and obtained his real estate license. He was one of his company's top regional sellers until retiring in 2012. He lives in Lawrenceburg (see the epilogue).

The other starters on Lincoln Institute's 1955 KHSAL state champions are deceased, and the fate of coach Herbert Garner is unknown.

John McGill, seventy-four, retired from International Harvester and lives in Louisville with his second wife and eight-year-old granddaughter (see the epilogue).

Randy Embry, seventy-three, played at the University of Kentucky for four years and then became a successful high school basketball and baseball coach. Embry coached at Daviess County High School from 1967 to 1980 and led his baseball team to the Kentucky state championship in 1971. He posted a 442–146 record as head basketball coach of Owensboro High School from 1980 to 1999, when he was hired by his former UK teammate Pat Riley as a scout with the Miami Heat. Embry still lives in Owensboro.

Arnold Thurman retired as athletic director of Shelby County High School in 1979 and had a second career with Kentucky Farm Bureau Insurance until he retired in 1995. Thurman died at his home in Shelbyville, Kentucky, on May 30, 2015.

Notes

1. New Journey on an Old Road

1. Details of the Tigers' trip to the state tournament came from interviews with former players, students, and teachers.

2. *Owensboro Messenger-Inquirer,* March 13, 1960.

3. "Senior High Wins Regional," *Owensboro Messenger-Inquirer,* March 14, 1960.

4. Hicks's scouting report was paraphrased from my interview with Randy Embry, July 18, 2015.

5. Game accounts were reconstructed from the March 18, 1960, editions of the *Louisville Courier-Journal, Lexington Herald,* and *Owensboro Messenger-Inquirer* and from interviews with the participants.

6. This chant and others made a lasting impression on a twelve-year-old white fan whose father took him to Lincoln games in 1960.

2. Prejudice versus Common Sense

1. Berea College website, https://www.berea.edu/about/history/.

2. The apostles Paul and Silas ministered to the biblical Berea in Acts 17:10–15.

3. John G. Fee, *Autobiography of John G. Fee, Berea, Kentucky* (Chicago: National Christian Association, 1891; digitized by University of North Carolina at Chapel Hill, 1997), 90–91.

4. Ibid., 137–38.

5. Ibid., 172–81; Camp Nelson Heritage Park website, http://www.campnelson.org/home.htm.

6. George C. Wright, "The Founding of Lincoln Institute," *Filson Quarterly* 49, no. 1 (January 1975): 57.

7. William E. Ellis, *A History of Education in Kentucky* (Lexington: University Press of Kentucky, 2011), 99.

8. Gerald L. Gutek, *A History of the Western Educational Experience* (Long Grove, IL: Waveland Press, 1995), 507–9.

9. Ellis, *History of Education in Kentucky,* 100.

10. George C. Wright, *A History of Blacks in Kentucky,* vol. 2, *In Pursuit of Equality, 1890–1980* (Frankfort: Kentucky Historical Society, 2001), 112–13.

11. *The Constitution of the Commonwealth of Kentucky* (Frankfort: Kentucky Legislative Research Commission, 1952), 30–31.

12. Kenneth C. Barnes, *Journey of Hope: The Back-to-Africa Movement in Arkansas in the Late 1800s* (Chapel Hill: University of North Carolina Press, 2004), 31.

13. "Whites Are Called Demons," *Chicago Record-Herald,* June 29, 1903, cited in Lottie Offett Robinson, *The Bond-Washington Story* (Elizabethtown, KY: Robinson, 1983), 29.

14. "Berea College," *Lexington Leader,* February 1, 1904.

15. James C. Klotter, *Kentucky: Portrait in Paradox, 1900–1950* (Frankfort: Kentucky Historical Society, 1996), 152–53.

16. *Berea College v. Kentucky,* 211 U.S. 45 (1908).

17. George C. Wright, *Racial Violence in Kentucky, 1865–1940* (Baton Rouge: LSU Press, 1990), 320–21.

18. Wright, "Founding of Lincoln Institute," 63–64.

19. *Shelby Sentinel,* September 3, 1954.

20. Dan McNichol, *The Roads that Built America* (New York: Silver Lining Books, 2003), 66.

21. Brian D. McKnight, *Contested Borderland: Civil War in Appalachian Kentucky and Virginia* (Lexington: University Press of Kentucky, 2006), 211.

22. In the interest of full disclosure, I proudly admit that my brother, Jerry T. Miller, rediscovered the incident that early newspapers called the "Skirmish at Simpsonville." His efforts resulted in a memorial consisting of twenty-two "In Memory Of" markers and headstones and a historical marker erected on US 60 near the site of the mass grave where local citizens reportedly buried the soldiers. The burial site became an African American cemetery administered by members of the Trim #2 United Brothers of Friendship Lodge in Simpsonville. When the last lodge member died in 1965, the untended cemetery became overgrown with weeds and trees and was neglected until its rediscovery in 2011.

23. "Fund for Lincoln Institute Complete," *Lexington Herald,* June 27, 1909.

24. Wright, *History of Blacks in Kentucky,* 62–63; "Site Is Bought for Lincoln Institute," *Lexington Herald,* May 7, 1909.

25. *Shelby News,* May 27, 1909.

26. *Shelby Record,* June 11, 1909.

27. Quoted in James W. Miller, "The Legacy of Lincoln," *Shelby News,* February 20, 2013.

28. "Holland Law Held to Be Unconstitutional," *Lexington Herald,* May 22, 1910.

29. "A Voice of Hope from Shelby," *Lexington Herald,* June 9, 1910.

30. "Value of Negro Population Evident," *Lexington Herald,* January 28, 1912.

31. Maureen Ashby, "Montclair," in *The New History of Shelby County, Kentucky* (Prospect, KY: Harmony House Publishers, 2003), 71–72.

32. "Mayor Gruber," *Lexington Herald,* November 4, 1912.

33. Wright, *Racial Violence in Kentucky,* 110. Several sources discuss the incident in detail, including *Louisville Courier-Journal,* January 16, 17, 18, 1911; *New York Times,* January 16, 17, 18, 1911; *Shelby News,* February 2, 1911; *Hopkinsville Kentuckian,* January 17, 18, 1911.

34. Wright, *Racial Violence in Kentucky,* 111; *Louisville Courier-Journal,* January 30, May 12, 1911; *Earlington Bee,* January 15, 1911; *Shelby News,* February 2, 1911.

35. Wright, *Racial Violence in Kentucky,* 111–12.

3. A Young Man of Substance

1. Notable Kentucky African-American Database, University of Kentucky, http://nkaa.uky.edu/subject.php?sub_id=147.

2. George C. Wright, "The Founding of Lincoln Institute," *Filson Quarterly* 49, no. 1 (January 1975): 67.

3. Wright, *History of Blacks in Kentucky,* 65–69.

4. Ibid.

5. Ibid.

6. *Lexington Herald,* September 30, 1912.

7. "People's Forum," *Lexington Herald,* January 16, 1922.

8. Eleanor Young Love interview, October 2, 1978, University of Louisville African-American Oral History Collection, digital.library.louisville.edu/cdm.

9. Whitney M. Young Sr. curriculum vitae, box 10, Whitney M. Young Sr. Papers, Special Collections, Paul G. Blazer Library, Kentucky State University, Frankfort.

10. Duanne Puckett, "Whitney Young," in *New History of Shelby County,* 628–29.

11. "Bars Ku Klux Klan," *Lexington Herald,* August 21, 1921; "Klan Speaker Is Fined $200 in Police Court," *Lexington Herald,* August 12, 1923.

12. Duanne Puckett, "Whitney Young Jr.," in *New History of Shelby County,* 629–30.

13. Dennis C. Dickerson, *Militant Mediator: Whitney M. Young Jr.* (Lexington: University Press of Kentucky, 1998), 25.

14. Ibid., 26.

4. Organizing Athletics

Epigraph: Quoted in Bob Kuska, *Hot Potato: How Washington and New York Gave Birth to Black Basketball and Changed America's Game Forever* (Charlottesville: University of Virginia Press, 2004), 90.

1. "Colored Basketball Teams in Big Contest," *Indianapolis Freeman,* November 30, 1907.

2. Robert Pruter and Project Muse, *The Rise of American High School Sports and the Search for Control* (Syracuse, NY: Syracuse University Press, 2013), 288.

3. "Colored News Notes," *Lexington Herald,* February 28, 1921.

4. Pruter, *Rise of American High School Sports,* 289.

5. Louis Stout, *Shadows of the Past: A History of the Kentucky High School Athletic League* (Lexington, KY: Host Communications, 2006), 10.

6. "Colored News Notes," *Lexington Herald,* November 19, December 14, 1922.

7. Stout, *Shadows of the Past.*

8. Pruter, *Rise of American High School Sports,* 275–78.

9. Ibid.

10. Ibid., 284.

11. Gerald L Smith, Karen Cotton McDaniel, and John A. Hardin, eds., *The Kentucky African-American Encyclopedia* (Lexington: University Press of Kentucky, 2015), 295.

12. *Kentucky Negro Educational Association Journal* 1, no. 4 (April 1931), http://kdl.kyvl.org.

13. *Kentucky Negro Educational Association Journal* 1, no. 3 (February 1931).

14. Ibid.

15. Ibid.

16. Smith et al., *Kentucky African-American Encyclopedia,* 295–96.

17. Stout, *Shadows of the Past,* 11–12.

18. Ibid.

5. The Faith Plan

Epigraph: W. E. B. DuBois, "Does the Negro Need Separate Schools?" *Journal of Negro Education* 4 (July 1935): 328–35.

1. George C. Wright, "The Faith Plan: A Black Institution Grows during the Depression," *Filson Quarterly* 51, no. 4 (October 1977): 336–49. See also Duanne Puckett, Vivian Overall, and Betty Matthews, "Lincoln Institute," in *New History of Shelby County,* 286.

2. Wright, *History of Blacks in Kentucky,* 65–69; "State Acquires Lincoln Institute," *Lexington Herald,* January 10, 1964.

3. Dickerson, *Militant Mediator* 26.

4. Eleanor Young Love interview, October 2, 1978, University of Louisville African-American Oral History Collection.

5. Stout, *Shadows of the Past,* 74.

6. Lincoln Institute Student Guide, 1958, Kentucky Education Collection, Margaret I. King Library, University of Kentucky, Lexington.

7. *Lincoln Log,* 1936–1937, Lincoln Institute publications, 1917–1966, Kentucky Department for Libraries and Archives, Frankfort.

8. Ibid.

9. See "Midway Bluejays Win Net Crown," *Shelby Sentinel,* March 26, 1937; "States [*sic*] Finest to Meet in Lexington," *Shelby Sentinel,* March 18, 1938; "Shelby's Masters Also Bite the Dust," *Shelby Sentinel,* March 25, 1938.

10. "Dunbar High School," *Lexington Herald,* March 8, 1937.

11. "Negro High School Basketball Meet Here," *Frankfort State Journal,* March 10, 1937.

12. *Louisville Courier-Journal,* March 14, 1937.

13. "State Champions Go South," *Lincoln Log,* 1936–1937, 11.

14. Ibid.

15. "Lincoln Retains Negro Net Title," *Frankfort State Journal,* March 14, 1938. Rosters of participating teams compliments of KHSAL Collection (box 1, folder 6), Center of Excellence for the Study of Kentucky African-Americans, Kentucky State University, Frankfort.

16. Stout, *Shadows of the Past.*

6. "Janitorial Engineering"

1. Puckett et al., "Lincoln Institute," 286.

2. Letter from L. N. Taylor, Kentucky Department of Education, to J. M. Tydings, Lincoln Ridge, Kentucky, November 9, 1938, Lincoln Institute correspondence and subject files, Kentucky Department for Libraries and Archives, Frankfort.

3. "Signal Corps Brings New Type of Education to State," *Lexington Herald,* August 30, 1942.

4. "State Acquires Lincoln Institute," *Lexington Herald,* March 27, 1947.

5. "Young Becomes Assistant State Supervisor," *Kentucky Negro Educational Association Journal* 16, no. 1 (January–February 1945), http://kdl.kyvl.org.

6. Albert Minnis Jr. and Dr. Bernard Minnis, interviews with the author.

7. "'Inequality' Scored as KEA Opens Convention," *Lexington Herald,* April 21, 1949.

8. "Appoint Urban League Executive Instructor at Two Universities," *Kansas City (KS) Plaindealer,* April 27, 1951. See also Puckett, "Whitney Young, Jr.," 629.

9. Obituary of Arnita Young Boswell, *Chicago Tribune,* July 11, 2002.

10. Albert Minnis Jr., interview with the author.

11. Jessie C. Smith, ed., *Notable Black American Women: Book II* (Detroit: Thomson Gale, 1996), 416.

12. Lincoln Institute 1953–1954 Student Guide, Lincoln Institute publications, 1917–1966, Kentucky Department for Libraries and Archives, Frankfort.

13. Legislative Research Commission, excerpt of a report reprinted in the Lincoln Institute 1953–1954 Student Guide.

14. Lincoln Institute 1953–1954 Student Guide.

15. Letter from Sam B. Taylor, October 23, 1953, included in Lincoln Institute Report to the Board of Trustees for the School Year 1953–1954, box 9, Whitney M. Young Sr. Papers, Special Collections, Paul G. Blazer Library, Kentucky State University, Frankfort.

16. Whitney M. Young Sr. curriculum vitae, box 10, ibid.

17. "Suit to Stop High School Filed in Shelby," *Louisville Courier-Journal*, July 1, 1948.

18. "Shelby Gets till June 30 to Improve High Schools," *Louisville Courier-Journal*, March 18, 1949.

19. "Shelby to Drop 5 High Schools, Retain 3 Others," *Louisville Courier-Journal*, May 12, 1949.

20. "School Surveys Cited in Educational Study by Citizens Group," *Shelby News*, July 15, 1954. See also *Kentucky Negro Educational Association Journal* 7, no. 2 (January–February 1937).

21. "School Merger Is Effected in Anderson," *Lexington Herald*, August 21, 1949.

22. Ibid.

23. John N. Cunningham, interview with the author, August 12, 2014.

24. Lincoln Institute 1953–1954 Student Guide.

25. Willetta Barnett interview, June 21, 2005, Lincoln Institute Oral History Project, Berea College.

7. "Inherited Tendencies"

Epigraph: Donna L. Franklin, *Ensuring Inequality: The Structural Transformation of the African-American Family* (New York: Oxford University Press, 1997), 131.

1. Random examples of student life came from interviews with students, faculty, and staff by the author and others cited herein.

2. Judith Taylor Cunningham interview, September 12, 2004, Lincoln Institute Oral History Project, Berea College.

3. William Mack interview, January 19, 2005, ibid.

4. Whitney M. Young Sr., "Philosophy," September 1, 1952, Lincoln Institute Collection, Kentucky Department for Libraries and Archives, Frankfort.

5. Lincoln Institute 1953–1954 Student Guide.

6. Mary Taylor interview, January 19, 2005, Lincoln Institute Oral History Project, Berea College.

7. Letter from Whitney M. Young Sr. to Robert B. Harrison, January 12, 1953, Lincoln Institute Collection, Kentucky Department for Libraries and Archives, Frankfort.

8. Dorothy Dow interview, November 1, 2003, Lincoln Institute Oral History Project, Berea College.

9. Jennie Williams interview, November 1, 2003, ibid.

10. John N. Cunningham, interview with the author, August 12, 2004.

8. "Inherently Unequal"

Epigraph: Quoted in "Bunche Lauds Court Rulings on Segregation," *Lexington Herald,* June 7, 1950.

1. Stout, *Shadows of the Past,* 12.

2. Ibid., 13.

3. Ibid., 116.

4. Ibid., 14.

5. *Plessy v. Ferguson,* 163 U.S. 537 (1896).

6. Ibid.

7. Unless otherwise noted, the discussion of events leading up to the Supreme Court's *Brown* decision comes from James T. Patterson, Brown v. Board of Education: *A Civil Rights Milestone and Its Troubled Legacy* (New York: Oxford University Press, 2001), 7–23.

8. Mark Tushnet, *Making Civil Rights Law* (New York: Oxford University Press, 1994), 155.

9. *Brown v. Board of Education,* 347 U.S. 483 (1954).

10. "Kentuckians Are Stoic on Desegregation Move," *Lexington Herald,* May 27, 1954.

11. Minutes of the Board of Control, Kentucky High School Athletic Association, August 6, 1954, box 008, folder 6, KHSAA Collection No. 1981-024, Crabbe Library, Eastern Kentucky University, Richmond, KY.

12. "Permanent Group for School Study Formed in County," *Shelby News,* July 1, 1954.

13. Author unknown, "Shelbyville Public Schools (1950–59)," 4, History of Education file, Shelby County Library, Shelbyville, KY.

14. Kevin Collins, "African-American Education," in *New History of Shelby County,* 283–84.

15. Gary Brown quoting Whitney Young Sr., interview with the author, August 14, 2014.

16. John N. Cunningham, interview with the author, August 12, 2014.

17. The unique dimensions of the floor at Hughes Hall were revealed in interviews with John N. Cunningham and Albert Minnis Jr.

18. Schedule cards are included in the Lincoln Institute archives at the Kentucky Department for Libraries and Archives, Frankfort.

19. "Dunbar Wins, 72–67, in Overtime Thriller," *Lexington Herald,* February 18, 1955.

20. Stout, *Shadows of the Past,* 13–14.

21. Providence of Region II, Columbia of Region IV, and Barbourville of Region VII are not listed among the fifty-two former KHSAL member schools that Stout profiles in *Shadows of the Past,* 3–4. According to Alicestyne Turley-Adams, *Rosenwald Schools in Kentucky* (Frankfort: Kentucky Heritage Council, 2005), the Rosenwald Foundation built schools in Providence and Columbia; these are likely the schools in the KHSAL regional breakdown.

22. Tournament brackets are from box 2, folder 7, KHSAL Collection, Center of Excellence for the Study of Kentucky African-Americans, Kentucky State University, Frankfort.

23. "Demons Lose in State Meet," *Lexington Herald,* March 18, 1955; "'54 Champion Eliminated in K.H.S.A.L.," *Louisville Courier-Journal,* March 18, 1955.

24. "Central Swamps Lynch," *Louisville Courier-Journal,* March 17, 1955.

25. "Lincoln Upsets Central Quint for Net Halo," *Lexington Herald,* March 20, 1955.

9. "With All Deliberate Speed"

Epigraph: *Tower Gazette,* November 1955, 5, Lincoln Institute Collection, Kentucky Department for Libraries and Archives, Frankfort.

1. *Brown v. Board of Education,* 349 U.S. 294 (1955).

2. Tracy E. K'Meyer, *From Brown to Meredith: The Long Struggle for School Desegregation in Louisville, Kentucky* (Chapel Hill: University of North Carolina Press, 2013), 23.

3. For reports of the two 1955 Kentucky-Indiana all-star games, see "Hoosier Stars Battle Kentuckians Tonight," *Evansville Courier and Press,* June 18, 1955; "Indiana Rallies to Sink Kentucky," *Lexington Herald,* June 19, 1955; "Hoosier Stars Overtake Kentuckians," *Evansville Courier and Press,* June 19, 1955; "Kentucky Stars Nip Indiana in Overtime Thriller, 86–82," *Lexington Herald,* June 21, 1955.

4. *Willis v. Walker,* 136 F. Supp. 177 (W.D. Ky. 1955). See also Ellis, *History of Education in Kentucky,* 280.

5. Author unknown, essay on "Shelbyville Public Schools (1950–59)," 5, History of Education file, Shelby County Library, Shelbyville, KY.

6. Ibid.

7. Kevin Collins, "African-American Education," in *New History of Shelby County,* 283.

8. "Shelbyville Public Schools," 5.

9. Victor Brown interview, June 21, 2005, Lincoln Institute Oral History Project, Berea College.

10. Pearl Washington Allen interview, June 21, 2005, ibid.

11. Veltra Moran Brown interview, September 12, 2004, ibid.

12. *Tower Gazette,* November 1955.

13. Lincoln Institute Report to the Board of Trustees for the School Year 1955–1956, 6–8, box 9, Whitney M. Young Sr. Papers, Special Collections, Paul G. Blazer Library, Kentucky State University, Frankfort.

14. Ibid., 15.

15. *Tower Gazette,* November 1955.

16. Kentucky Superintendent of Public Instruction Biennial Report 1917–1919, 171–84, cited in *Experiment Station Record,* vol. 43 (Washington, DC: Government Printing Office, 1921), 695.

17. *Tower Gazette,* November 1955.

18. Ibid.

10. At the Highest Level

Epigraph: Quoted in "Negroes Will End Boycott of Buses," *Richmond (VA) Times-Dispatch,* December 21, 1956.

1. Charles J. Ogletree Jr., *All Deliberate Speed: Reflections on the First Half Century of* Brown v. Board of Education (New York: W. W. Norton, 2004), 138–39.

2. Stout, *Shadows of the Past,* 14.

3. Minutes of the Board of Control, Kentucky High School Athletic Association, July 29, 1955, box 009, folder 6, KHSAA Collection No. 1981-024, Crabbe Library, Eastern Kentucky University, Richmond, KY.

4. Agenda and program of the National Federation of High School Athletics, June 26–30, 1955, box B-012, folder 4, KHSAA Collection.

5. K'Meyer, *From Brown to Meredith,* 15–16.

6. Minutes of the Board of Control meeting, December 21, 1955, box B-009, folder 6, KHSAA Collection.

7. "Negro School Is Told to Admit All Races," *Lexington Herald,* September 30, 1955.

8. Lincoln Institute Report to the Board of Trustees for the School Year 1955–1956, 29, box 9, Whitney M. Young Sr. Papers, Special Collections, Paul G. Blazer Library, Kentucky State University, Frankfort.

9. Ibid., 19.

10. Michelle Gilliard Sheehan, interview with the author, April 18, 2015, and subsequent conversations with the author.

11. Walter Gilliard to Theodore A. Sanford, April 18, 1956, and Sanford to Whitney M. Young, April 19, 1956, box S-080, KHSAA Collection.

12. Young to Sanford, April 23, 1956, and Sanford to Young, April 25, 1956, ibid.

13. *The Kentucky High School Athlete*, October 1956, publication of the Kentucky High School Athletic Association, KHSAA Collection.

14. "232 Kentucky Schools Integrated This Year," *Lexington Herald*, October 21, 1956.

15. Ellis, *History of Education in Kentucky*, 283–84. See also Tracey E. K'Meyer, *Civil Rights in the Gateway to the South, Louisville, Kentucky, 1945–1980* (Lexington: University Press of Kentucky, 2011), 52–54.

16. Ellis, *History of Education in Kentucky*, 284.

17. Ibid., 284–86.

18. Ibid., 283.

19. Wright, *History of Blacks in Kentucky*, 203–5; K'Meyer, *Civil Rights in the Gateway to the South*, 49–52.

20. James C. Klotter, *A New History of Kentucky* (Lexington: University Press of Kentucky, 1997), 388; Wright, *History of Blacks in Kentucky*, 204.

21. "Louis Stout: A Barrier-Breaking Athlete Sets Example for Others," *Kentucky Monthly*, February 2007, 48–49.

22. Don Smith, interview with the author, July 17, 2015.

23. "Dunbar Pulls away to Beat Fee, 60–51," *Lexington Herald*, February 20, 1954.

24. "Bulldogs, Santa Claus Share Conversation around Maysville," *Lexington Herald*, December 16, 1956.

25. Dwayne "Nug" Faris, former Maysville High School student-athlete, interview with the author, January 6, 2015.

26. *The Kentucky High School Athlete*, January 1957, 3–10, KHSAA Collection.

27. Minutes of the Board of Control meeting, March 15, 1957, box B-009, folder 7, KHSAA Collection.

28. Stout, *Shadows of the Past*, 56.

29. "The Kean Brothers," *Louisville Courier-Journal*, July 3, 2007.

30. Stout, *Shadows of the Past*, 14. Stout, who later coached at Lexington Dunbar, became the KHSAA's first African American commissioner in 1994.

31. Jeff Bridgeman, *Kentucky High School Basketball Encyclopedia, 1916–2013* (Morley, MO: Acclaim Press, 2013); Stout, *Shadows of the Past*, 3–4.

11. In Front of the Parade

1. Eleanor's influence in Gilliard's promotion was mentioned in numerous interviews I conducted with former students and staff members.

2. Donald Steinberg, *Expanding Your Horizons: Collegiate Football's Greatest Team* (Pittsburgh: Dorrance Publishing, 1992), 172.

3. *The Southern Workman* 59 (1930): 234 (publication of the Hampton Normal and Agricultural Institute, Hampton, VA); Bridgeman, *Kentucky High School Basketball Encyclopedia,* 629.

4. Milton S. Katz, *Breaking Through: John B. McLendon, Basketball Legend and Civil Rights Pioneer* (Fayetteville: University of Arkansas Press, 2007), 11–19.

5. Scott Ellsworth, "Jim Crow Loses: The Secret Game," *New York Times Magazine,* March 31, 1996.

6. Katz, *Breaking Through,* 75–78.

7. Unless otherwise noted, Arnold Thurman's insight and comments were expressed during interviews with the author on November 4 and December 5, 2014. Also see Tom Chase, *B for Berea: The Amazing Story of Berea College Basketball in the Words of the Men Who Played It* (Johnson City, TN: Overmountain Press, 2000), 226.

8. Roy K. Young, *My Old Kentucky Home at War* (Birmingham, AL: Cliff Road Books, 2009), 127.

9. "Lincoln Institute Senior of the Week," *Louisville Defender,* March 10, 1960.

10. William Ben Spalding, interview with the author, November 25, 2014.

11. Daniel E. Thomas, interview with the author, December 4, 2014.

12. Jewell Logan, interview with the author, November 14, 2014.

13. "Kentucky Schools Take Another Step toward Racial Integration," *Lexington Herald,* November 7, 1957.

14. Patterson, Brown v. Board of Education, 109–10.

15. "Faubus to Obey U.S. Court," *Washington Evening Star,* September 15, 1957.

16. Patterson, Brown v. Board of Education, 111.

12. "A World Uncertain"

Epigraph: Eleanor Roosevelt, "My Day," *Lexington Herald,* August 5, 1957.

1. Arnold Thurman, interview with the author, December 5, 2014. Subsequent quotes from Thurman are from this interview.

2. The two local newspapers, the *Shelby News* and the *Shelby Sentinel,* both of which published two editions per week, began to report the scores of Lincoln's home games during the 1957–1958 season.

3. The thirty-ninth eligible former KHSAL member, Mayfield Dunbar, did not participate in the KHSAA tournament until 1959, perhaps because the Terrors lost all forty-four of their games during the 1956–1957 and 1957–1958 seasons, according to Bridgeman, *Kentucky High School Basketball Encyclopedia,* 627.

4. "Negro Flees . . . ," *Shelby Sentinel,* March 17, 1955; "Negro Killed . . . ," *Shelby Sentinel,* June 22, 1956.

5. Whitney M. Young Sr., address to 1958 graduates, *Lincoln Log,* Lin-

coln Institute publications, 1917–1966, Kentucky Department for Libraries and Archives, Frankfort.

6. John N. Cunningham, interview with the author, August 12, 2004.

13. An Accepted Way of Life

Epigraph: Brad Folsom, "I'll Never Forgive Them; Oscar Robertson Comes to North Texas," www.Historo.com.

1. John K. Cunningham, interview with the author, March 16, 2015.

2. Wayne Drehs, "The Forgotten Hoosiers," ESPN.com, February 26, 2009, http://sports.espn.go.com/espn/blackhistory2009/news/story?id=3932017.

3. Bob McDowell, interview with the author, November 20, 2014.

4. "Lincoln Institute Cagers Get Tough; May Be Headed for 30th District Crown," *Shelby News,* February 26, 1959.

5. "Tigers Defeat Waddy in First District Game," *Shelby News,* March 12, 1959.

6. Klotter, *New History of Kentucky,* 237.

7. US Census Bureau, "Population of Counties by Decennial Census: 1900 to 1990," http://www.census.gov/population/cencounts/ky190090.txt.

8. Earl Cox, "Quickest Thinking State Coach? He's Gallatin Co.'s Suther-land," *Louisville Courier-Journal,* January 12, 1958.

9. Quoted in Billy Reed, *Transition Game: The Story of S. T. Roach* (Lexington, KY: Host Communications, 2001), 116–17.

14. A "Progressive and Enlightened" State

1. "Court Orders Owen Elementary Schools Integrated This Fall," *Lexington Herald,* February 17, 1959.

2. "Christian County Will Integrate Schools Next Year," *Lexington Herald,* September 2, 1959.

3. "Orderly Integration Reported at Sturgis," *Lexington Herald,* September 2, 1959.

4. "Super 'In Kentucky' Gives Kentucky Progress Report," *Lexington Herald,* March 6, 1959.

5. "Local Burley Market Hits $66.30 Average in Sales This Week," *Shelby News,* December 3, 1959; "Calving Season Problems Discussed by Veterinarian," *Shelby News,* December 10, 1959.

6. "Lincoln Netters Again Bidding for Eighth Regional Crown," *Shelby News,* December 10, 1959.

7. "Central after Revenge against Lincoln 11," *Louisville Courier-Journal,* October 22, 1955; "Central Romps 34–6 over Lincoln Institute," *Louisville Courier-Journal,* October 23, 1955.

8. Ben Spalding, interview with the author, November 25, 2014.

9. "Lincoln Netters Again Bidding for Eighth Region Crown," *Shelby News,* December 10, 1959.

10. Albert Minnis Jr., interviews with the author.

11. Billy Collins, interview with the author, July 13, 2015.

12. "Lincoln Shaves Them Close," *Shelby News,* December 17, 1959.

13. Ibid.

14. "Lincoln Institute Wins Eminence Meet," *Shelby News,* January 7, 1960.

15. Homeless Tigers

1. "Fire Levels Lincoln Building; $400,000 Damage," *Louisville Defender,* January 14, 1960; "Lincoln Institute's Loss Has Been Estimated at $400,000, *Shelby Sentinel,* January 14, 1960; "Fires Wreck Lincoln H.S. Building and Drug Store in Shelbyville," *Shelby News,* January 14, 1960.

2. Lincoln Institute Report to the Board of Trustees for the School Year 1959–1960, 27–28, box 10, Whitney M. Young Sr. Papers, Special Collections, Paul G. Blazer Library, Kentucky State University, Frankfort.

3. Jewell Logan, interview with the author, November 14, 2014.

4. Daniel Thomas, interview with the author, December 4, 2014.

5. "Lincoln's Tigers Down Fighting Bobcats to Win the County Band Tournament," *Shelby News,* January 29, 1960.

6. Ben Spalding, interview with the author, November 25, 2014.

7. Ellis, *History of Education in Kentucky,* 289.

8. WLAC Radio website, http://wwns.com/wlac/history.html.

9. Gary Brown, interview with the author, August 14, 2014.

10. Victor Brown interview, June 21, 2005, Lincoln Institute Oral History Project, Berea College.

11. Bob Fay, "Around and About," *Shelby News,* February 18, 1960.

12. "Bagdad, Lincoln Co-favorites in 30th District Basketball Meet," *Shelby News,* February 18, 1960.

13. Stout, *Shadows of the Past,* 54–55.

14. Clem Haskins and Marc Ryan, *Clem Haskins: Breaking Barriers* (Champaign, IL: Sagamore Publishing, 1997), 36–42.

16. Out of the Ruins

1. *Shelby News,* March 10, 1960.

2. David Van Meter, letter to the editor, *Shelby News,* March 10, 1960.

3. Evan Settle to Theodore A. Sanford, March 2, 1960, Lincoln Institute, 1956–64 file, box S-080, folder 7, KHSAA Collection, Crabbe Library, Eastern Kentucky University, Richmond, KY.

4. "Lincoln Rallies to Win District," *Shelby News,* March 10, 1960.

5. Sanford to Settle, March 9, 1960, Lincoln Institute, 1956–64 file, box S-080, folder 7, KHSAA Collection.

6. Whitney M. Young, "Out of the Ruins of Yesterday," *Shelby News,* March 10, 1960.

7. Lincoln Institute Report to the Board of Trustees for the School Year 1959–1960, 14, box 9, Whitney M. Young Sr. Papers, Special Collections, Paul G. Blazer Library, Kentucky State University, Frankfort.

8. "Oldham Colonels Lose Heartbreaker to Lincoln," *Oldham Era,* March 18, 1960; "Lincoln in State Tourney Today," *Shelby News,* March 17, 1960.

9. Bill Chenault, "Lincoln 8th Region Champs," *Shelby Sentinel,* March 17, 1960.

10. Daniel Thomas, interview with the author, December 4, 2014; Billy Collins, interview with the author, July 13, 2015.

11. "Carrollton Put on Probation," *Oldham Era,* April 1, 1960.

17. Secret Ballot

Epigraph: William S. White, "Senator Johnson Keeps a Promise," *Richmond Times-Dispatch,* February 18, 1960.

1. Unsigned letter to Theodore A. Sanford, March 3, 1957, box T-012, KHSAA Collection No. 1981-024, Crabbe Library, Eastern Kentucky University, Richmond, KY.

2. Letters to Theodore A. Sanford, ibid.

3. J. D. Craddock Jr. to Louisville Chamber of Commerce, copy to Theodore A. Sanford, March 20, 1957, ibid.

4. "Tournament Should Be Held Here," *Lexington Herald,* March 20, 1957.

5. Minutes of the Board of Control, July 28, 1958, summer meeting, box B-009, folder 8, KHSAA Collection.

6. Minutes of the Board of Control, April 17, 1959, annual meeting, box B-009, folder 7, KHSAA Collection.

7. KHSAA administrative folder, box T-012, KHSAA Collection.

8. Luther Adams, *Way up North in Louisville: African-American Migration in the Urban South, 1930–1970* (Chapel Hill: University of North Carolina Press, 2010), 130–32.

9. "Leaders Disappointed in Aldermen's Action," *Louisville Defender,* March 3, 1960.

10. Minutes of the Board of Control, January 23, 1960, winter meeting, box B-009, folder 7, KHSAA Collection.

11. "Flaget Stuns Central 58–49, Gains Final," *Louisville Courier-Journal,* March 12, 1960.

12. John McGill, interview with the author, March 18, 2015.

13. Pew Research Center, "Religion and Public Life," http://www.pewforum.org/religious-landscape-study/religious-tradition/catholic/.

14. Notable Kentucky African-American Database, University of Kentucky Libraries, http://nkaa.uky.edu/record.php?note_id=1208.

15. Ibid., http://nkaa.uky.edu/subject.php?sub_id=94.

16. John E. Kleber, ed., *The Encyclopedia of Louisville* (Lexington: University Press of Kentucky, 2001), 876.

17. Dr. Robert Walter Johnson, "Trailblazers in Virginia History," http://www.lva.virginia.gov/public/trailblazers/2011/johnson.htm.

18. A Whistle from Midcourt

1. Game accounts were reconstructed from the March 18, 1960, editions of the *Louisville Courier-Journal, Lexington Herald,* and *Owensboro Messenger-Inquirer* and from interviews with the participants.

2. Jewell Logan, interview with the author, November 14, 2014; Bob McDowell, interview with the author, November 20, 2014.

3. Sanford to Young, March 23, 1960, box S-080, KHSAA Collection, Crabbe Library, Eastern Kentucky University, Richmond, KY.

4. Young to Sanford, March 28, 1960, ibid.

5. Lincoln Institute Report to the Board of Trustees for the School Year 1961–1962, 15, box 9, Whitney M. Young Sr. Papers, Special Collections, Paul G. Blazer Library, Kentucky State University, Frankfort.

Epilogue

1. "Vocational School for All Races Urged at Lincoln Institute," *Lexington Herald,* April 22, 1960.

2. Kleber, *Encyclopedia of Louisville,* 876.

3. John W. Brown to Theodore A. Sanford, December 12, 1962, box S-080, folder 7, KHSAA Collection Crabbe Library, Eastern Kentucky University, Richmond, KY.

4. "George Conley, Ex–State Senator, Dies," *Bowling Green (KY) Daily News,* January 2, 1992.

5. Quoted in Rey L. Gillespie, "Community Relations," *Cleveland Plain Dealer,* September 10, 1961.

6. Reed, *Transition Game,* 50.

7. "Arson Reward in DuBois School Fire Posted," *Lexington Herald,* September 4, 1964.

8. "Kittens Whip IBM 98–59," *Lexington Herald,* January 3, 1965.

9. Whitney M. Young Sr., Report to the Board of Regents, April 1966, Lincoln Institute Collection, Margaret I. King Library, University of Kentucky, Lexington.

10. Acts of the Commonwealth of Kentucky, 1966, chapter 112 (H.B. 89), 542–45.

11. Joseph McPherson, interview with David Cline, December 9, 2004, Civil Rights Movement Project, Southern Oral History Program, University of North Carolina–Chapel Hill.

12. "Advisory Committee for Aiding Racial Desegregation Urged," *Lexington Herald,* September 13, 1955.

13. David Wolfford, "Louis Stout: A Barrier-Breaking Athlete Sets Example for Others," *Kentucky Monthly,* February 2007, 49–51.

14. *Holland Evening Sentinel,* June 10, 1964, 6.

15. Michelle Gilliard Sheehan, interview with the author, April 18, 2015.

Bibliography

Books and Articles

Adams, Luther. *Way up North in Louisville: African-American Migration in the Urban South, 1930–1970.* Chapel Hill: University of North Carolina Press, 2010.

Barnes, Kenneth C. *Journey of Hope: The Back-to-Africa Movement in Arkansas in the Late 1800s.* Chapel Hill: University of North Carolina Press, 2004.

Bridgeman, Jeff. *Kentucky High School Basketball Encyclopedia, 1916–2013.* Morley, MO: Acclaim Press, 2013.

Bullock, Henry Allen. *A History of Black Education in the South from 1619 to the Present.* New York: Praeger Publishers, 1970.

Chase, Tom. *B for Berea: The Amazing Story of Berea College Basketball in the Words of the Men Who Played It.* Johnson City, TN: Overmountain Press, 2000.

Cloud, Olivia. "The Kean Brothers." *Louisville Courier-Journal,* July 3, 2007.

The Constitution of the Commonwealth of Kentucky. Frankfort: Kentucky Legislative Research Commission, 1952.

Cox, Earl. "Quickest Thinking State Coach? He's Gallatin Co.'s Sutherland." *Louisville Courier-Journal,* January 12, 1958.

Dickerson, Dennis C. *Militant Mediator: Whitney M. Young Jr.* Lexington: University Press of Kentucky, 1998.

Drehs, Wayne. "The Forgotten Hoosiers." ESPN.com, February 26, 2009. http://sports.espn.go.com/espn/blackhistory2009/news/story?id=3932017.

Dudziak, Mary L. *Cold War Civil Rights.* Princeton, NJ: Princeton University Press, 2011.

Ellis, William E. *A History of Education in Kentucky.* Lexington: University Press of Kentucky, 2011.

Ellsworth, Scott. "Jim Crow Loses: The Secret Game." *New York Times Magazine,* March 31, 1996.

Fee, John G. *Autobiography of John G. Fee, Berea, Kentucky.* Chicago: National Christian Association, 1891. Digitized by University of North Carolina at Chapel Hill, 1997.

Franklin, Donna L. *Ensuring Inequality: The Structural Transformation of the African-American Family.* New York: Oxford University Press, 1997.

Gutek, Gerald L. *A History of the Western Educational Experience.* Long Grove, IL: Waveland Press, 1995.

Hall, Wade. *The Rest of the Dream: The Black Odyssey of Lyman Johnson.* Lexington: University Press of Kentucky, 1988.

Hardin, John A. *Fifty Years of Segregation: Higher Education in Kentucky, 1904–1954.* Lexington: University Press of Kentucky, 1997.

Harrell, Kenneth E., ed. *The Public Papers of Governor Edward T. Breathitt, 1963–1967.* Lexington: University Press of Kentucky, 1984.

Haskins, Clem, and Marc Ryan. *Clem Haskins: Breaking Barriers.* Champaign, IL: Sagamore Publishing, 1997.

Hulbert, Archer Butler. *Historic Highways of America.* Vol. 2, *Pioneers {?}Roads and Experiences of Travelers.* Cleveland, OH: Arthur Clark, 1904.

Jones, Faustine Childress. *A Traditional Model of Educational Excellence.* Washington, DC: Howard University Press, 1981.

Katz, Milton S. *Breaking Through: John B. McLendon, Basketball Legend and Civil Rights Pioneer.* Fayetteville: University of Arkansas Press, 2007.

Kleber, John E., ed. *The Encyclopedia of Louisville.* Lexington: University Press of Kentucky, 2001.

———. *The Kentucky Encyclopedia.* Lexington: University Press of Kentucky, 1992.

Klotter, James C. *Kentucky: Portrait in Paradox, 1900–1950.* Frankfort: Kentucky Historical Society, 1996.

———. *A New History of Kentucky.* Lexington: University Press of Kentucky, 1997.

Kluger, Richard. *Simple Justice: The History of* Brown v. Board of Education *and Black America's Struggle for Equality.* New York: Knopf, 1975.

K'Meyer, Tracy E. *Civil Rights in the Gateway to the South, Louisville, Kentucky, 1945–1980.* Lexington: University Press of Kentucky, 2011.

———. *From Brown to Meredith: The Long Struggle for School Desegregation in Louisville, Kentucky.* Chapel Hill: University of North Carolina Press, 2013.

Kuska, Bob. *Hot Potato: How Washington and New York Gave Birth to Black Basketball and Changed America's Game Forever.* Charlottesville: University of Virginia Press, 2004.

McCoy, Robert B., and John T. Strachan, eds. *The Midland Trail.* Glorieta, NM: Rio Grande Press, 1916.

McKnight, Brian D. *Contested Borderland: Civil War in Appalachian Kentucky and Virginia.* Lexington: University Press of Kentucky, 2006.

McNichol, Dan. *The Roads that Built America.* New York: Silver Lining Books, 2003.

Miller, James W. "The Legacy of Lincoln." *Shelby News,* February 20, 2013.

Mjagkij, Nina, ed. *Organizing Black America: An Encyclopedia of African-American Associations.* New York: Garland Publishing, 2013.

The New History of Shelby County, Kentucky. Prospect, KY: Harmony House Publishers, 2003.

Ogletree, Charles J., Jr. *All Deliberate Speed: Reflections on the First Half Century of Brown v. Board of Education.* New York: W. W. Norton, 2004.

Patterson, James T. Brown v. Board of Education: *A Civil Rights Milestone and Its Troubled Legacy.* New York: Oxford University Press, 2001.

Pruter, Robert, and Project Muse. *The Rise of American High School Sports and the Search for Control.* Syracuse, NY: Syracuse University Press, 2013.

Reed, Billy. *Transition Game: The Story of S. T. Roach.* Lexington, KY: Host Communications, 2001.

Robinson, Lottie Offett. *The Bond-Washington Story.* Elizabethtown, KY: Robinson, 1983.

Smith, Gerald L., Karen Cotton McDaniel, and John A. Hardin, eds. *The Kentucky African-American Encyclopedia.* Lexington: University Press of Kentucky, 2015.

Smith, Jessie C., ed., *Notable Black American Women: Book II.* Detroit: Thomson Gale, 1996.

Sowell, Thomas. "Patterns of Black Excellence." *Public Interest* 43 (1976).

Steinberg, Donald. *Expanding Your Horizons: Collegiate Football's Greatest Team.* Pittsburgh: Dorrance Publishing, 1992.

Stout, Louis. *Shadows of the Past: A History of the Kentucky High School Athletic League.* Lexington, KY: Host Communications, 2006.

Turley-Adams, Alicestyne. *Rosenwald Schools in Kentucky.* Frankfort: Kentucky Heritage Council, 2005.

Tushnet, Mark. *I Dissent: Great Opposing Opinions in Landmark Supreme Court Cases.* Boston: Beacon Press, 2008.

———. *Making Civil Rights Law.* New York: Oxford University Press, 1994.

US Census Bureau. "Population of Counties by Decennial Census: 1900 to 1990." http://www.census.gov/population/cencounts/ky190090.txt.

US Department of Transportation, Federal Highways Administration. *America's Highways 1776–1976.* Washington, DC, 1977.

Walker, Vanessa Siddle. *Their Highest Potential: An African-American School Community in the Segregated South.* Chapel Hill: University of North Carolina Press, 1996.

Wolfford, David. "Louis Stout: A Barrier-Breaking Athlete Sets Example for Others." *Kentucky Monthly,* February 2007.

Wright, George C. "The Faith Plan: A Black Institution Grows during the Depression." *Filson Quarterly* 51, no. 4 (October 1977).

———. "The Founding of Lincoln Institute." *Filson Quarterly* 49, no. 1 (January 1975).

———. *A History of Blacks in Kentucky.* Vol. 2, *In Pursuit of Equality, 1890–1980.* Frankfort: Kentucky Historical Society, 2001.

———. *Racial Violence in Kentucky, 1865–1940.* Baton Rouge: LSU Press, 1990.

Young, Roy K. *My Old Kentucky Home at War.* Birmingham, AL: Cliff Road Books, 2009.

Special Collections

African-American Oral History Collection, University of Louisville. digital.library. louisville.edu/cdm.

Civil Rights Movement Project, Southern Oral History Program, University of North Carolina, Chapel Hill, NC.

Kentucky High School Athletic Association Collection, Crabbe Library, Eastern Kentucky University, Richmond, KY.

Kentucky Negro Educational Association Journal. http://kdl.kyvl.org.

KHSAL Collection, Center of Excellence for the Study of Kentucky African-Americans, Kentucky State University, Frankfort, KY.

Lincoln Institute Collection, Kentucky Department for Libraries and Archives, Frankfort, KY.

Lincoln Institute Collection, Margaret I. King Library, University of Kentucky, Lexington, KY.

Lincoln Institute Oral History Project, Special Collections, Hutchins Library, Berea College, Berea, KY.

Whitney M. Young Sr. Papers, Special Collections, Paul G. Blazer Library, Kentucky State University, Frankfort, KY.

Interviews and Oral Histories

Interviews by the Author

Gary Brown, Versailles, KY
Billy Collins, Oklahoma City, OK
John Kavanaugh Cunningham, Lawrenceburg, KY
John Norman Cunningham, Lawrenceburg, KY
Randy Embry, Owensboro, KY
Dwayne "Nug" Faris, Maysville, KY
David Hawpe, Louisville, KY
Jewell Logan, Portland, OR
John McGill, Louisville, KY
Albert Minnis Jr., Simpsonville, KY
Dr. Bernard Minnis, Shelbyville, KY

Jim Richards, Bowling Green, KY
Michelle Gilliard Sheehan, Silver Spring, MD
Don Smith, Indianapolis, IN
William Ben Spalding, Tucson, AZ
Daniel E. Thomas, Frankfort, KY
Arnold Thurman, Shelbyville, KY

Interviews by Professor Andrew Baskin, Lincoln Institute Oral History Project, Berea College

Pearl Washington Allen, June 21, 2005
Bettye Banks, January 19, 2005
Willetta Barnett, June 21, 2005
Veltra Moran Brown, September 12, 2004
Victor Brown, June 21, 2005
Wanda Warren Brown, July 29, 2003
John Kavanaugh Cunningham, September 12, 2004
John Norman Cunningham, June 21, 2005
Judith Taylor Cunningham, September 12, 2004
Rose Washington Cunningham, June 21, 2005
Herbert Dorsey, November 1, 2003
Dorothy Dow, November 1, 2003
Jacqueline Burley Fleming, September 24, 2004
Willie C. Fleming, September 24, 2004
Jewell Logan, July 31, 2004
Eleanor Young Love, November 15, 2003
Robert Luney, January 19, 2005
William Mack, January 19, 2005
Estelle Marshall, September 24, 2004
Dr. Bernard Minnis, November 1, 2003
Vivian Warren Overall, July 29, 2003
Hattie Mae Cottrell Payne, September 24, 2004
William E. Smith, July 31, 2004
Mary Taylor, January 19, 2005
Daniel E. Thomas, July 31, 2004
Anna Warren, July 29, 2003
Jennie Williams, November 1, 2003

Civil Rights Movement Project, Southern Oral History Program, University of North Carolina–Chapel Hill

Joseph McPherson interview, December 9, 2004

University of Louisville African-American Oral History Collection

Eleanor Young Love interview, October 2, 1978

Index